FOOTBALL, CU - STYLE

A laughingly informal look at the last 25 years of University of Colorado football as seen through the irreverent eyes and told through the impudent typewriter of Fred Casotti, who has watched it all happen, part of the time as a student, for a brief period as a sportswriter, most of the time as CU's sports information director and, most recently, as assistant athletic director.

Casotti takes you on a casual stroll through the past quarter-century of CU football with his impressions of the coaches and the players who dominated the period and the games which he has selected as the top 25 CU victories during that span of time.

FOOTBALL, CU*-STYLE

*Casotti Uncensored

by
Fred Casotti

Pruett Publishing Company
Boulder, Colorado

© 1972 by Fred Casotti

All rights reserved, including those to reproduce this book, or parts thereof, in any form, without permission in writing from the Publisher.

ISBN: 0-87108-067-2

Pruett Publishing Company
Boulder, Colorado

Printed in the United States of America
by Pruett Press, Inc.
First Edition

CONTENTS

1. In the Beginning — Jim Yeager 1
2. Out of the Hills — Dal Ward 5
3. Enter the All - American Boy — Sonny Grandelius 13
4. A Year to Forget — Bud Davis 19
5. Enter the Messiah — Eddie Crowder 27
6. The Constant Parade — The Assistants 37
7. A Good Bench is Important, Too 91
8. Buffaloes I've Worked With 107
9. My All-25 Year Platoon Teams 145
10. The Captains 201
11. Some of the Others 213
12. The 25 Sweetest Saturdays 219
    Epilogue 281

LIST OF ILLUSTRATIONS

Alumni Squad, May, 1963 viii
This is My Lady x
You've Got to Have Talent 9
A Very Serious Head Table 32
It's Great to be Well-known 95
Two Coaches and Friends 95
Eddie Dove 139
Frank Bernardi 139
Viva La Victory 148
Bob Anderson 205
A Very Special Piece of Persimmon 221
I Never Did Measure Up Too Well 222
It Was A Very Grim Year 276

INTRODUCTION

I considered calling this book, "Love Story." But that title was taken. And, anyway, this book has a happy ending. Then I thought I might try something like "A Rocky Mountain Love Story." But that sounded like it might be about a couple of mountain goats, coupling somewhere up behind the Flatirons. So I scrapped that. And then I thought about calling it, "My Love Affair With the Buffaloes." And that was even worse. So I junked the whole idea about using "love."

But, despite the absence of the word in the title, this book is basically a love story. And it IS about a love affair between an impudent little Italian and a herd of Buffaloes. Golden Buffaloes, that is. University of Colorado style. And it's all clean and wholesome and pure and wonderful.

Anyway, this is a very personal look at the last 25 years of CU football as seen through the wide-open, often-glazed, sometimes-unbelieving, occasionally bleeding and always-prejudiced eyes of a short, dumpy, near-sighted, enthusiastic escapee from the state of Iowa who wandered onto the CU campus, almost by accident, in the fall of 1947 and fell in love, at first sight, with the Colorado Buffaloes.

Not with the CU campus even though its beauty was, and still is, sufficient to produce at least a degree of infatuation. And not with the impressive mountain setting. Even though those imposing Flatirons which stand in stately guard over the campus and its city are certainly beautiful enough to arouse ardor in even the coldest stoic. And certainly not with my professors, even though enough of them were sufficiently kind and understanding to not block my progress toward a degree.

But with the Buffaloes! Shabby as they might have been in those dreary old gold uniforms and those battered old headgears. With those sagging bellies hanging down over their belts. (College football teams were still cluttered with those World War II returnees who had escaped with their lives but lost their muscle tones somewhere along the way.) I guess it just didn't take much to arouse my amorous instincts in those days. (Except in the very important area of choosing a wife and, in that one, it took a tremendous combination of beauty, intelligence and understanding.)

So I graduated and didn't go any farther away than I had to and came back the first chance I got. And my union with CU has been as enjoyable and rewarding and passionate as the one with my wife. (I'm sure there have been a whole lot of moments in our marriage that she

ALUMNI SQUAD, MAY, 1963

has rated my two greatest loves in exactly that order: CU first and her second.) But it has always been a photo finish.

And now I have tried to describe some of the men and the events which have made the football part of my association so thoroughly great. This is a completely prejudiced work. As any good love affair should be, complete and totally prejudiced. If it seems at times to be rambling and unorganized and over-enthusiastic and over-written, that is probably because I am a rambling and unorganized and over-enthusiastic and over-writing person. Especially when it comes to Golden Buffaloes.

All I can say about the last 25 years is that if I could do it all over, I'd do it exactly the same way. I've worked with a lot of great people, many of them Buffaloes and just as many of them not Buffaloes. Many of them are mentioned in this book. Many of them are not. Just being great wasn't enough to make this meander down memory lane. You had to occupy a special section of the Casotti cerebrum, that inner-cranial grotto where the memories of very special Buffaloes are carefully stored.

Here, then, is the record of my recollections, portrayed through my impressions of the people who made some of the best things happen in the last 25 falls and told through my memories of the greatest days of those falls. It's basically a happy book, sometimes an impudent one, always, I hope, a fair one and, above all, an honest one. I am sure there is such a thing as honest prejudice. If an occasional dart gets under your skin, don't take it sitting down. Rip this book in two and throw it in the trash can. Then go out and buy another copy. It's good therapy and you will have contributed a double share in helping us make back our expenses.

In closing this opening, I'd like to dedicate this book to:

(1) My wife, Darlene, for her patience and understanding and willingness to perform in the background as I've sailed through the first 25 years of our marriage, too often pushing her off to one side while I've over-lavished my attention on the Buffaloes. Behind every great man there is a great wife. But a lot of us who weren't great still had great wives.

(2) My daughters, Candy and Chris, who have made it all worthwhile. Loving Buffaloes and a wife can go just so far. You've got to have children, too. And I have two great daughters.

(3) All those Buffaloes, on and off the field, who have made my work such a joy.

(4) And, lastly, to all you people who share my feeling about Buffaloes enough to have bought a copy of this book. That's real love, friend. May you enjoy the pages which follow.

THIS IS MY LADY

I've made a lot of dumb moves in my life but marrying my wife wasn't one of them. This is my lady, Darlene, and she is very nice and very pretty and very understanding. And she can carry lots of junk in her arms. This was a very nice trophy that the Buff Club presented me in 1968. For having a very nice and very pretty wife, I think.

IN THE BEGINNING—
JIM YEAGER

My introduction to CU football was uninspiring, to say the least.

The first game I saw was the opening home game of the 1947 season. Jim Yeager's last campaign as a head coach. The Buffaloes were handled rather routinely by Missouri, 21-0. The next Saturday, John Zisch had to kick a late field goal to produce a 9-7 victory over a BYU team which entered the game a big underdog.

Big deal, CU football! To someone coming out of Big Ten territory and having followed some good Iowa teams coached by Eddie Anderson, Colorado was as far back in the bushes as I had suspected it might be before I enrolled.

But it was football and it's pretty tough for anyone to screw up such a great game. Lots of people have tried it in the past and they haven't even come close. I'd guess, though, if anyone can do it, it will be the pros of today with their all-out mercenaries on both sides of the line of scrimmage as well as on both sides of the bargaining table. But this is projecting into the future which is today and this section is about CU coaches I have known (most of whom I've loved) and we're talking about 1947.

And if football is a game you can't screw up, the same holds true for a victory. No matter how it comes, no matter how tough or miserable or hairy or lucky or whatever, a victory is always palatable and digestible. You don't need Alka Seltzer to settle it in your stomach...although lots of Alka Seltzers are required to settle down everything else that goes in stomachs on Saturday nights after the games. And there's always an exception to every rule and the one for this one is that victories are frequently unpalatable to the gamblers whose teams didn't make the point spread. But these guys don't count. They ought to be at a dog track somewhere. Running. And getting bet on themselves. And getting the abuse from bettors who lost on them. That's about all I have to say about gamblers except that they foul up a church picnic.

My favorite gambling story takes place in Oklahoma during the

1950's when Bud Wilkinson's dynasty was rolling over the world and the only issue at doubt Saturday after Saturday was whether the Sooners would make the point spread.

My good friend, Jay Simon, now sports information director at Kansas was then a member of the Oklahoma City Daily Oklahoman sports staff and called the gamblers,"Chinamen." One called the sports department late one Saturday afternoon and asked for the Oklahoma score. "The Sooners won, 28-7," replied Jay. The point spread was 27. And the gambler, who obviously had lost his bet, was appropriately furious and expressed his fury and disgust with the Sooners to Simon. Jay put down his phone and groaned in his soft drawl, "How much rice can a Chinaman eat?"

But, getting back on track, I include Jim Yeager on my list of CU coaches even though I didn't work with him as a member of the staff. I did, however, watch his Iowa State teams play, as a knotholer in the late 30's, as well as his last CU team in 1947. And, more importantly I got to know him fairly well as a friend after he got out of coaching and bought and managed the Brooks-Fauber store in downtown Boulder until his death of a heart attack in 1970.

His nickname was "Gentleman Jim" and it couldn't have been more fitting. If you'll pardon the expression, he was a sweet guy, a gentle man. And a good football coach whose teams ran and screen-passed from the short punt formation — and did them very effectively.

His 1938 Iowa State team was undefeated until the last game of the season, losing to Oklahoma at Ames in the game which decided the Big Six championship and sent the Sooners to the Orange Bowl (where they got the hell kicked out of them by Tennessee.)

Jim came to CU in 1941 and a year later had a 7-2 team and was 5-2 in 1943 before going into the navy. Most of his men returned after the war and a continuation of those successes was anticipated.

It didn't happen. The service returnees were fat, sassy . . . . and horrible. The linemen were big and slow and lazy. They might have been a good tug-of-war team. But not much else. And they'd been through the great war with its invasions, mass bombing raids, A-bombs, massive doses of penicillin, etc. and it was tough for them to get real excited about a schoolboy game coached by a gentle person who didn't believe in using the whip. And a whip was the only thing which might have gotten the 1946 and 47 teams moving.

So the Buffaloes floundered and Yeager's coaching career faded into women's lingerie and all those other exotic wrappers which make some females into such exciting packages.

We used to talk about the old days, B.S. (before scholarships.)

"It was much more fun coaching then," he'd smile. "Most schools gave some help to some men but it was almost always in the form of jobs and most of the jobs included work although you always heard a lot about good halfbacks winding up 8-day clocks for their tuition. We never had any of those where I coached, though. Football today is much more aggressive, both from a player's and coach's standpoint. It's a much better game. But I preferred it the way it was in my day."

One of the last memories of a conversation I have with Jim, typifies his personality, his philosophy and his sense of humor. It was during the fall and pre-season practice was underway and football was back in the news. I stopped in at his store to sell him a program ad. While he was signing the contract, I asked him if he ever missed coaching.

"Sure I do," he smiled as he looked up. "It's a great job, working with young men and, you like to think, helping to make them better men. And enjoying the wins and suffering through and after the losses but, always, doing it together with your men. It was a great life. And I'm glad that I could settle down in Boulder where I have the opportunity to see the three schools which have meant the most to me — Kansas State, Iowa State and Colorado.

"But every once in a while I recall some of the unpleasant memories. The painful ones. The times when you think people weren't fair with you. Most of the time your memory pulls out the good things. But not always. Let me tell you a story which might illustrate the painful part of coaching. Not long ago, some of us were fishing up in the mountains north of here. I woke up in the middle of the night with a bad stomach ache. For a moment, I thought it was a Saturday night after a losing game. Then my senses cleared and I realized it was just the chili I'd eaten for supper. I guess I'd have to say I'm getting along without coaching very well."

So much for "Gentleman Jim" Yeager. May he rest in peace. A nice man. And a good coach. Most of them are.

OUT OF THE HILLS—
DAL WARD

With Yeager out of the CU picture, the search for a new coach to take over simultaneously with the Buffaloes entering the Big Six conference (to change its name to, surprise, Big Seven) in 1948 began with such then-current luminaries as Carl Snavely and Dudley DeGroot prominent in the pre-hiring guessing.

But the somewhat-surprising selection turned out to be Dallas Ward, a top assistant to Bernie Bierman at Minnesota and a key man in helping Bierman produce the Golden Gopher dynasties which made a shambles out of so many Big Ten races during the pre-World War II days.

Although Ward's selection came as a surprise to most non-informed observers (and most observers of football are non-informed), it was quite understandable if you realized that Ward had served in the navy with such influential CU personalities as Kayo Lam, George Lesser and Lu Monroe — the latter the extremely-interested-active-and-influential business manager of the Boulder Daily Camera, a Boulder native, CU graduate and athletic activist who covered all the CU games despite his high administrative post with the daily newspaper.

At any rate, Ward got the job and the already-graying disciple of the Minnesota unbalanced single-wing came riding out of Big Ten country to lead Colorado out of the bushes and into the big time.

At this point in CU history, a young and clever Denver Post sports writer-cartoonist, Bob Bowie, gave the Buffaloes a cartoon characterization they were never to lose — Big Time Cholly.

It was somewhat unfair. Most caricatures are. But it was somewhat authentic in that it represented the feelings of many sports fans in the Rocky Mountain West who felt that CU was deserting its friends and old allies in the Mountain States conference to go "bigtime," if you will. But most of the CU loyalists called it progress.

Some of the small-thinkers clustered around whatever passed for a CU band-wagon at that time (and there are always a lot of mini-thinkers around a program — they normally trot along after the bandwagon, never jumping on until it is roaring downhill nearly out of control: then they complain because they don't get the seat they want!) felt the Buffaloes were moving out of their class. Oklahoma, Nebraska, Missouri, Kansas, etc. instead of Colorado Mines, BYU, New Mexico, Wyoming, Colorado A&M? Horrors! They'll never make it, they cried.

The job of building CU into a major power, quickly (no group of football fans, no matter how small the program, ooze with patience), was in Ward's hands. And the hands were relatively unknown.

If my introduction to CU football under Jim Yeager was unimpressive, I'd hate to have to come up with the proper adjective to describe Ward's debut in Folsom Stadium. Before 20,000 fans including the governor, Ward's dingy-gold-clad Buffaloes played like 11 mounds of Buffalo chips, losing to New Mexico, 9-6. There was distant baying and some I-tole-you-so yips from the wolves. After the next Saturday, even the jackals were snarling. The Buffaloes lost to Kansas, 40-7. The only good thing about that game was that it was played in Lawrence and those were the days before television and if you couldn't get KOA and Starr Yelland you mercifully missed the description. Until the papers came out on Sunday morning. (If you subscribed to the Boulder Camera only, you were spared until Monday evening because it didn't publish on Sundays at that time.)

But I have a firm belief that a man — or a coach — will show you something early. If he has anything to show. Most coaches insist on 4-year contracts to take a new job, particularly one which requires a good bit of rebuilding (and most do or there wouldn't be a new coach coming on.) A dog will be a dog right from the start. But a good man will lay something good on you fairly soon. At least somewhere along the way during the first season. No matter how bad the program he has inherited.

Ward gave CU fans a taste of what was to come in his third Saturday, a 19-6 victory over a heavily-favored Nebraska team which swaggered into Boulder, led by its All-American center "Trainwreck Tom" Novak, with all kinds of Big Ten scalps and wampum belts and hymens and whatever dangling from their belts.

The runty Buffaloes, with such mastodons as Malcolm Miller and Don Hagin leading the way, took it to the Cornhuskers right from the start. There was nothing fluky about the win. And Ward was on his way. The Buffs were only 3-6 that year. But in his third season, Ward was 7-3 and never went below 6-4 in the final nine years of his 11-year career at CU.

What kind of coach was Ward?

A great offensive coach. Despite the totally-unfair and completely-inaccurate label of "horse-and-buggy offense" slapped on his single wing attack by his detractors — and he had many (Dal could irritate some people almost as easily as his offense could roll up ground yardage.) His offense was skillfully designed, simple to watch from the stands (football fans always seem to think that if something looks simple from the stands it must look just as simple from across the line of scrimmage; and, as they so often are, they're very wrong), and mercilessly efficient.

His pass-run option off the single wing sweep may have been the toughest play in football to stop. It made an All-American out of a player like Bob Stransky, who couldn't run very hard and barely could throw a spiral. But he could do what had to be done on those single wing sweeps which was follow the interference, throw the short pass to the quarterback drifting out into the flat and, most importantly, know when to do what. Most single wing tailbacks were run or pass-oriented on the option. Stransky's greatest asset was that he wasn't. You knew a Zack Jordan would pull up and pass if he had any kind of a chance. And you knew a Carroll Hardy would pull in the ball and run. Both were much better athletes than Stransky. Neither was as effective a tailback.

The trap blocking which opened such gapping lanes for the fullback spin series was another easy-to-watch-but-tough-to-stop feature of Ward's single wing. Especially with guys like John Wooten doing the trapping and bulls like John Bayuk busting up and through with the ball.

And, when Ward, after repeated threats which generally didn't materialize, finally did go to a multiple offense, his attack got even better. The man whose presence convinced Ward that the time had come to really go to a multiple offense (previously, Ward's version of the multiple was to line up out of the huddle in a T then shift to the single wing) was Boyd Dowler, a 6-5 stringbean who could throw and catch well, run adequately and, as a blocker, occassionally tangle up a defender by falling somewhere in his path. A good T-formation ballhandler and dropback passer off that formation and a great receiver as a single wing blocking back, Dowler led the Buffaloes to an Orange Bowl championship as a rookie. A year later, in 1957, the Buffs led the nation in rushing offense with an average 322.4 yards per game and were second in total offense at 415.2.

So offense was never a problem for Ward despite the increasing mutters of discontent about his "horse-and-buggy single wing" which grew and grew and grew and finally helped get him fired.

No coach is perfect and Ward certainly wasn't an exception to that rule. He had two glaring weaknesses which finally did him in.

He didn't pay as much attention to the defense as he did to the offense. His defenses weren't poor, certainly. But they didn't measure up to his offense.

He could have remedied this by having a good defensive coach on his staff, giving him the assignment to do that job and then letting him do it.

But Dal's approach to coaching was pretty much a one-man show. He coached and the assistants stood around and didn't speak unless they were spoken to — by the boss. It was frustrating for them because he had some good ones who wanted to do more. But he believed in his system and assistants were there basically to be seen and not heard.

So, at the end of 11 years — and that's about as long as a coach can last unless he does some spectacular things in the last half of that period — Ward was fired.

Unfairly. Because you're supposed to get fired if you don't win. And Ward won. Pretty consistently. The reasons set forth by the CU board of regents were vague. Like "for the good of the team and program." Nothing definite. You could read any character attack you wanted into the board's charges. Ward could have been whatever bad thoughts you wanted to believe. Because you couldn't find any reasons from his players, past and present. And you couldn't find any reasons from his fellow staff members. And you still can't today!

So what kind of a man was Ward?

Not what he seemed, but not in the typical tradition of today's Madison Avenue-image-oriented person who always shows a good face to the public no matter what his private personality might be.

Ward, to the contrary, was a gruff, blunt, undiplomatic man who shot straight from the hip. No baloney. He said what he thought and, if what he thought wasn't what you thought, he didn't try to soften it for you. You could call him abrasive, if you didn't like him.

But not many people who knew him disliked him. Because he was an honest person. He was hard to get to know. Didn't warm up to strangers quickly. Not many people do — and most of them are fools or salesmen.

Once Dal accepted you as a friend, though, you could do no wrong insofar as he was concerned. Slow to accept you, yes. But once you made it, you had a life membership in his club. And, conversely, if he didn't like you, you could do nothing right so forget about trying to win your way into his circle.

One example of this personality trait of Dal's which stands out vividly in my memory, and which illustrates it perfectly, involved two sophomore fullbacks on his 1954 team. Bayuk, a stocky, powerful blockbuster from Salida, and Jack Becker, a big, rangy ramrod

YOU'VE GOT TO HAVE TALENT

A group of his Boulder friends chipped in and bought Dal Ward a color TV following the 1957 season and to keep the presentation ceremony from being too sentimental I was asked to do an imitation of Dal on the sideline. This particular gesture was some kind of a signal to the quarterback but I can't remember what it was. Or maybe his shorts had gotten twisted.

from Yankton, S.D. Both were cocky, confident athletes. Neither hesitated to tell anyone who would listen how good they were. And both were good running fullbacks — Bayuk with more power, Becker with more speed and breakaway threat.

Neither was a subtle young man, either as a runner or conversationalist. I don't know how and where Dal formed his personal opinion of both but he liked John and didn't like Jack. (And don't let anyone tell you personal likes and dislikes don't sneak into all head coaches' evaluations of their personnel!)

Bayuk, to Ward, could do no wrong. Becker could do no right. Especially in practice where the head coach is all-powerful. Whenever Bayuk made a mistake, Dal would take off his cap, scratch his head and gently reproach John thusly, "No, no Johnny. That's not right. Do it this way." And he'd show him. Whenever Becker made a mistake, it produced a roar of rage and the prompt command, "Start lapping!" Laps around the practice field were the penalties of making mistakes and my memory of Jack Becker's career at CU was an endless succession of laps around the practice field. To Jack's credit, he accepted his role and did his jogging with a minimum of complaining — although he never understood why he was always jogging and Bayuk wasn't. Neither did Bayuk but he was too smart to wonder out loud.

But this was Ward's way. There were no in-betweens with him. You were either his friend. Or he didn't recognize you. And this can produce a lot of non-friends and if you have enough of these you don't need any real enemies.

The major rap against Ward by his detractors was that he was a bigot. Didn't have enough blacks on his squad. But Frank Clarke was a regular in 1955 and John Wooten came along the next year and became an All-American after three years as a regular. Both think highly of Ward today and I doubt that you could get either to acknowledge one bad thing about Dal.

But Ward, as I have tried to point out, didn't believe in tokenism, either insofar as friendship was concerned or insofar as darkening the roster of a football squad. He didn't have many blacks on his squad and this opened the door for his enemies to fire him.

One incident which occurred during the 1957 Orange Bowl trip was certainly used against Dal and, in my opinion, it was unfair. The post-game team party was held then, as it still is today, at the Indian Creek Country Club in Miami Beach. Until Jan. 1, 1957, no black had ever entered that club except as an employee. Clarke and Wooten were on the CU team and were the first blacks to ever enter Indian Creek as guests. But Orange Bowl committee members urged Ward to ask the two men to leave as quickly as possible and even arranged for a prominent black Miami doctor to arrange for their entertainment once they had left the country club. Ward went along with the request and passed it on to the two players. They weren't really excited about staying in a place that included 1948 Dixiecrat presidential candidate Strom Thurmond as a member of the welcoming line. So they went to the club and left as soon as the awards ceremony was over. And had a great time being shown much brighter parts of Miami Beach than Indian Creek Country Club. But time has a way of distorting incidents and by firing time in 1958, the story was that Ward personally kept these two players out of the club. Untrue? Completely! But it had an impact on the regential considerations which were to affect Ward's life so drastically in February of 1959.

So what kind of man is Dal Ward?

He acted tough but was soft inside. When you first met him, you were half scared of him. I'm sure all his freshmen and sophomore players were. But once you got to know him, he was easy. In fact, one of his coaching weaknesses was that once his men recognized this — and most of them were smart enough to absorb this knowledge by the time they were seniors — they took advantage of his kindness. Ward's best teams were sophomore-dominated. Like his 1956 club which went to and won the Orange Bowl. Some of his most disappointing were senior-dominated. Like the same group when they were seniors in 1958 and finished 6-4, losing their last two games to Colorado A&M and Air Force in big upsets and being the straws which finally broke Dal's back.

He's the kind of guy who didn't much recognize me for most of the first two years I was sports information director at CU. But once he accepted me as a friend, I had it made. The only name he knew me by during those first two years was, "Shorty." He still calls me that occasionally. I call him one of the best friends I've ever had and one of the finest men I've ever known and I'm proud to go on record with this statement.

So much for Dal Ward. He was called upon to lead CU out of the bushes and he did. It wasn't exactly a Hiroshima or Nagasaki he bequeathed to his successor, Sonny Grandelius. Instead, it was the best freshman squad in the history of the school to that time, one which was to include two All-Americans and form the nucleus of a Big Eight championship three years later.

So much for Dal Ward. A damned good coach and a hell of a great guy. Most of them are!

ENTER THE ALL-AMERICAN BOY—SONNY GRANDELIUS

Dal Ward had led CU out of the wilderness and almost to — but not into — the big time. The Buffaloes were on the verge of national prominence several times but always got shaded by Oklahoma in a cliff-hanger so it was always almost-but-not-quite and that wasn't good enough.

So the search began for the man who could take the program all the way. A search committee made up of athletic director Harry Carlson, assistant to the president Don Saunders and business school professor Bill Stanton didn't have to search very hard. Because the man found them. And ended the search almost before it began, leaving such promising candidates as Dave Nelson, Bob Blackman and Bill Yeoman at the starting gate waiting for it to open.

The young man, wearing the armor and good looks of a white knight, was Sonny Grandelius and he had what the hungry CU fans wanted. The perfect image. Boy from the wrong side of the tracks who made good in a big way at the state university. Good looking. Modest. Some professional playing experience. An impressive assistant coaching record at his own school. The committee didn't waste any time interviewing anyone else. It was Sonny's job and let's all hear it for the All-American boy who is going to lead us into the throne room and do it in a big time way that all of us CU fans will hail. Hail the conqueror! Here comes Sonny! Gangway, Big Eight! (by now Oklahoma State was a member.)

Sonny was out of Michigan State by way of Muskegon, was an All-American halfback for the Spartans in 1951, swept all the major awards at that school for athletics and academics and made all the proper post-season scenes like the Shrine East-West game, Hula Bowl and College All-Star game. After a hitch in the army in the Korean War, he played one year for the New York Football Giants then joined the Michigan State staff and had been backfield coach for four years before taking the CU job.

Sonny didn't waste any time introducing the CU faithful to the big time. Big time contributing, that is. In Ward's final year, the Denver Buff Club, determined to help their coach reach the summit, held an emotional meeting in Denver in which they pledged their massive support to give CU enough money to afford the scholarships which were necessary to produce the team which could defeat Oklahoma, not just come close. After appropriate remarks from the leaders of the meeting, a Denver stockbroker and one of Ward's closest friends jumped to his feet and pledged $100. Big deal! He spent more than that to park his car just off Seventeenth street each month. That set the tone of the pledges and the whopping amount of $9,000 was pledged that night. About two pumps of an oil well produced that much for Oklahoma and there were a lot of oil wells behind Wilkinson's all-winning program. To add insult to injury, barely more than $6,000 of the $9,000 was ever collected.

At Sonny's first meeting with the CU men of means, he calmly and authoritatively told them about the Michigan State program, why it was one of the nation's finest, how the same thing could be done at CU and what it would cost them — $50,000. The few oldtimers who had remained aboard after the Ward dismissal turned white but the new faces who had rallied to the cause of the new leader laid a lot of "Here, Heres" on Sonny and everybody took the rubber bands off their billfolds and $38,000 was pledged in a few weeks. And collected. The surge to the summit was underway and that calm, confident, handsome figure in the front of the boat was Sonny Grandelius. He knew where he was going and how to get there.

What kind of a man was Sonny?

First of all, I want it understood that I admired him. I never had the same feeling of warmth for him that I had for Ward and others who followed. But I admired his confidence and his ability to think and act big. He knew how to work with those "Chinamen" they still talk about in Oklahoma. I have always preferred to call them "Big Cigars."

I think that the first characteristic about Sonny which impressed me was his ability to use a negative approach, (which should have turned off the recipient completely,) to his advantage. For example, early in his CU career at a typical get-together at the coach's house following a home game, one of the biggest of the Big Cigars walked up to Sonny who had taken up a position in his kitchen and dropped a couple of coaching cliches on Sonny. Sonny, with a proper sneer, promptly told the Big Cigar that he didn't know what he was talking about and would he just leave the coaching to the coaches. The man, who should have been horribly offended, accepted the rebuke almost gratefully.

Same thing happened with a Denver sportswriter who quoted Sonny, accurately, in a post-game comment as saying a man had played a "helluva game." Don't ever use profanity in any remarks you attribute to me, exploded Sonny the following Monday. The writer, who normally would have been driven into a rage by this type of reproach, apologized and obeyed the order.

And in contrast to Ward, who seemed tough but wasn't, Grandelius had the public image of a cherub but actually was a tough, demanding coach. No player took advantage of him. Nobody was good enough that he had his job secured no matter what did or did not happen.

Some examples? The weather was horrible during Sonny's first spring practice. Rain and-or snow for much of the first two weeks. When the first Saturday came, Folsom Stadium was in no condition for the first full scrimmage of the spring. So, call it off, right? Wrong!

Sonny took his squad into the fieldhouse where he'd had the groundskeepers plow up the first two inches of the concrete-hard clay and dirt. The game scrimmage went as scheduled and it was one of the roughest ever for a CU squad. But it set the tone of Sonny's coaching approach and his teams were always excellently conditioned and extremely tough, physically and mentally.

Example number two. The star fullback of that 1959 team was Chuck Weiss, a big, tough junior from Minnesota who had been the starter for Ward as a sophomore the year before. Weiss banged up a knee early in the 1959 campaign. Not a bad injury but painful enough to keep him out of practice for a week. He missed a game and when he returned to practice the following Monday he was on the third team and stayed there all week and didn't play the next Saturday even though he was ready. That example let everyone know that he'd better be prepared to have to battle his way back up the depth chart if he ever missed practice for any reason. "Take a salt tablet and gut it out," was Sonny's philosophy on injuries. He got his opportunity to start at Michigan State when the regular ahead of him injured a leg. Sonny never gave up the starting job.

Sonny lost his first three games at CU, the third one by 42-12 to Oklahoma. No CU coaches ever seem to get off well. There was a feeling of panic setting in among Sonny's young assistants. One of the older ones even went so far as to suggest the development of a "disaster defense" designed to hold the score down. Sonny almost killed him on the spot. And maybe should have. Our way will win, so let's forget about everything else and start winning, he growled. His only concession was to switch to a shotgun formation to give his young quarterback, Gale Weidner, more time to find his receivers.

By the end of the season the Buffaloes, en route to a 5-5 finish, were in contention for an Orange Bowl bid - the conference runnerup got the nod that season. But the Buffs lost a bitter 14-12 game to Nebraska on a bitterly-cold day at Lincoln to end that bid.

No matter. Grandeluis' program was off to an excellent start.

What kind of a coach was he?

Probably not as deeply skilled in the technical aspects of coaching football as any other CU head coach, before or since. Sonny was an administrator. He assembled an outstanding staff — as good a one as we've ever had at CU. And let them do the coaching. He prowled the practice field, checking out every coaching area constantly. But he had time to visit with any Big Cigar or press member or faculty member who visited practice. His practices were tough, excellently organized. So were his teams. He was a good coach.

So where did he break down? How could a coach who was that good get fired less than three months after winning the only Big Eight grid championship in the school's history?

Sonny's biggest shortcoming was his impatience. He was a young man in a hurry. He'd always achieved every goal he'd set for himself, within his own time schedule. At Colorado, he stepped on some toes — of some administrators and of other coaches around the nation. He was going to be a great coach with a great program within a short period of time. Get out of my way, everybody, because here I come! And so the sniping began. From other coaches who lost recruits to Sonny's staff. From CU officials who were frightened about the cold efficiency of this young man in a hurry. And Sonny was in too much of a hurry to stop and take stock of the situation. Had he eased off slightly, he'd have continued on target at nearly the same timetable. But there was no slowing down and the result was that his program was being investigated by the NCAA while his team was in the process of winning the Big Eight championship in 1961. Rumors were running wild as the Buffaloes prepared for the Orange Bowl game with Louisiana State. You'd have thought CU was the worst culprit in the history of NCAA investigations. It wasn't, by a good margin. But the CU administration which by now was frightened, almost horrified, by the machine that Sonny was establishing, as he had been directed to by them, decided it was time to be rid of this All-American boy who, to them, had taken on some of the characteristics of Attila the Hun. They appointed their own investigator to supplement the NCAA's.

And so when the fairly modest charges were proven, instead of the "bravos and well-dones" which penalized football coaches who have won normally receive, Sonny got fired. Coldly and mercilessly and almost jubilantly. Get out of here, young fellow, you gave us more than we wanted.

Don't get me wrong. Sonny had faults. He wasn't perfect by a long way. None of us are.

I guess what I'm trying to say is that Sonny Grandelius was hired to do a job, did it and got fired. Got fired because a lot of people got frightened because he was too good at getting what he wanted. And who knows what he might have wanted next?

One last comment about Sonny. He was somewhat lucky in his arrival into the Big Eight. You have to be lucky in some ways to accomplish a lot in a hurry and Sonny was fortunate in that he was in the Big Eight when both the Oklahoma and Nebraska football programs were at their lowest ebb in post-World War II history. CU's chief contenders for the Big Eight championship during Sonny's three years as head coach were Missouri and Kansas, coached by Dan Devine and Jack Mitchell. Both these coaches were adept at assembling very good groups of talent. Neither, however, was very adept at winning championships.

So much for Sonny. He was asked to bring CU into the big time and he did. Right smack in the middle of it with a nationally ranked team and the makings of a dynasty. But he was a victim of his own impatience. So he won the championship and lost his job. Not many coaches have got that achievement on their service records. It takes a lot of doing.

So exit Sonny. Leaving the CU football program like the atom bomb left Hiroshima and Nagasaki. A smoking pile of ashes and a lot of charred bodies. And there wasn't any saviour in sight!

A YEAR TO FORGET—
BUD DAVIS

In contrast to the previous two coaching searches, this one never left home. There was no seeking out a tough, seasoned warrior like Dallas Ward or a bright, young Lochinvar like Sonny Grandelius. No more of that stuff right now. Let's just lie here and lick our wounds, was the general attitude of the administration. Maybe we'll die, thought some administrators, hopefully. But it turned out that the football program lived to flourish again. Although many of those administrators' CU careers died. And those deaths helped breath the football program back to life. A fitting irony.

So the administration reached into its own ranks for the man to lead CU's post-Grandelius football program as the skies, so Sonny a few short months earlier, now had turned to battleship gray. And a sinking battleship at that. Giving the job to Bud Davis was like making an aviation cadet solo in a burning plane. There was no way he could land safely: the only question was how bad would the crash be.

It was worse than it needed to be. Because of a combination of several things, all of them bad. First of all, the Big Eight conference had to jump in and pump some more bullets into the dead body, wiping out some players who hadn't been wiped out by the NCAA. Then CU got into the act and made some peculiar eligibility interpretations which were tougher than the Big Eight rules. Exit some more men.

Then Bud Davis finalized the fiasco by going almost exclusively into the high school ranks to put together his coaching staff. Maybe he couldn't have done anything else in view of the circumstances. The CU football program, in 1962, wasn't exactly the brightest spot on the map for anyone to jump into.

But it has always been my impression that if you shake a tree, ring a bell, blow a whistle or shout, "Who needs a job?" the one thing you'd get the most of would be assistant football coaches. Bud didn't do any of these things. Due in part because it was getting late in the winter. Spring practice was only a few days away. A staff had to be assembled and Bud's friends were the most available people. And most of them had fine coaching backgrounds. But they were practically all totally high school oriented and there is simply too much difference in the two types of coaching for an all-high school staff to be effective in college. The only man on the staff with college experience was Dal Ward, Bud's old CU coach, who was the first assistant named. But Dal had been in exile in the physical education department for three years and, understandably, lost some of his fire during that time. Besides, Dal had been a head coach for 11 years and it's tough to return to being an assistant after being the boss. So he didn't help as much as he might have. And, anyway, he was constantly and completely overruled by the other assistants who saw him merely as a good friend of Bud's whom Bud had rewarded by bringing him out of the obscurity of the volley ball courts and handball classes.

And, furthermore, this was a bright young coaching staff that was going to revolutionize CU football through the use of the forward pass, a weapon that Ward will suspect to his dying day and one which he used only on third-and-longs and then it was mostly a short dump-off to the blocking back slipping out into the near flat. Oil up your eyeballs, CU fans, exuded the new CU coaches. You are gonna see that old ball flying through the air like you been wanting and like you ain't never seen before! And it did. It flew through the air. And into the ground. And into other teams' arms. And, occasionally, into the stands. But very seldom did it get carried into the end zone, which is, the old conservatives and even some new liberals say, really what it's all about.

Two other members of Bud's staff, Ed Farhat and Don Stimack, were carryovers from Sonny's staff but they had been hired in the late winter just before the holocaust hit so they really had had no college experience except having been through a firing almost before they got their bags unpacked. Which, you've got to admit, is a vital piece of experience in the life of any college coach. But it's like a preparation for death not life and is not recommended as part of a young coach's early training. In fact, this experience should be delayed as long as possible.

So it was a brand new look to CU football. The pitchers were way ahead of the hitters in spring practice. And stayed ahead of them through the fall. Which might be okay in baseball. But it's a disasterous way to run a football program.

Let me interject something else at this point. It is a modern college tradition that everything must change when a coaching change has been made. Scrap Dal Ward and you must also scrap the single wing(even though it led the nation in offense a year earlier) and the quick kick(even though it may be the most effective offensive play in the history of football.) You must also scrap those crumby-looking old gold uniforms. So enter Sonny Grandelius and the winged-T. And no more tailbacks and quick kicks. And new black jerseys with metallic silver headgears and pants. And modernistic horns on the headgears, more like something created by a Detroit automobile designer than by a buffalo connoisseur. But the uniforms were a marked improvement even though the offense may not have been! The Buffaloes did a lot of punting — but on fourth down, which the fans will grudgingly accept most of the time — and they certainly didn't lead the Big Eight, let alone the nation, in offense. But the important thing was that changes had been made.

When the Buffaloes opened their 1960 home season against a Baylor team coached for the first time by John Bridgers, who had come to Waco from the Baltimore Colt staff, Bill Henderson, the wise old Bear business manager who had watched a lot of head coaches come and go in one of college football's all-time great gridiron graveyards, chuckled as he sat in Folsom Stadium with Kayo Lam, whose credentials were similar in experience and longevity to Henderson's, "There are two things a new coach has got to do," said Henderson. "Change the uniforms and make his men run out of the huddle."

And so the Buffaloes of 1962 emerged from their dressing room for the season opener clad in bright yellow. Bright yellow all the way, I mean. Headgears, jerseys, pants. Sunflower gold, the sporting goods salesman called it. But I've seen a lot more yellow sunflowers than I have gold ones.

True to the promises of their coaches, the Buffaloes came out throwing. And even though Davis' debut matched those of Ward's and Grandelius' (he got whipped by Utah, 37-21), he had a much more sensational beginning — Buffalo Bill Harris took a first quarter kickoff at Salt Lake City and ran 97 yards into the Redskin end zone.

The Buffaloes should have ended the season on that one play. But they still had nine games and more than 50 minutes left to play. And most of those minutes were to be tough ones. Davis did, however, have a shorter opening losing streak than either of his more illustrious two immediate predecessors. Luck again played a part in this achievement. Through a scheduling quirk, CU played a Big Eight opponent on the second Saturday of the season. The luck was that it was Kansas State, a team busy taking its coach, personable Doug Weaver, to an early grave and one which was more ept at losing than CU. After all, K-State had been losing for eons and CU was just an upstart at this business — it only had a two-game losing streak. And one of those was in a bowl.

K-State had always had the capability to go a decade without winning although the Wildcats really never got that proficient. But they were un-losable-to on that opening day in Boulder in 1962 and the Buffaloes, with Harris carrying the ball on almost every running play — 35 times for 156 yards, the most carries by a back in the nation that season — managed to nip the 'Cats, 6-0. K-State played a big role in the loss, however, as they inevitably did in those days, failing to score on three different occasions in the fourth quarter when they launched all 18 of their plays from inside the CU 20. It took an almost superhuman effort by their quarterback to prevent one score. On third-and-goal at the one, he somehow managed to take the snap, back out one step and fall flat on his back, leaving K-State with a fourth-and-goal at the five and there was no way they could make that kind of yardage, even against a CU defense which was to turn into a sieve a week later for the rest of the season. But, hang the future! For the moment, Bud Davis' CU sunflower-type Buffaloes were the undefeated and untied and unscored-upon leaders of the Big Eight. Thanks to the schedule and the Kansas State offense.

If I tend to be both over-humorous and over-sarcastic about the 1962 season, it is through the blessing of time which has erased most of the unpleasant memories and all the pain. Bud Davis was, and still is, one of my dearest friends. He was, and is, a great guy. Super-intelligent. Ambitious. Effective. And he's a better writer than I am, too. Bud got a bad rap on his coaching ability. He was one of the few thoroughbreds on his own staff. Subsequent events and careers have proven this. He is the only member of his staff to have moved onward and upward once out of the debris of the 1962 football season. The rest of those coaches, for the most part, returned to where they came from or to a similar level somewhere else and remain there today. Davis, as this was written, was the very effective and respected president of Idaho State University and I, among a great many people both athletic and non-athletic, would love to welcome him back to CU as our president some day. Assuming, of course, that college presidents continue to move in and out with almost the same frequency, and in some cases, more, as football coaches. (No offense to you, Dr. Thieme, you're a good guy and I hope you're with us a long time. But if you do decide to leave, I'd hope Bud Davis gets the next shot at the job.)

I would also like to mention at this point that there is not — and certainly was not then — much compassion in the world. For example, CU president Quigg Newton and the CU board of regents thought they were doing the right thing — and, naively, thought they were blazing a trail which would produce responsibility in future football programs the nation over — in firing Sonny Grandelius because he had wronged and been caught. A lofty thought. And a totally idealistic one. Hey, colleges, start firing those cheating coaches and we'll have a lot better situation in a hurry! But it was not to be. CU was the object of scorn among the nation's college administrators, including those in the athletic departments. To my knowledge, Quigg Newton received only one letter from another college president congratulating him for being part of a courageous action. But no other president wrote. But, then, so many of them are like so many athletic directors — they sit in their offices and quiver and shake and tremble at the thoughts of what this afternoon or tomorrow or next week or next month or next year might bring in the way of problems which they really don't want to cope with. Being a college president is supposed to be a nice job. As a reward for being a good old professor of humanities. Or for being a hot-shot fund-raiser. Or whatever. But it's supposed to be a Mr. Chip-sy form of retirement from the wars, not a re-introduction to the firing line at an age when the fires of passion have been banked rather than re-fueled. And the same thing goes for athletic directors, doubled.

At any rate, Newton and CU were looked upon as fools for doing the unexpected. Not only did they not give their errant coach a raise and enshrine him as a martyr, they actually had the ingratitude to fire him!

Let's talk about Bud Davis as a coach. First of all, he had been a highly-successful football coach after serving as a reserve quarterback on Dal Ward's early CU teams. Davis has some funny experiences about those undergraduate days but he has written about them already and he's a better writer than I am and, besides, he's going to write his autobiography some day and I don't want to beat him into print with anything. And, also, he just might be my president some day and I'd hate to have him holding that kind of a grudge against me. He's going to have enough of one against me because of what I'm writing about 1962 right here.

Bud's teams at Rapid City, S.D. were ranked second in that state for three straight years and his 1959 Greeley team won the Colorado state championship. In post-season playoffs not via a poll. His 5-year prep coaching record was 32-10 and he left coaching to become alumni director at CU in 1960 when Ken Penfold, a fine director and Dal Ward loyalist, couldn't take it any longer and left his alma mater to become a prosperous business man in Boulder. Bud returned to CU for two reasons: (1) to become alumni director (and he became a fine one), and (2) to complete work on his doctorate in education administration. In earning his doctorate, he wrote a comprehensive history of CU which ranks as one of the finest books written about any university anywhere.

So he had proper credentials although coaches and critics the nation over, sounding like the salesmen in the opening scene of "The Music Man," kept trumpeting, "But he doesn't know the territory!" He *did* know the territory! But he didn't know how to assemble a college coaching staff. And that, more than anything else, did him in.

However, in the eyes of college coaches all over the country, Bud was a dirty dog who had helped kill a fellow coach, never mind the charges, Sonny couldn't have been all that bad and, besides, there but for the grace of the NCAA could have gone I. Then he compounded the crime by stepping into Sonny's shoes almost before the body had grown cold. We'll show this upstart what it's all about, they muttered. Doug Weaver was probably too nice a guy to join this chorus and, besides, his team didn't have the wherewithal to destroy anybody except their loved ones and even those deaths were caused more by sorrow and malnutrition rather than by violence.

The 1962 Big Eight scores tell how effectively Bud Davis and his Sunflowers got it poured to them. Kansas, 35-6. Oklahoma State, 36-16. Iowa State, 57-19. (Iowa State!!!) Nebraska, 31-6. Oklahoma, 62-0. Missouri, 57-0. To give you an idea of how faint the quality of mercy was that fall, Bud Wilkinson raced the clock to make it 35-0 at the half! And he wasn't going for any national championship. In fact, he might have been better off not to have been so impressive because then he might not have got called to play Bear Bryant and Lee Roy Jordan and Alabama in the Orange Bowl and wouldn't have gotten tromped by them. Wilkinson poured it to a lot of Iowa States and Kansas States and Bud Davis' and J.B. Whitworths during his reign but he never beat Bear Bryant in a bowl.

And so Bud Davis got his come-uppance from the coaching fraternity. You might say he got initiated and black-balled at the same meeting.

But what kind of a man was Bud Davis?

A good man. Maybe a great one. Intelligent. Articulate. Literate. Honest. Naive.

Maybe the other coaches were jealous of him.

There's an old saying that you make steel by torturing iron. Bud Davis came out of that 1962 smelter with a lot of blue steel showing in him. His career since then has proven it.

What kind of a man is he? My friend. A hell of a man. And a

good coach. Most of them are!

Fittingly, Bud, unlike most fired coaches, went out on a winning note. His team finished the season with a glorious triumph over Air Force. This was one nice guy who didn't finish last! And we'll talk about that Air Force game, more, later on in this book.

ENTER THE MESSIAH— EDDIE CROWDER

Bud Davis inherited a football program which had just been atom bombed and promptly produced a hydrogen bomb which he then managed to explode accidentally. CU football at this point was Valley Forge, the first days of the Battle of the Bulge, Roy Riegels in the open in the Rose Bowl, Wake Island without John Wayne, Little Big Horn before the ground turned white after all those Indians kept coming and coming and coming. It was a delivery in which the doctor lost the baby but saved the afterbirth. It was nothing but a heap of ashes. Without even any smoke coming out of the pile.

At this point in its football life, CU didn't need a coach. It needed Christian Barnard. With a heart transplant. And a kidney transplant. And a lung transplant. And a few other transplants which hadn't been invented yet.

What it got was a Messiah. Waiting in the wings was the man who could save it all. Without a surgeon's instruments. Without miracles. Without new techniques. But with what CU had been looking for all along. The proper combination of intelligence, motivation, super-energy, fantastic determination and the right playing, coaching and personal background. There was nothing miraculous about the CU recovery. It was almost never needed because Eddie Crowder was Harry Carlson's first choice for the head job in 1959 but had taken himself out of consideration because he didn't feel he was old enough. Ironically, he was only a year younger than Sonny Grandelius, who was two months short of being 29 when he got the job but gave his age as 29 because it sounded better than 28 and little things like that can make a difference with a screening committee.

Eddie Crowder wasn't Dal Ward. He was too young, at 32. He wasn't Sonny Grandelius. He wasn't that good looking. And he certainly wasn't Bud Davis. But he had parts of all three of them in him. Like Ward he had been schooled under a great head coach. In fact, under two great coaches, Earl "Red" Blaik at Army and Bud Wilkinson at Oklahoma, the latter having been schooled by Ward and

Bierman at Minnesota. Like Grandelius, Crowder had been an All-American as an undergraduate and still is considered one of the finest ball-handling and playcalling quarterbacks in the history of modern football after a superb career at Oklahoma at the beginning of the Wilkinsonian dynasty. And like Davis, Crowder had superior intelligence and savoir faire. He knew what to do and when and how to do it. The time was here. And so was Crowder. Hallelujah! We are saved!

But there was no miracle ahead for the Buffaloes. Eddie got off to the same start as the other three coaches I've worked with who preceded him. But he did have a few more extenuating circumstances. In the first place he had inherited the worst disaster of anyone. And, in the second place, he got a bad scheduling break. CU's first opponent, Southern California, which had been wallowing in the depths when the 2-game series was put together seven years earlier, was now the defending national champion. And, thirdly, the Kansas State game had moved back a notch, to the third Saturday of the CU season.

So Crowder was properly inducted, 14-0 by USC in the rain and tall grass in Folsom Stadium then, 41-6 by Oregon State in the gloom and near-darkness of Portland's Multonomah Stadium which would make a better mausoleum than a football stadium. But just when things were getting grim, up jumped - or rather, up laid down - good old Kansas State. And the Wildcats after uncharacteristically going in front 7-0 in the first quarter, reverted to form and lost, 21-7.

A week later, the Buffaloes stomped Oklahoma State, 25-0, and it looked as though Crowder, indeed, was a miracle man. But CU ran out of Kansas States and Oklahoma States and into the grim reality of the Nebraskas and the Oklahomas and the Missouris. But there at the end of the line was Air Force, a team the Buffs could always match physically, even in down years. Crowder, however, as we've already discussed in mentioning his opening game, has never been blessed with great luck and just as he was getting his Buffaloes primed for the Falcons and an upbeat finish to the season, Lee Harvey Oswald pulled the trigger on John Kennedy and the whole thing got postponed for two weeks while the nation immersed itself in grief and funeral paggeantry. Grief, hell! Anyone who hadn't gone through the 1962 season, Saturday after Saturday, death after death, didn't know the real meaning of grief. All that stuff coming out on the television tubes was just a lot of superficial sorrow compared to the miseries of 1962. Anyway, by the time they got the never-to-be-extinguished gas jet lit in Arlington, nearly everybody except Pete Rozelle's Hessians had forgotten about football. And Rozelle's mercenaries didn't count because they didn't even take time off for the grieving. So we closed the

1963 season with a unique doubleheader at Air Force, a varsity football game at 1:30 followed by the opening game of the basketball season at 4:30. I suppose the Air Force had more going for it than we did. Maybe they were winning it for their dead commander-in-chief. Whatever, they scraped it out 17-14 but we had to give them a lot of help. Like a Larry Portis starting a fight when he wasn't even on the field and getting our best defensive back, Leon Mavity, who wasn't even in the fight kicked out in the melee which ended the first half. And we still weren't dead even after Air Force's great competitor Terry Isaacson punctured the zone vacated by the early-departed Mavity with a series of third and fourth-down completions to lead the Falcons to a touchdown and the final score late in the fourth quarter. But CU, with Noble Milton eating up big chunks of yardage, roared right back to the AFA 34 with plenty of time left to score and win. But on a first down play from there, QB Frank Cesarek came up with one of the great fumbles of all time. He not only bobbled the snap, he threw it right over his center's hands and into those of an unsuspecting Air Force linebacker named Joe Rodwell's arms. Rodwell, who was finishing a completely undistinguished career which saw him begin as a quarterback then work his way down to middle linebacker, reacted in true Air Force style. He juggled it and fell down. But it was his ball and Air Force's game and he was a hero. Like, for example, Colin Kelly. Oh, where have you gone, Crazy Legs Cesarek? And Left Hook Larry Portis? And all those other heavy-legged stalwarts who suffered through a 2-and-8 1963 but who helped plant the seeds which were to grow into a strong, healthy program in a few short years.

So what kind of man, then, was Eddie Crowder? Or, is Eddie Crowder. He's still here, you know. And, as such, is the most difficult of my coaches to discuss objectively. Not that I've been objective about any of them. But this one is still signing my pay checks! He's the only one who took over as athletic director, too. Dal Ward wouldn't have wanted to be bothered and, besides, he was an organization man who worked within the structure. And he pretty much got everything he wanted without having to deal with the nitpicking daily details which clutter the lives and careers of most athletic directors. Sonny Grandelius was too impatient. Wouldn't wait for his turn and lost his own job before the other one came open.

Bud Davis, I'm convinced, would have stepped up into the athletic director's job in 1965 when Carlson retired and would have been content to give up coaching. After all, he'd given it up once before and discovered that he could live without it. Most coaches think they can't but a lot of them would really be better off if they discovered this before they get too old. Davis might even have re-appointed Dal Ward head football coach at this point but it would have required one regent to die before that could have happened. That regent has since died but it's pointless to speculate about Ward's re-incarnation as a head coach because Bud's plans never got off the ground and Ward suffered a near-fatal heart attack in 1965 just before Carlson's retirement.

Eddie Crowder, then, was in the right spot at the right time. And that was not necessarily an accident since he was the right man at the right time and I feel that he could have had the CU head job in 1959 had he elected to go after it hard. Had he taken the job then he might not have been the right man at the right time because the man who took over in 1959 had to bear the cross of enmity from the many Dal Ward followers who were rightfully bitter after their hero was ousted.

But Crowder had the proper mentality and outlook and perception to take advantage of being the right man in the right place at the right time when the athletic directorship opened. There was nothing revolutionary about his getting the job. Two deserving old-timers in the CU athletic department, Lam and track coach Frank Potts, who had been Carlson's closest advisors for a long time, were both nearing retirement age. It would have been a token appointment, though, in recognition of long and loyal and effective service and tokenism wasn't what CU needed at that point. Leading the department was a young man's job and Crowder was the young man who had the credentials. After all, hadn't he led CU out of desolation and into a 6-2-2 season in three years? So Eddie took over with the complete approval of practically everyone. Sure, there were some nervous people who feared the consequences which might accompany the directorship getting into the hands of the football coach. But, let's face one basic fact of intercollegiate athletic life: whether you like it or not, or whether you approve or not, or whatever, the football program and the football coach dominate an athletic department. Athletic directors who aren't head football coaches do a lot of shaking and twitching and worrying about their jobs. About whether or not their football coach is cheating. If he is they can't do anything about it except maybe get fired, before or after the fact. If his coach isn't cheating, and isn't winning, he might get fired right along with his losing coach. Especially, if he's had to help appoint more than one football coach and if none of them has been very successful. Whatever the situation, the life of an athletic director isn't a very rewarding one and not many men who have been successful head football coaches are going to be happy relinquishing the spotlight and the accompanying adulation of the football job for the out-of-the-limelight paper-shuffling, committee-infested existence of a director.

So Eddie Crowder became head coach-athletic director in 1965 and solved his paper-shuffling, committee-clogged, administrative-anthilling problems by a string of guys named Jack Mills and Fred Casotti, who could cope with those minor details, freeing the boss for the big decisions, like recruiting and coaching football players whose accomplishments have a far greater bearing on the life and prosperity and security of an athletic department than the greatest pure administrator who ever lived or drew up a terrific table of organization or dazzled a committee meeting with eloquence even more effective than a mainline shot of caffeine. And no one has suffered from his dual role. Some coaches, in fact, have prospered more than they deserved because of Crowder's great pains to avoid being called a mono-minded football man, oblivious of other and lesser sports.

What was there about Eddie Crowder in the beginning that impressed me — and obviously I was, and continue to be, impressed with the man. His most impressive accomplishment, I believe, was the manner in which he brought all the hostile factions together in a few brief months in early 1963. There were four fairly identifiable factions. First, there was the Dal Ward faction, still somewhat sullen because of the treatment their man had received from the board of regents and, equally infuriating, the manner in which he had been treated as a "non-person" by the administration and Sonny Grandelius (at the requirement of the administration) after he was fired. Secondly, there was the Sonny Grandelius faction, similarly furious because their man had gotten fired after winning the Big Eight championship which, after all, was what he had been brought in to do, wasn't it? Thirdly, there was the Bud Davis faction, the smallest of the four, which didn't appreciate the hasty exit he had been forced into when it became obvious that his way wasn't producing any quick results and which felt that he hadn't been given a fair chance. And, fourthly, there was an Ivy-leaguish element which didn't really care one way or the other just so long as football was suffering and down and, hopefully, maybe enshrouded in a terminal illness.

Eddie brought them all together. And made them love it! Face it, three of these four groups wanted something good to happen. The fourth didn't have sense enough to realize the positive influences a healthy and productive football program can have on a university's existence but they were smart enough to recognize that Eddie was a

A VERY SERIOUS HEAD TABLE

This was Eddie Crowder's first press conference, at the Denver Press Club, after taking the CU head job in January, 1963. On Eddie's right was his chief assistant, Rudy Feldman. On my left was Wayne Duke, who was the fairly new Big Eight Conference commissioner at the time. I am smiling because I am a fool and didn't realize it was a very serious occasion.

good man and, accordingly, one they could live with and accept once they recognized that football was too big to succumb so easily.

Eddie, naturally, had great respect for Dal Ward as a coach from the several CU-Oklahoma collisions when Dal was head man for the Buffs and Eddie was an assistant under Wilkinson. He had great respect for Dal as a man because his own coach, Wilkinson, had this same respect from his acquaintance with Dal, first as a player under him, then as a fellow head coach in the Big Eight. So Eddie welcomed Dal back aboard the CU football party. Gave him back his self-respect. Showed the world what he thought of Dallas Ward. Nobody has done more for Dal Ward than Eddie Crowder and he continues to do it today. Dal has been an assistant athletic director under Eddie and their relationship has been excellent and it has been valuable to both men. Just as any good relationship should.

And what about the new guard? The men of affluence, not allowed on the Ward wagon, who were welcomed with open arms by Sonny. There was a prominent place on Crowder's team for them, too. But bygones had to be bygones! There was no room for any old dissensions or problems on this team. There was too much to be done and not enough time to do it in to permit any petty differences. So, make peace, you Ward and Grandelius people. This is now the Crowder team and there's room on it for everybody but you've all got to pull together. And contribute together. And work together. If we are to win together. And that's what it's all about! So, welcome aboard.

The same philosophy applied to the Bud Davis people. But, realistically, there weren't any new Big Cigars in this movement. There hadn't been enough time - or victories - to produce any stampede to Bud Davis country. But there were a few converts and the new temple was open to them, too.

And what about the anti-athletics types? Most of these people were won over by Crowder quickly. An extremely intelligent and articulate person, Eddie could speak their language as well as they could speak it themselves. Here was a coach they could accept. He not only spoke the English language, he spoke it fluently. And could carry on an intelligent conversation with anyone, including them! This wasn't a sweat-shirt type coach who wore a baseball hat turned sideways. And spoke only in X's and O's. Nor was he a pretty-boy All-American type who could charm your wife at the same time he was lifting your billfold. To the contrary, this fellow looked more like a professor than a football coach. And spoke more like one than a lot of professors! Not much hair. Long, winding nose. Horn-rimmed glasses. Even smoked an occasional pipe of tobacco. Maybe he even sometimes dozed behind the clouds of smoke, as a lot of solid, dreamy professors - and an occasional athletic director - do.

So everybody could find something they liked in Eddie Crowder. And Eddie Crowder could find something he liked - and needed - in everybody. It was a perfect multi-marriage. Instant unity. Forget the past and let's four-barrel ahead. Damn the torpedos, get on with it! The CU machine is finally on track and in the right hands. There ain't nobody gonna stop us now! Hosannah! Here we come.

What kind of a man was this Crowder who had pulled everything together so quickly? A super-intelligent man. Super articulate. Super-motivated. Super-everything. He knew where he was going and how to get there. There was no quick, easy route. And once you got there you didn't stay there without expending the same day-and-night effort which got you there. It's tough to get there and tougher to stay there. Nothing that's worth anything comes easily or cheaply. That was - and is - the Crowder creed.

Any flaws in the man? Surely there must be one or two. (Be honest, Casotti. Even if he is your leader!) Sure he has some flaws. Again, there has only been one perfect man in the history of the world and He got nailed to a cross. If Eddie has one major flaw, and who is to say this has to be a flaw except a lazy man, which most of us basically are, it might be that he's too intense. Not many people can keep up the pace he sets as a normal way of life. Not many men have that big a motor in them, one without an "off" key. Most men, I feel, believe that if they can accomplish 90 percent results with 95 percent, or less, effort, they have done a very good, maybe a great, job. Eddie Crowder isn't happy with that kind of effort. He'd prefer 100 percent, or more, effort even if it meant only 91 percent results. That extra one percent of results is worth the extra effort. It might be the difference between first and second. Or something and something, no matter what. The potential improvement of results is worth the extra effort, no matter how pointless or repetitious or unpromising it might appear. This kind of personal philosophy doesn't necessarily produce a lot of affection among his staff or team members. But it produces a tremendous amount of respect and admiration and those are the basic things a leader must create if he is to be an effective leader.

Another Crowder flaw is that he might be too articulate. The average person, be he a player or an assistant coach or anybody, has a tendency to distrust anybody who is noticeably smarter than he is. Especially if the person is more articulate than him. This quality, I feel, more than anything else helped keep such a great and intelligent man as Adlai Stevenson out of the White House. It may have kept

Eddie Crowder from establishing a line of communication between himself and some of his men. And the harder he tried, the wider may have grown the credibility gap.

Intensity was a favorite Bud Wilkinson word. It probably describes Eddie Crowder better than any other single word.

And what kind of a coach is Eddie Crowder? Again, he has a little of everybody in him. His practice organization is as good as was Sonny's. He, like Ward did, does a lot of jaw-to-jaw instructing - to both players and assistants. He has a brilliant grasp of the game's strategy. A lightning-quick mind and tongue. Is more offensively concerned. After all he was an All-American quarterback, not a safety or a linebacker. But he is sharp enough to hire good defensive co-ordinators and let them co-ordinate. He spends most of his time in the offensive war room. But he can charge into that defensive room and light fires when he has to. What he does best, though, is just plain lead. He can lead in a lot of ways. By being more motivated. By being smarter. By being willing to work harder than anyone he is leading. By being able to size up a situation better than anyone else. By just plain wanting to win more than anybody else around him. By just being more intense than anybody else.

He's a great guy although, like a lot of great guys, he doesn't expose his insides to many other men. And he doesn't go around beating on his chest and telling the world what a great guy he is. To the contrary, he'd rather have you think he's a cold-blooded, hard, driving man. And he can be when the situation demands. But inside he's a soft gentle man. Like Ward was. And, like Ward, if he has a fault as a man, it's that he's too soft-hearted and too gentle once anyone gets to him. And he's more accessible than any other coach I've seen, spends more time counselling people - players, coaches, casual acquaintances, almost anybody - than he really ought to. But that's his nature. He is fanatically interested in people, their viewpoints, their problems, their lives. Will do anything he can to help anyone he knows. He's a man of contrasts. Is as quick to collect a dollar as any head coach. And they are the modern masters of that art. But, unlike a lot of today's coaches, he's generous almost to a fault. I've seen him take one of his employees - not a player, Mr. NCAA Detective - to The Regiment, one of his favorite Boulder haberdasheries - and buy him a couple hundred dollars worth of clothing almost on the spur of the moment because that man has shown him something special in the way of effort or loyalty or whatever. Not many lord masters do that for a lackey. A lot of lord masters don't even do those kinds of things for their wives.

So this is a good man. And a hell of a good coach. And a great human being. Most of them are. But not as much as this guy!

THE CONSTANT PARADE—
THE ASSISTANTS

Just as important, in their own way, to the CU football program as the five head coaches I've discussed are the assistants, most of whom have served so faithfully, some of whom have served semi-faithfully, and a few of whom have served maybe unfaithfully. But they've all served and, for the most part, served well. Assistant coaches are like cleats and hash marks and jock straps and all the other things that go along with the great game of football. You've got to have them and they have to be good or you ain't got much of a program. They're often a frustrated lot, basically satellites clustered around the perimeter of their head coach who is their sun and moon and whose good fortune is their good fortune and whose bad fortune is their bad fortune. They're the children in the coaching family and the head coach is the father and he has the option of being a tyrant, a benevolent despot, a nice guy, a buddy, God, or just about whatever he chooses to be.

The assistants do what they're told, make an occasional suggestion which may or may not be accepted, percolate or seep (depending upon their personality and-or motivation) through endless staff meetings clustered around the feet of their leader who sits serenely (most of the time) and all-powerful on his throne, go through the pleasures and pains of raising a family (in absentia most of the time because today's football season begins in mid-August with the first day of fall practice, extends through the recruiting season which begins the day after the last game and takes a semi-break only for spring practice, and ends with the last day of the recruiting season which is the day before fall practice begins), revel in the jubilation of victory, writhe in the torture of defeat, and dream of that day when they become a head coach and sit on that throne themselves, by hell, and be a really nice guy with only occasional meetings, all short, lots of victories, good, loyal and faithful and understanding supporters and all that crap.

Most of them will never make it but you've got to have a dream and all assistant coaches nurse that dream of being the boss some day in a program which produces joy and victory. Probably the best thing about assistant coaches, over and above the fact that they do important - and, for the most part, good and vital - work, is that some of them do grow into head coaches and a few of them grow into fine head coaches like Dal Ward and Eddie Crowder and other fine ones who I don't know well but who I've admired from the distance like John Bridgers, John McKay, Tommy Prothro, Jack Curtice, Lloyd Eaton, Joe Paterno, Ben Martin and a whole lot of others — these are just some of the good coaches whose paths we have run across, sometimes painfully insofar as the scoreboard was concerned but always pleasantly in that these are basically good people who make living in the world of intercollegiate football a nice experience.

I guess I've seen as many assistants flow through a program in the past 20 years as anyone in the country. It would be unfair, and incomplete, to let them pass without a mention. Some of them have been great friends, most have been good friends, and all have been dedicated men - dedicated to the great game of football and to the University of Colorado. So starts the great parade. At the last count, the number of assistant football coaches I've worked with at CU was 45. But the pace has picked up in recent years and by the time this work gets printed the number might be up to 55. You assistants who miss this book will be the first ones in this section of the next book so hang tough, don't be late for any of the meetings, and, for God's sake, don't go to sleep when they turn the lights off and start the film.

1. MARSHALL WELLS

They called him "Jumbo." Or "Big Man." Or "Marsh." He was as close to a number one assistant as Dal Ward ever had and that was because Marsh came to CU from Minnesota with Dal and in the early days at CU was Dal's closest confidant. A huge player in his undergraduate days at Minnesota (6-4, 240), Wells was a striking sight at the CU games as he prowled the sidelines like an elephant right out of Pogo, limp cigar dangling out of his mouth.

My first memory of Marshall was when I was a senior at CU in 1948, the first year for Ward and his staff. Occasionally, when a CU player was injured and needed to be helped off the field, Marshall would lumber out, gather up the wounded Buffalo in his arms and carry him off the field like a mother cradling a baby. I guess Marshall was a multi-talented coach. Maybe the only combination line coach-ambulance in the history of football.

Marshall, like his boss, was out of the old school. Football was a way of life. But life was an easy-going, pleasant affair to be lived and worked at at one's own pace. With lots of smelling the flowers stuffed into the process. Marshall loved to fish. And hunt. And play poker at the Elks Club. And coach big, hulking, linemen. But there was time for each of those activities along the way. None of this 18-hour day, 7-day week, 12-month year silliness where football is concerned. Coach like hell in the fall, go at it just as hard in the spring, recruit a little once in a while. Have a good program. And have a good time. Not a bad philosophy and it didn't produce horrible gridiron results, either.

As the big elephant on the staff, and also because he was a gentle-natured giant as most giants, thankfully, are, Marshall always took a lot of kidding from other staffmembers. Most of the time he took it with a grin. Had he not been good-natured, there might have been a lot of dead people strewn in his wake. Like Ray Jenkins. And Frank Prentup. And Fred Casotti. Among others.

I remember in 1957 when we opened the season against Washington at Seattle. Marshall worked and planned all summer long to set up a salmon fishing excursion in the Pacific after the game. Back in those days, teams stayed overnight at the scene of the road game and some sort of educational activity like a sightseeing trip up the Columbia River Basin or along Puget Sound or to Nogales, Mexico was arranged for the team after church on Sunday. The return flight home was made on Sunday afternoon. It was a good deal for everyone and I miss it somewhat but that was back in the days when football was a more casual way of life. Now it's wilder and more organized and more frantic and more everything but I love it just as much and maybe it's what might keep a man from growing old. Or looking like he's growing old. My illustrious ancestor, Count Casotti, used to say, "Wear out from the inside out. Nobody will ever know it's happening and you won't have to accept the responsibilities of growing older because you won't look like it. And you'll make a hell of a fine-looking corpse when you do hang it up."

Anyway, Marshall Wells worked his tail off getting that fishing trip lined up. Got with a fishing tackle salesman from Denver who knew the Seattle area well and got a fishing boat chartered for early Sunday morning then assembled a crew of fishermen and would-be fishermen and drunks and so forth. Did a lot of work. But, of course, it was going to be worth it because a lot of us who were chipping in to pay for the charter weren't going to get much out of it except a boat ride and seasick and stuff like that while ole Marsh was gonna haul himself in a couple of nice, juicy, take-homeable salmon.

The game went reasonably well, we thought. Washington was favored by a couple touchdowns but had to scramble to tie us, 6-6. We were pleased with the tie (Jim Owens wasn't: it was his first game as a head coach and he called it "like kissing your sister") until Monday when the coaches studied the films and realized that we should have won by a couple of touchdowns at least. But, anyway, we were in a festive mood and, since the cars for Westport where we were to board our flagship were scheduled to leave the Olympic Hotel at 4:30 a.m. some of the hardiest of us-like Chester the Red Nelson (who was still covering CU, the Broncos hadn't been born yet and he was still four years away from learning the joys and raptures of going 4-9-1 with them for the next decade), Starr Yelland (who had spent two hectic days and nights in Seattle preparing for his KLZ broadcast), Marshall (the master planner) and myself (master of nothing and general all-around jack and certainly not a fisherman or a potential one but a pleasant little parasite who always seemed to latch onto programs, most of them bad.) So we roamed the streets of Seattle, probed the pubs, leered at the ladies of the evening, watched Chester's eyes slowly begin bulging out of their sockets as our bourbon level rose steadily like the Missouri river during the spring thaw and other things which my memory has mercifully blotted out.

Most of the excursionists bolted down their Ovaltine and went to bed at 9 o'clock with their fishing togs carefully laid out at the foot of their beds so they'd be bright-eyed, well-rested and ready to roll at dawn. Marshall's motley crew assembled in the pitch-black of Seattle 4:30 a.m. and crawled into three cars and sluggishly slipped away from the sidewalk in front of the Olympic. Look out, salmon, here we come! With Marshall Wells and his stinking, black cigar in the prow of the first car.

The rest of us all-nighters were assigned to the rear car so that we wouldn't obstruct the vision of any of the other drivers in case we threw up before we got to breakfast. And so we lurched into Westport, ate our breakfast, met our captain, boarded our ship and bounced over the waves westward, the growls of our tortured stomachs almost drowning out the noise of the sputtering motor. Marshall hadn't rented this boat from Avis or Budget and it not only had dirty ash trays in it, it had dirty spark plugs, dirty anchors, dirty screws, dirty everythings except the pilot and he was clean. And gentle. And perservering. And nice. And I don't think he'd ever seen a salmon before. Most nice guys finish last, you know.

There was a slight swell swelling or whatever swells do and we did a lot of bobbing and weaving before we got out of sight of the dock. Not the kind of moves which ought to be laid on a lot of systems full of Jack Daniels, Gibsons, Vodka Tonics, Seven-and-Sevens and all that kind of wonderful stuff. Miraculously, though, most of us inlanders made it all the way with only an occasional muffled, and cautious, burp marking our progress through the waves. All except Dr. John Little, the dean of our summer school and a special guest faculty member on the trip. John, a proficient dry fly trout fisherman who had been an ardent outdoor sportsman since his childhood days in Colorado, had been the first to bed and he was probably the guy who bought the Ovaltine. But there ain't no real justice in this world, you know, and poor John was hanging over the fantail pouring out his insides to Lar, the god of the sea, before we had even passed through the great barrier reef or whatever rough water we had to pass through before we got into the calm of the Pacific. John spent 90 percent of the trip hanging over that fantail and he may still have its marks creased in his abdomen to this very day. Which ought to tell us something about clean living.

To drive towards the end of this story, we reached the spot where the king salmon were waiting for our bait, dropped anchor and let it all hang out . . . lines, poles, John Little's lunch from-day-before-yesterday . . . everything! But about the only exciting thing that happened all day was when Chester hooked onto what the skipper screamed had to be the biggest salmon in the history of the northwest. Chester, who had earlier caught a smaller salmon and had been duly unimpressed by the experience, was slumbering in a semi-stupor on a bench in the middle of the deck when the jerk on his line almost unseated him, no small task inasmuch as a sodden, sleepless sportswriter who has just had his life saved by a brace of coffee royales is a pretty solid mass of inertia. Chester, a proud man, battled his giant salmon for 20 minutes. It was kind of like watching the movie, "The Old Man and the Sea." Except Hemingway didn't create Chester and, besides, Chester wasn't an old man. Just a too-heavy, out-of-shape man whose method of staving off emphysema was alternating regular and menthol cigarettes. Everybody was clustered around Chester, offering to relieve him at the reel but he wasn't having any of that. He was gonna pull in this big mother all by himself and everybody just stay out of my way and would you please pop my eyes back in if they break loose. And Chester was winning his battle with the monster from out of the deep. Slowly the line shortened. The group grew silent. Even the skipper stopped screaming about world records and would Chester be sure to mention the name of his boat when he wrote about it in his columns. Finally the thing gave up and Chester wrestled it to the side of the boat. And it was just a skate. A junk fish. A nothing. Ten years of watching the Denver Broncos. But worse than anything, a skate has a wide body. Even dead it can put up a lot of resistance through the water. Pulling one in, dead or alive, is sort of like dragging a car body through the water. But a car body might be worth more on the open market than a dead skate. And it for damned sure would make a better picture. I could see it all clearly - Chester casually leaning along the side of the hoist, cigarettes (one regular, the other menthol) dangling out of each side of his mouth, flanked by the upright body of an old Chevrolet with the proud little skipper beaming in the background. But one of the minor tragedies of life is that a lot of the gripping little vignettes never get filmed while a lot of the ungripping big ones do. So the picture of Chester and his catch never got taken. And what about Chester after the collapse of his dream? Well, I'll say this for Chester. He's got a lot of class. He didn't moan or wail or lament to the high heavens or to the goddess of the catch or whoever was working the beat that day. He just made sure that those pains shooting down his arms were from the rigors of the battle and not coronary thrombosis, laid out his two packs of cigarettes where he could reach them quickly when he awoke and stretched out on the hard bench and went to sleep and never stirred again as we carried him off the boat, into the car, out of the car and onto the plane. A real thoroughbred. And a great skate!

All of which gets us around to Marshall Wells. We caught about six or seven salmon all told. Plus the skate. And I hauled in a woman-eating shark, a heterosexual one, and there ain't many of those in the waters off the west coast. But guess who didn't get a bite? From a salmon or a skate or a smorgasbording shark or anyone? Marshall Wells. Crestfallen, crushed, mocked-at, jeered-at, internally-raging, outwardly-dying Marshall Wells. The longest thing he had in his hands all day, I suppose, was his cigar. And even it kept going out in the saltwater breeze.

Marshall was a gentle man despite the violence of his calling. He had to be. Or he'd have killed a half-dozen of us on that salmon boat that Sunday morning in September of 1957 off the waters of Seattle. Whatever, he was the first assistant to appear in my long parade. And he'll always have a special place in my memory. Stay with 'em, Jumbo. You were a good man and they did you wrong.

2. FRANK PRENTUP

Frank Prentup was like Zane Grey. The blood of real Indian chiefs ran through his veins. (Nobody ever told what ran through Zane's arteries, did they? So everybody called Frank Prentup, "Chief," and he was as smart an Indian as ever got his heart buried at Wounded Knee. A great guy. As I've said before, and as I'll keep saying throughout this work, most of them are. Chief was Dal's backfield coach and had been a great all-around athlete in Kansas by way of Fort Riley, (he was an army brat) and Kansas State, excelling in football, baseball, basketball, golf, boxing and swimming. A legitimate sextuple-threater. Chief was also baseball coach at CU for many years and a good one although he tended to overcoach somewhat because he was so good and so quick to learn that he assumed, erroneously and he never got over this, that everyone could be as quick and good as he had been as a youth. I can still remember Chief pitching batting practice in his coaching uniform— black jacket, grey twill pants, rubber-cleated shoes and regulation baseball cap — and striking out good hitters with his junk even though he was more than 50 years old. And I saw him pick up a golf club one morning in Pearl Harbor during the only baseball trip I ever made as sports information director - a week in Hawaii in March of 1968 - and knock a 5-iron 150 yards dead to the stick. And he hadn't played golf for more than 10 years.

Chief was a great guy to travel with. Lots of fun. Knew a lot of interesting things about a lot of interesting subjects. I guess when you've knocked around the country as the son of a career army officer, you get exposed to a lot of things and experiences and if you're as bright as Chief you learn a lot. And I don't think I've ever been around a coach or physical education professor who knew more about his sports or subjects. You had to be a special sort of person, though, to hold up under Chief's constant barrage of coaching instruction. If you wanted to be nasty, you could call them criticisms. But they were authentic and honest and well-meant. The average human being, however, can just absorb so much instruction in a certain amount of time and that was way less than the Chief expected. So if you were a nervous type you could get bugged, and eventually destroyed, by the Chief's coaching. But if you were a hell-for-leather kind of a guy with a thick skin and a good sense of proportion he was a great coach because he gave you a lot of great coaching if you were the kind of guy who knew when to turn your receiver on and off. Like Tom Brookshier, the wildest righthand pitcher I ever have seen. Chief used to have a description for guys like Tom which was beautiful in its simplicity of description. "He throws right and thinks left," grinned Chief. That's the type of comment Count Casotti would have made had he ever been a baseball coach. Anyway, one afternoon in a game at old Varsity Park (we re-named it Sparrow Beach in co-honor of the Dodgers' Florida training grounds and the birds who used to roost in the trees right behind the stands) Tom was pitching with nobody on. He accepted the sign, wound up and fired his fastball. Right over the thirdbaseman's head. About 10 feet over his head. Tommy, who was never at a loss for words until he interviewed Duane Thomas in the Cowboy dressing room after Super Bowl VI, looked over at the grimacing Prentup and shouted quickly and loudly, "I know, I know,

Chief! But did you notice my follow through? Exactly like you show us in the fieldhouse!'' And Chief just rolled his head over on his shoulder and howled. With everybody else. So if you were a Tom Brookshier-type you could take Chief and love him and flourish under him. But if you were a Joe Puleo or a Darrell Higman or a Bob Pomeroy or a thousand others, you suffered and worried and stewed and didn't really flourish. Or if you were a Carroll Hardy, with so much talent you could do anything you wanted to do and ignore any coach in the world and still be better than most of the men on the team, you could be a regular for four years under Prentup both in football and baseball and still come sliding into thirdbase in the final baseball game of your college career and whiplash to your feet and look your own man right in the eye - he had gotten from first to third just a thousandth of a second ahead of the tripling Hardy - and still draw a bonus for signing with the San Francisco 49'ers and the Cleveland Indians and go on to become the only man in the history of the Boston Red Sox who ever pinch hit for Ted Williams (Williams got hurt while he was at bat and Hardy, who was Williams' late-inning legs anyway, got the call to go down in baseball history.) Frank's football coaching career got hung up along with Dal Ward's in the 1958 firing and he continued to coach baseball for 11 more years before retiring to his sanctuary in the P.E. department.

So much for Frank Prentup. A good guy. And a good coach. And a good Indian. If there were any Italian Indians in my family tree, I'd want them to be just like Frank Prentup.

3. BOB SNEDDON

Bob Sneddon was the new end coach on Ward's staff when I got the job as sports information director in October of 1952. He had just come down the road from Ft. Collins where he had been a valued assistant to wily Bob Davis, one of the sharpest college coaches in the west, at Colorado A&M. Sneddon was a hard-working, conscientious assistant, the kind who needed a lot of work and responsibility and he picked the wrong place to come to so was never very happy under Ward and left after his second season. Sneddon was a good coach but an impatient one. I suppose he felt like he could come right in and be a top hand on Dal's staff. But take another guess, Bob. You had to serve your apprenticeship. The only difference in his status and mine back in 1953 was that Ward didn't call him, ''Shorty.'' Sneddon did, however, volunteer to help coach basketball under Bebe Lee who had also come to CU from Colorado A&M and the two of them produced a Big Eight co-champion in the 1953-54 cage season. But Bob was never very happy working for Bebe, either. I guess he just wasn't a very happy man in those days. But I thought a lot of him, still do, and consider him as good a coach as I've ever been around. In the spring of 1953, Bob set an all-time CU record for miles put on a school car during a recruiting trip. His territory was northeast Colorado and he was working on a gimp-legged sprinter-halfback from Holyoke. Bob left on a Friday morning to watch the prospect in a track meet that afternoon. When he checked back in at the office on Monday morning, the car had more than a 1000 miles on it, a fact which did not escape the eagle eyes of Kayo Lam, our eagle-eyed business manager and okayer of travel expense vouchers.

Lam, who could move along that nocturnal trail pretty good himself, had a pretty good idea of what had happened but nobody ever found out because Sneddon had a very suspicous wife and he wasn't saying anything except that maybe he took the wrong fork in the road a couple of times between Holyoke and Boulder, about a 200-mile trip and you can't hardly make that many wrong turns in that distance. If you drew a circle from Boulder with a 500-mile radius in it, you could reach Lincoln, Neb., Salt Lake City, Utah, Amarillo, Texas or Casper, Wyoming. That's as close as Lam ever came to pinpointing Sneddon's marathon recruiting trip. By the way, we got the gimp-legged sprinter-halfback from Holyoke and he never amounted to much and the only thing he ever did for CU was to jump the gun a couple of times and get that old knee injury operated on at our expense before jumping ship and transferring to a smaller school. Maybe Bob and CU would have been better off if he hadn't stopped off at Holyoke at all on his way to wherever he went. And, besides, what were a few extra miles on a school car, Kayo?

4. *RAY JENKINS*

The nickname for Ray Jenkins that described him best was "Earthquake McGoon," the caveman in Little Abner. He was a rough, tough guy who did whatever he was doing to the hilt, an ex-CU football and track great from tiny Cheraw in southeastern Colorado who picked up the tricks of the big cities, like Denver and Louisville, real fast and real good once he arrived at CU with his cardboard suitcase and his admissions acceptance. He and his sidekick, John Pudlik, an equally-wild and big young man from north Denver, quickly made their marks on the competitive fields and in the Boulder County play spots. So often, the men who were wildest as undergraduates turn out to be the most demanding coaches and Ray Jenkins was one of these. He was tough. Man, how he was tough! First as a freshman coach, then as the end coach after Sneddon left. But he had that unique ability to be extrenely tough and nasty on the practice field, yet never make any enemies among the men he was coaching so roughly. Only a few of the coaches I've watched have had this ability and I guess it is a mysterious combination of believing in what you're doing and how you're doing it and transmitting this feeling to the men you're working so hard. Anyway, Ray Jenkins had it and his players respected him and played extremely well for him. And he was good for them. He had the two All-Big Eight ends in 1956, Wally Merz and Jerry Leahy, and that hasn't happened many times in the history of the conference. Neither, by the way, was a gilt-edged prospect when Jenkins took them in hand, especially Leahy who had been tried at just about every position on the team before he found himself at end under Ray.

Like a lot of big men, Ray was an intense person who really got worked up emotionally for a key game and whose only real release was a physical one. Like hitting the other team when he was a player. Or bellowing with rage and pounding a press box counter or slamming a press box phone to the floor after a frustrating play. As an undergraduate, he'd work himself into his greatest rage for Colorado A&M. His feeling about that intra-state rival remained so strong that Ward wisely let him make the pre-game pep talks before most Aggie games. Jenks didn't always get the Buffaloes worked up too red hot but he always left that locker room in a rage! As a CU assistant, Ray's most frustrating moments came against Oklahoma, CU's most frustrating opponent by far because they were always supposed to kill us but inevitably ended up by just barely beating us on a Merrill Green counter or a Clendon Thomas touchdown or a Prentice Gautt gallop or something. Mostly because, I still think, they had more football players and were fresher at the finish. Anyway, Ray would always get ripped off into a gigantic rage about every Friday evening before the Oklahoma game. The Buffaloes had lost the most frustrating game of the entire series of Ward-Wilkinson confrontations in Boulder a year earlier, on Nov. 3, 1956 — my 33rd birthday, incidentally — losing 27-19 after leading a Sooner team which had flogged Paul Hornung and Notre Dame 40-0 a week earlier by 19-6 at the half. Oklahoma started the third quarter with a touchback when Frank Clarke kicked off over the end zone then came right up to a fourth-and-a-yard-and-a-half at their own 28½, went for it and made it by half-a-yard and went on to win, with the help of a key holding penalty against the Buffs in the third quarter which nullified a long CU gain deep into Sooner territory. I think it was end Les Lotz, a tough, lean competitor, who got called for letting an arm slip through his man's legs on his initial block but Marshall Wells never could find any holding on anyone in the movies all next week. Anyway, the Buffaloes charged into Norman a year later to see if they couldn't get some revenge in what Missouri's Don Faurot or Hoot Betty or somebody had named, "The Snake-Pit." There's a "snake-pit" in every conference, I know, but this one just happened to be the number one snake-pit of all time at that time and CU was about the only Big Eight team that didn't die of pre-game terror in Norman. I can remember my first trip to Norman, in 1953. We were staying at the Biltmore Hotel in Oklahoma City and my room was just down the hall from Dal and Kayo's and I walked in on that Saturday morning while Dal was shaving and Kayo was stuffing his clothes and tickets and money and stuff into his suitcase. Oklahoma was contending for the national championship that year and was a heavy favorite over our CU team which had lost three straight games to Missouri, Kansas and Kansas State (one of only two times Ward ever lost to K-State which had a pretty good team under Bill Meek that year.) Leonard Cahn, in his Monday morning column that week, wrote a facetious column on the Buffaloes' plight in having to play in the snake-pit after having embarrassed the Sooners with a 21-21 draw at Boulder the year before during which Don Branby had spent most of the afternoon clubbing Eddie Crowder with forearms, backhands, straight rights, left hooks — just about every kind of a human weapon a man can muster with the possible exception of a kick or two to the groin and Branby would probably have tried that except that (1) Crowder never gave him that much of a standing target and (2) Branby really wasn't very nimble with his feet and was more of a slugger than a dancer. The guy who put the headline on Leonard's column, wrote "On to Norman!" Sure! on to Norman, as 21-point underdogs and without a healthy tailback on the team: Carroll Hardy had got his ribs bruised at Seattle and he was a very slow healer; Ronnie Johnson had been struck down by an asthma attack after returning a kick for a touchdown against Kansas two weeks earlier in Boulder (that Boulder chinook wind did raise a lot of dust on that track in the old days and Ronnie nearly choked to death in it after running back a KU punt 92 yards) Homer Jenkins had broken his leg in the end zone trying to corral the opening kickoff at that same Kansas game. And to top it all off we had a converted guard, Roger Hunt, playing quarterback for us that season.

So I walked into the room and said something bright and original, like, "How we gonna do, Coach?" Ward just looked at me in the mirror, ripped off another row of whiskers, shrugged his shoulders and grinned, "Hell, I don't know, Shorty. But we'll get after them. They aren't any different than anybody else and I think they pull their pants on one leg at a time just like we do." Dallas could always come up with dazzlers like that old one-leg-at-a-time deal. And he was always calm before a game, no matter how big it was. And so were his teams.

But we were talking about Ray Jenkins and his pre-game rage which always started somewhere on Friday night. The catalyst on this Friday night at Norman in October of 1957 was basically the same group which had gone on that historic salmon-fishing trip off Seattle's shores after the opening game of the season. Most of us had been to Harold Keith's fine press party in the Skirvin Hotel where Harold's little boy, Johnny, had played the banjo in a dixieland band like he always (and still does) had a habit of doing. But this was a full-fledged case of nepotism cause Harold was paying them to entertain the local and visiting press, most of whom were too busy swilling down that free whiskey in bootleggers' paradise to hear John Phillip Sousa and his 1000-piece marching band, let alone John Keith and Robert Adams and Howard Robinson and Bobby Scott and some kids from Greeley who were named Jim and Margaret Ann Peterson and Don Royer and Gordon Ellinger who called themselves the Jada Quartet and were good enough that they had played on the Perry Como television show among other ones. Anyway we had a great time and Chester the Red Nelson exploded with pride when he discovered later in the evening when the hotel manager invited all of us including the musicians to be his guests in the hotel's private key club that the Jadas were from Greeley right up the road from Denver. And Hamilton B. Maule, who was to become a world famous football writer for Sports Illustrated but who in 1957, along with Sports Illustrated, was a relative unknown and in-between wives and busily trying to hustle the hotel manager's wife and Margaret Ann and just about anything that came by our table. Totally ineffectively, I might add, much to the delight of us country folks who took great consolation in seeing this Texas-drawling dude from New York City striking out just as futilely as most of us always did. Anyway, we stayed in the key club until Maule's fingerprints started showing up on everybody, including some of the barmaids, and the manager finally closed up the place and we all headed for Norman and the Lockett Hotel, Norman's finest and the top hotel in the world as far as paper-thin walls are concerned. One of our former basketball near-greats and ex-assistant basketball coach, Bruce Conway and his lovely wife, Sue, had wandered in from somewhere in Texas for the game and didn't have a hotel room (there was only one hotel in Norman and we had it full and Oklahoma hadn't discovered motels yet) so were waiting for me in the lobby and there wasn't anything else to do but to order in a couple of rollaways and a chastity belt from room service and invite them to be guests in my room. I forget who my other roommate was but I think it was Chester the Red. Anyway, we had to retreat up to my room to get Bruce and Sue organized and somebody found a bottle. There was still a pretty good crowd of us and we drew a couple of hanger-onners in the lobby so we were rippling the air pretty good with our loud talk and laughter as we chortled about the old days and Chester discovering the Jadas but too late to be of any consequence because they'd already been on national television several times. And things like that when in shattered the door and filling up its jagged outline was...you guessed it...Earthquake McGoon, in his earthquakingest, raginest, insanest, I'll-fight-every-sonofabitch-in-the-room-if-you-don't-get-quiet-est rage. Among our group now was Kayo Lam and he was competitive, to say the least, and he jumped up to calm Ray. They didn't have too much of a calming effect on each other and pretty soon they were drawing a line and the first one that crossed it was going to set off a 2-man war which might have been just as destructive as the War of the Roses or one of those old time jousting wars where everybody got coated with inch-thick armor and rode full speed at each other on their horses except that their horses were so weighted down with all that armor their riders were wearing that nobody hardly ever got knocked off their horse let alone killed. No momentum, you know.

So I jumped up with a witty remark to quiet things down. Like, "For God's sake, Ray, go back and put on your robe before you come charging in to the privacy of my palatial suite which was filled with levity and revelry before you broke down the door and cast a pall on our gathering?" Something like that. But it didn't work and The Earthquake turned on me with the kind of language that the Italian Anti-Defamation League would go crazy hearing today. But coming from an old PT-Boat commander, it was awful impressive to me. And to everybody else but Lam, who was an old Landing Officer from the Enterprise who PT-Boat types didn't scare too much. It was going to be a 2-man war without any spectators because all the rest of us were looking for a door that didn't have Jenkins in the middle of it so we could escape to anywhere. Just about that time, a voice from down the hall roared softly (there were no players on the floor, just coaches and staffmembers and camp followers), "What the hell's going on down there? Quiet down!" It was Ward, who had been awakened by the noise. Jenkins turned as white as I already was, backed out through the hole in the wall that had once been a doorway and disappeared into the night. So did the rest of us. Fortunately, the Buffaloes played a tremendous game the next afternoon. It took the Oklahoma marching band to beat us, finally. (Wilkinson could come up with all kinds of ways to whip you!) We were ahead 13-7 in the fourth quarter and about third-and-two at the Sooner seven and going in for the clincher. We had our number two quarterback, Ralph Herbst, in the game and we were down at the end of the field where the Sooner band sat. They were screaming and beating on their drums and making all kinds of noises, just like all those drunk Chinamen in the stands who were gonna lose their bets by now no matter what the final score was because it wasn't gonna be OU by the spread.

Anyway, no one had instructed Herbie that he could get a free official's timeout if the noise from the stands was too loud and he tried to call a snap signal and somebody couldn't hear it and jumped offside and before it was all over, we were having a substitute center named Charlie Brown, who wasn't even our extra point kicker but had the strongest leg, we thought, on the team, trying a field goal from the 26, a 36-yarder. He didn't get the ball out of the end zone and Oklahoma came crunching back with a scoring drive and beat us, 14-13. God only knows what Jenkins might have done to us if the game hadn't been so close and his rage diverted toward the Oklahoma band.

Ray later became head coach at Montana and if he thought he knew frustration and rage while on Ward's CU staff, he had another think coming. But he was still a good coach and didn't get a fair chance at Montana. So many right guys pick the wrong places to become head coaches at. Ray Jenkins was one of those and his coaching career was short and unlamented by anyone except his family. As a fitting irony to the end of his head coaching career, he was fired on Nov. 22, 1963. So nobody but his family ever knew about it because that was the day that Lee Harvey Oswald shot President Kennedy and nothing else but that got into the news for a week. But I'm happy to say that Earthquake McGoon is still alive and living in Boulder where he headquarters as a talent scout for the New Orleans Saints. And he's too smart to come over and kill me for writing this book because he knows he'd be one of the top suspects. Maybe the top one. You're still a good guy, Earthquake, but I still fear that your bite is just as bad as your bark so don't take anything personally.

5. HUGH DAVIDSON

When Bob Sneddon resigned to enter private business in Utah, his native state, at the end of the 1953 season, Ray Jenkins moved up on the staff as end coach and Hugh Davidson, an ex-CU fullback under Ward in 1949-50-51 joined the Buffaloes as freshman coach. Davidson was a gritty, determined little guy who had been a pretty fair single wing fullback despite weighing only 163. He was a tenacious player who made up for his lack of overwhelming physical ability by being extremely tough and determined. The same credentials applied to him as a coach. He worked very hard and forced his own improvement as a coach just as he had as a player. If Hugh had a shortcoming as a freshman coach, it was one which most freshman coaches everywhere have...he wanted to be part of the varsity staff where most of the glamour was. Young freshman coaches see their jobs only as stepping stones to the varsity and that's completely understandable. If they didn't have that ambition they'd certainly never make it. But a freshman coach in a college program is a tremendously vital member of the staff. The frosh need lots of attention, both on and off the field. Most of them have been highly recruited and charmed and oversold on their abilities. It's the product of a system which forces coaches to go into the open market after talent. All schools offer basically the same scholarship so the schools which make the biggest impression on the high school seniors get the most and best rookies.

Once the young man enrolls in college and draws his freshman gear, the picture changes completely. Suddenly he becomes a "greenie" with so much to learn, about college life, study habits and his new level of football, that it's almost too much for him. Thus the need for a lot of fatherly advice, including close supervision over his study hours, during that critical first year in college.

So Hugh Davidson was a good, but not a great freshman coach — the only great one I've seen is Dan Stavely who is the current CU coach and who will show up later on this list twice. Stavely succeeded Hugh as freshman coach when the latter went to Montana with Ray Jenkins as backfield coach. Hugh later succeeded Ray as head coach at Montana when Ray was fired in 1963 and got the same treatment himself a few years later.

Hugh was a good friend, still is. We spent a lot of pleasant moments sneaking in nine holes of golf over the noon hour at the old Boulder Country Club and for a scrawny little guy he could whack a golf ball as far as anyone I've played with. He was a good guy, a good coach. Most of them are.

   6. *WILL WALLS*

There were no changes in the staff in 1955 but a fifth assistant, and the first fulltime football assistant in the history of CU — all the previous ones had duties as physical education instructors — was added and what an addition he was! His name was Will Walls and he was one of the wildest and gentlest and craziest and best and most delightful coaches I've ever been around. You name it, he'd done it — and done it well. An outstanding end on the great Sammy Baugh — led TCU teams of mid-30's fame, he'd gone on to star with the New York Giants in the NFL, was on his way to being a Hollywood star when he decided he didn't want to be a moving picture cowboy — he was a natural for the role, tall, dark and looking not unlike Johnny Cash. One of Walls' Hollywood running mates in those days in the early 1940's was Robert Mitchum and they must have made a swashbuckling pair as they worked their way through a never-ending line of eager starlets.

But when Hollywood told Walls his future as an actor lie in cowboy roles, he saddled up and rode off into the sunset. To become a college football coach. And a good one. He returned to the Los Angeles area in 1946 as head coach of the Kilgore, Texas JC team which played in the Little Rose Bowl at Pasadena. Walls came to CU from Louisiana State where he had been fired along with his head coach there, Gaynell Tinsley and the rest of the staff. They were one of the few staffs in the history of Baton Route who failed to win consistently. But Walls, one of the finest judges of talent who ever coached, was busily recruiting Billy Cannon, Johnny Robinson and Jimmy Taylor for the Tigers when he got his walking papers.

Walls coached the tackles for Dal Ward and promptly helped Dick Stapp and Ken Schlagel develop into a pair of stalwarts as CU went 7-2-1 to earn an Orange Bowl berth where they whipped Clemson, 27-21.

Walls was a wild man who couldn't sit still. Every time he heard a train whistle, he instinctively packed his suitcase. He was always on the move and Dallas and the Travis Hotel there always managed to find their way onto his itinerary. No matter where his assignment took him, he'd always find an excuse to go by way of Dallas. His masterpiece of routing came one season when he was assigned to scout Missouri which was playing at Lincoln that Saturday and he went through Dallas — coming and going. Will had a lot of things going on the road and whatever was going for him in Dallas must have been good because it sure kept calling him back. And, remember, this was a big, good-looking guy who had been around the horn a couple of times, at least, in Hollywood!

But in fairness to Willie, he did a lot of recruiting in Dallas and the adjoining area and got a lot of good players for CU out of there, including a pair of runts, end Bill Elkins and defensive back Reed Johnson, who became fine regulars for the Buffaloes.

Walls liked to travel by any means, but had a passion for big, high-powered cars. Liked to get out in the open and floorboard them. You could always tell when Will was driving a car...you could see his foot sticking through the front end, about two feet in front of the bumper, pawing for the footfeed. He totalled two cars that I know of and was almost killed in the first, doing a Ben Hogan as he lay unconscious in the sagebrush alongside a west Texas highway. Found with a broken back, totally paralyzed and near-death, Walls was rushed into surgery. He was paralyzed and couldn't talk but he could hear and comprehend. As two doctors hovered over the operating table, one asked the other who was going to do the surgery. It doesn't make any difference, replied the other, this guy hasn't got a chance anyway. Which infuriated Walls so much that he lived just so he could tell that doctor what he thought of him. And, at the proper time, he did. Out of danger, Walls was lying in bed a few days later when the doctor walked in and greeted him. "You'd make a great coach," Walls exploded. "You give up before the game starts!" Will's favorite expression, one he blurted out almost with a sneer in answer to a question which had an obviously positive answer, was, "Has a cat got an ass!"

Was Will Walls a good coach? Has a cat got an ass?

7. BOB BEATTIE

Signing on with CU as a frosh assistant in 1956 was a young man from New England named Bob Beattie whose primary assignment was as head ski coach.

Beattie, who was to become the leading American ski coach and the nation's head man in the 1964 and 1968 Winter Olympics, had been a single wing guard as an undergraduate at Middlebury College in Vermont and had a deep-seated love of the game. He volunteered to join the CU grid staff as an unpaid freshman line coach, a move which, incidentally, paid him big dividends as it lifted him out of the obscurity of being an unknown and unloved ski coach and moved him onto center-stage even though his part was a relatively small one in the overall production.

The same characteristics which were to make him a brilliant ski coach made him an extremely effective football coach and he could have been a fine grid coach had he ever overcome one glaring defect which would undoubtedly have done him in some day. Beattie, a dawn to midnight worker, inevitably went to sleep within seconds after the lights were turned off in the movie room. And reviewing the films has always been a big thing with football coaches — and even Beattie used this technique to his advantage with his ski team. There's an old story about a football coach getting married and returning to work after his honeymoon and being asked, how was the honeymoon by his fellow staffmembers upon his return. "I don't know, I haven't seen the movies yet," replied the coach. We'll never know whether Beattie could have eliminated his problem, I suspect he could have because he's accomplished just about everything he's ever wanted to, because he hung up his football career in 1960 when

Sonny Grandelius issued him an edict, become a fulltime football coach or a fulltime ski coach, one or the other. Beattie chose his first love, skiing, and it was a wise choice because he was busy winning NCAA championships in 1959 and 1960 as Grandelius was full-speed-aheading down the road to destruction. Beattie was among the mourners at Sonny's demise. But he was alive and doing very well, thank you, as the brightest young ski coach in the country.

What were Beattie's coaching secrets? No secrets! His abilities and strengths were familiar ones. Ones which all good coaches have. Boundless energy and a love for coaching which transcended even his personal family life. Nothing ranked above coaching with him. Not his wife. Or his children. Or anything. He had a one-track mind...be a great coach. And so he became one, but in skiing rather than football. There was no doubt in any of the young men who played in CU's freshman lines under him, though, that he wouldn't have been a great one in football had he elected to remain in the game.

Beattie's ski coaching career is worth a book in itself and should be written someday. I'll close with one brief anecdote which involved Bob's introduction to Boulder in the fall of 1956. The Buffaloes opened at home that year against an unheralded Oregon team which contained a lot of good sophomores who as seniors two years later were to take a heavily-favored Ohio State team right down to the wire before losing in the Rose Bowl. Oregon wiped out the favored Buffaloes. Humiliated them, 35-0. We had a wake at our house that night and a lot of assistant coaches and other friends gathered at the trough and before we knew it the wake was out of control and a stranger walking in at midnight would have thought the Buffaloes had just whomped Oklahoma. Beattie, who could go with the flow, was going with the flow. Every so often, as he was refilling, he'd shake his head and mutter, "If this is what you do when you lose, for God's sake what happens when you win?"

Bob, who had been schooled in the shelter of tiny Middlebury and the sleepy under-emphasis of a league labeled the "Poison Ivy", was just getting his introduction to the big-time. Hey, Bob! You just had to learn sometime that you got to drink the hardest when you've just gotten tromped.

As a coach, Bob believed in tough practices and he made his young Buffaloes work hard and like it. All good coaches do. There's something about sincere enthusiasm that is contagious and one of the most important coaching assets is to have this enthusiasm and to be able to transmit it to your men.

One last key to Beattie's success was his total devotion to his men. His primary assignment in his first season was as head ski coach. But as a member of the grid staff he and his wife were eligible to go to the Orange Bowl and two weeks in the mid-winter sun and sand and sea of Miami Beach. Beattie didn't bat an eye as he turned down the attractive trip while his wife almost wept. But he was getting his ski team ready for the winter and he didn't feel that he could desert them for the pleasures of Miami Beach and still command their complete respect. In his first meet as CU's head coach, his skiers upset mighty Denver. And three years later they were the national champions.

That was Bob Beattie. A tremendous guy. And a tremendous coach. I loved the guy. I still do. Enough said.

8. *JACK NELSON*

When Ray Jenkins moved on to Montana as head coach in early 1958, his replacement as CU's end coach was a young man who had been a graduate assistant with us in 1954, Jack Nelson. But the handle he preferred was Jocko and anybody who preferred that name deserved to be called it. Jocko had signed on with Utah State and been a solid member of that staff and Dal Ward was delighted to get him back four years later. For Jocko, though, it was a case of bad timing because he joined the Ward wagon just before it got rolled over the cliff. With Jocko's timing, had he been born 50 years earlier, he'd have probably gotten a job as a physical education instructor on the Titanic the day before it sailed.

So we really never got to see enough of Jocko to give him a fair judgment. But he was a good coach and has proved it since his brief encounter with CU in 1958, going to Michigan as an assistant then to his alma mater, Gustavus Adolphus, as head coach and building an excellent record there which almost got him the head job at Iowa and when he just missed out on that position he joined the Minnesota Vikings as linebacker coach.

Jocko was a personality boy, a real charmer who was a fine recruiter and warmed the hearts of many a mother and father in the midwest, the territory to which he was primarily assigned. On the field, he was an enthusiastic, effective, coach who communicated well with his men. He was a good man. Most of them are.

9. *DAN STAVELY*

Coming aboard to replace Hugh Davidson as freshman coach when Hugh went to Montana with Ray Jenkins was Dan Stavely, a career freshman coach who had fashioned an enviable record at Washington State. Proof of his value to a staff was that he had survived four head coaches at that school, almost an unheard of accomplishment since somewhere along that many firing or quittings you're almost bound to get pulled down or out. But Dan stayed on because he was an unusual frosh coach — a mature, dedicated Christian who relished the life of being a father-confessor, Indian guide, counsellor to class after class of rookies, showing them the way out of their individual wildernesses and providing a service to a program which can't be measured for its importance.

Dan Stavely has probably had a more important influence on more young football players in this country than any other man. A strong statement but one which I believe to be totally true. But the law of averages caught up with him at Boulder and he got wiped out in less than a year. I guess he left his security in Pullman. But a man as good as Dan never has trouble finding a job and he quickly was snatched up by Pappy Jack Curtice who had just taken over as boss man at prestigious Stanford.

Never a bitter man, Dan laughed in 1958 at the situation involving his finding out he'd just been fired. He still laughs about it today and he has the last laugh because there isn't a member of that 1958 board of regents still on it and most of the administration which gave Ward's firing its blessing is also gone, by one manner or another while Dan, like good wine, gets better each year of his second CU hitch.

Anyway, he was in Seattle on a recruiting mission that February day in 1958 when the ax was lowered. He was, in fact, in a Seattle hotel room extolling the virtues of CU to a bright young high school senior named Charlie Mitchell. And, incidentally, praising the stability of the CU football situation which had had Ward as its head man for 11 consecutive years, in contrast to the turbulence which marked the Washington University scene, the school which was battling CU the toughest for the services of Mitchell. Dan had the radio on in his hotel room and he and Charlie listened together to the sports show which included in its log, the story of Ward's firing. With his entire staff. Stavely smiled weakly, shook Mitchell's hand, wished him luck and drove to the airport and caught the next plane to Denver. Mitchell went to Washington, became an All-American there and eventually got to within 30 miles of Folsom Stadium, starring for several seasons with some of the early Denver Bronco clubs in the AFL.

Before closing this first section on Stavely, and he'll be back in more detail later in this sequence, it should be noted that his hiring in 1958 marked a significant breakthrough. For Dan was a graduate of Denver University, the long and hated rivals of the Buffaloes. And worse than that, Dan had been a 2-sport star for the Pioneers and, as such, a constant thorn in the side of CU. But quality outranks provincial and petty rivalries and Dan, despite his shady background, was welcomed into the CU family with open arms by such a one-time bitter on-the-field foe as business manager Kayo Lam, an athletic contemporary in the same two sports, football and wrestling.

So, Dan Stavely came and went with more speed than he had ever shown on the gridiron or wrestling mat. But he was to be back at CU in five years, a stroke of great fortune that CU didn't really deserve during those black days of early 1959.

10. JOHN POLONCHEK

With the arrival of Sonny Grandelius came a brand new staff — Stavely came the closest to being retained before getting carried downstream in the flood. Beattie remained but he was a free coach, drawing his entire salary as ski coach. Number one aide to Sonny was a smallish Michigan State ally, John Polonchek, who came in that spring of 1959 as backfield coach. John had lettered three years at Michigan State as a tailback and defensive back and was a tough little banty rooster of a guy who probably should have been on the midget team. He weighed only 145. But he was wiry and wily and as good a little man as ever wore the green and white at East Lansing.

And John was a Grandelius man through and through despite taking some bad raps for his complete devotion to his leader. CU's players, for example, referred to John as "Tweety Pie." Behind his back of course. The reference, in case you aren't a movie fan, was to the cartoon bird. Some of the players felt that John wasn't positive enough, preferring to echo Sonny's orders. But that was unfair criticism. He was a smart, creative coach. But Sonny's system was power-oriented and he had the brutes to make it work so the offense was a grind-it-out winged-T which looked like a flying wedge in comparison to the variety of attack which Ward had been producing with his "horse-and-buggy" single wing.

Polonchek played his role to perfection under Sonny as an almost invisible, unheard chief assistant. But an effective one. When Sonny went down, John went with him. Without a murmur. Unlike some other members of the staff. Polonchek had class. He went to work with Samsonite in Denver and soon had worked his way into an important echelon with that internationally-oriented organization. But football was in his blood and, as it is so often, an addiction which can't be expelled. So John went back in, as an assistant with the Oakland Raiders where he was part of that pro team's surge to the top of its league.

I was a Ward loyalist who mourned bitterly when he was fired. But CU still ranked first with me and the new men who came in were our new leaders and we who stayed on pulled for them just as hard as we had for Dal and his men. Polonchek more than measured up to the level of his predecessors on CU staffs and I am proud to still have him regard me as a friend. As I do him. He was a good man. Most of them are.

11. CHUCK BOERIO

Chuck Boerio, or Charlie if you prefer, was a dynamic leader of linebackers and one of the chief reasons why I still regard Sonny's original staff as one of the finest, if not the finest, ever assembled at CU. Boerio had it all. An outstanding linebacker at Illinois where his head coach, Ray Eliot, one of the master orators of all time still gets emotional when he tells of the exploits of Boerio, an All-American center for Eliot's 1951 Rose Bowl champions. Boerio had been a tightly-wound 185-pounder for the Illinois, such a ferocious hitter that he was held out of most scrimmages as a senior for fear that he might wreck himself smashing down his own teammates. He was just as intense as a coach, a man who enjoyed throwing himself into the action at practice to put across a point. He was an impressive figure in the bright gold coaching jackets which Sonny introduced to CU, a black-curly-haired, good-looking Italian with the personality of an organ-grinder, alternately shouting and laughing his way through practice. His men loved him and he loved them and they formed an impressive combination. Need any for-instances? Try Joe Romig, Walt Klinker and Tom Wilscam on for size. Like Boerio, none of these men were physical giants. But, like him, they were all tightly-wound tigers who were more than matches for men much bigger than they. With the firing, Boerio got out of college coaching and college football was the poorer for his withdrawal. But he remained in Boulder, an area which he quickly came to love and returned to coaching after a lengthy absence in the relatively obscure position as head coach at Nederland high, a tiny high school in a small mountain town 20 miles up Boulder Canyon west of Boulder, a school so small it was playing 8-man football when Charlie became head coach. Needless to say, he was an instant success at Nederland, leading his team to the state finals in his second year. It was good to see him return to coaching. He's the type of man who should be guiding young men. May he long continue!

12. BOB GHILOTTI

When Ghilotti was named as end coach, we figured we almost had enough Italians around to form a campus chapter of the Black Hand. But Bob Beattie, even though his name rhymed with mine and Ghilotti's, turned out to be a Scotsman so we couldn't get our charter from international headquarters in Sicily and had to give up that project. Ghilotti was a rarity, a quiet Italian, and first impressions of him as a coach weren't really impressive. He was quieter on the field than Polonchek, if that was possible. Almost stuck his mouth in an end's ear to give him advice. He looked more like a man passing along a hot tip at a racetrack than a coach imparting some coaching. But Ghilotti was a good coach and a staunch advocate of the passing game — most end coaches are, if they have any brains. But Grandelius, like Ward and most other sound coaches, appreciated the ground route more than the air and Ghilotti, consequently, was more often than not over-ruled and out-voted in the offensive strategy sessions. But his receivers were a brilliant crew — Gary Henson, a glue-fingered roue; Jerry Hillebrand, a do-everything-when-he-felt-like-it giant; Chuck McBride, a gritty redhead with less ability but more guts than most of his mates; Bill Elkins, scrawniest of the scrawny but a great competitor; and others.

With CU operating from the shotgun through much of the latter part of the 1959 season, these men constantly came up with fantastic catches of Gale Weidner fireballs. Weidner who had been recruited by Ward to be a single wing tailback, and he'd have been a great one, had a sensational sophomore season when the Buffaloes switched to the shot gun, spread if you prefer, completing 100 passes for 1200 yards and seven touchdowns. Weidner threw the ball extremely hard with, for the most part, fairly decent accuracy although he'd fire a sideline pitch into the stands occasionally, and that was in the days when you had to throw it over the track to get it to the spectators. But he needed lots of big catches from his targets to reach that record-breaking 100. And he got them. Men like these helped make his job a relatively happy one for Ghilotti, who had been a fine receiver himself as an undergraduate at Stanford. Had Grandelius' successor been chosen from his staff, Bob would have been the man. But the regents, now thoroughly disenchanted with the men they had welcomed so eagerly three years earlier, evicted the whole crew. With the purge went Ghilotti's chances to become a head coach and after serving on staffs with the Kansas City Chiefs and University of California, he left coaching in 1971 to go into private business in the San Francisco area. An intelligent, perceptive and gentle human being, he'll be successful in whatever field he selects. I think he could have become a good head coach. I know he'd have come out of the dressing room throwing. And the fans would have loved that. Provided he was completing them. And winning. Passing alone ain't enough, you know! As Bud Davis and his men were to learn to their sorrow in 1962.

13. BUCK NYSTROM

Multiple-cross a bulldog and a tiger and a mole and you'd probably come up with Buck Nystrom. A squatty, tenacious, gregarious, tough blockbuster of a guard at Michigan State and probably the best line coach I've ever been around. Bobby Anderson, who was to explode on the CU scene a few years later, called the down linemen, "trench-hogs." It was a label of love not of derision...Bobby knew who the guys were who were doing the important work with very little of the glory. Buck Nystrom was the trench-hog to end all trench-hogs, totally dedicated to life in the middle of the line, entangled in the arms and legs of the opposing trench-hogs, clawing out a path over which the glamour guys in the backfield galloped to glory. Buck had served his apprenticeship as a player in the area in which he was to coach so outstandingly. And he had earned the proper credentials to impress any young lineman who reported to his classroom on the grass. All-American captain of the 1955 Spartans who won the Rose Bowl, Buck was just as able in the classroom, gaining All-American Academic honors and probably the ultimate honor an athlete can win, aside from being voted captain of his squad by his teammates, and becoming the outstanding combined scholar and athlete of his graduating class.

So Buck came rumbling into Boulder, complete with his private torture chamber for aspiring young offensive linemen — board drills and bull-in-the-ring exercises, all barked out in his muffled roar. Buck had a hoarse, rasping voice which never lasted more than the first week of practice. The rest of the fall he sounded like a man who was heading for a case of throat cancer. But how he did communicate with those young linemen. CU's line crew loved their jobs. But they didn't necessarily know it at the time. Fact is, most of them dreaded going out to practice each afternoon.

But the physical problems they encountered daily in Buck's brawling, sprawling sessions on the practice field next to the stadium were lessons in survival. I can remember only one game in which CU's linemen took more punishment than they gave and that was the second game of the 1961 championship season when Jack Mitchell's equally-physical Kansas Jayhawks kicked the living hell out of the Buffaloes for three quarters in an early season game which would decide the Big Eight champion. The Jayhawkers put it to the Buffs about as good as you can put it to anyone and led 19-0 after three periods. But this was a Colorado team which didn't die easily and they rallied to win it, 20-19, on a furious Gale Weidner-led aerial comeback. I can remember huge "Baby Huey", 6-4, 240-pound All-American end Jerry Hillebrand, lying in the training room the next morning, still exhausted.

But normally the Buffaloes gave more than they received, thanks to the demanding practice sessions of Sonny and his staff and, in particular, Buck Nystrom. Buck lived his job, believed in his way completely. And when you are unconditionally dedicated to your work, you quickly become a master craftsman. He was. And the men who may have dreaded putting on the pads and reporting for another day of drudgery in the pits didn't realize it at the time but they were learning to love their dumpy drillmaster.

Two memories of Buck Nystrom's coaching job come quickly to my mind. The first was a pre-season practice session in 1961 and Buck was working his guards on a pulling assignment in which they were to pull and lead the play to the outside. None of the guards was getting out quickly enough to clear out his man effectively. After a few moments of this inefficiency — and, please understand, the players were somewhat weary after several days of two-a-day practices in the hot September sun — Buck shoved the defensive player aside and stepped into the play himself, challenging his men to "knock down an old beat-up coach, if you can; I don't think you're tough enough or quick enough!" Frustrated and furious, the guards gritted their teeth and determined to annihilate their loud leader. And they were a pretty fair crew — led by two-time All-American Joe Romig and including Ken Vardell, Dave Young, Larry Cundall, Al Hollingsworth, Cliff Houk and Tim Monczka. One-by-one, they assaulted Buck who bounced them away like they were nothing. There were eight guards in the drill and it was well down the list the second time around before one of them, and it was an obscure sophomore, who just happened to catch Buck at the proper point of exhaustion and finally toppled him. Buck, clad only in his gold jacket and cotton twill pants, was so bruised and battered that he could barely walk the next morning. But, by going into the trenches and working with his men, he had driven his point home. By the way, you'd have thought the rookie who flattened him had just won the Heisman trophy, the way Buck leaped to his feet and congratulated him.

The second incident occurred after Buck had left CU. A few years later he was on Darrell Mudra's staff at North Dakota State and doubled in the spring as tennis coach (Buck wasn't a bad tennis player, by the way, even though he didn't look the part.) He brought his North Dakota State net team into Colorado for some duals with local schools during spring vacation. His meet in Boulder was scheduled for Friday before the annual Varsity-Alumni game and he arrived on Thursday, the night of the annual dinner and party for the Alumni team. Buck, of course, was invited to attend and as the night drew on, the reminiscing got thicker and wetter and before long, Buck and some of his old guards and centers were down on the floor exchanging coaching techniques. Just wallowing all over the hard, wooden floor of the old Boulder Country Club. And before long they were talking about the old days and crying and just having a heck of a good time. They may not get the glory, but I don't think any group of men get the same deep camaraderie as the interior linemen. You can't get closer to each other than down underneath all those people in the middle of the line. And for working with those guys in the trenches, where 99% of all football games are won, you could never find a better man than Buck Nystrom. A great coach and a great guy! Most of them are.

14. FRANK JOHNSON

Teaming up with Buck Nystrom to form a tandem of squat, dumpy coaches was Frank Johnson, who came in with Sonny as freshman coach. Frank was a Notre Dame graduate and had served his apprenticeship under Frank Leahy as a reserve lineman. As I remember it, there were two men named Frank Johnson on the Irish squads he played on so they called one "Whitey" and our Frank, "Blackie." Because of his black hair and dark beard, I suppose. Certainly not for the color of his heart because he was a nice guy with one of the sharpest senses of humor I've ever come across and I've always appreciated good senses of humor and they're not necessarily predominant in the personalities of football coaches, most of whom are grimly devoted to their work. And, besides, most football coaches are either big guys or little guys who have achieved success far beyond their physical qualifications and neither of these types are often humorists - they've earned their success by either brute strength or brutal effort or both and not by the sharpness of their wits.

Frank was sort of the ugly duckling of the staff, the last man chosen and, as most people felt then and still do, in the least important position on the staff. Let me go on record once again, though, that I consider the freshman job the most important job on the staff next to the head coach. Frank was an adequate freshman coach who did a good job, neither more nor less than was required. A good journeyman coach, and I use the word in a complimentary sense. But probably his best talent was that he could do a tremendous imitation of Leahy. I can still see him, gritting his teeth and squinting his eyes and, in the voice of his old master in almost perfect mimicry, showing a young lad how it should be done, the Notre Dame way! Frank went to Canada after leaving CU in the exodus of early 1962 and eventually helped build the Toronto Argonauts into a first-rate power in the CFL. One of Frank's major contributions to that program was picking up Bill Symons, a high-voltage chunk of raw material who Frank had helped recruit for CU out of Nucla but who got caught in the unusual situation of having three head coaches in three years of college so that he never really had a chance to develop into the super star he'd have become under normal coaching conditions. Symons, who had been knocking around on the fringe of the NFL, became an instant star for Toronto and one of the best running backs in the Canadian pro league. Justice often arrives late. But it arrives most of the time. And it was true justice that saw Frank Johnson and Bill Symons finally make it big in Canada. They were both great guys.

15. ROLLIE DOTSCH

There were no changes on Sonny's staff in 1960 as the Buffaloes continued to build up to their championship season of 1961. But in 1961 Roland (Rollie) Dotsch, another recent Michigan Stater, came onto the staff to help John Polonchek with the backs. John, by this time, was getting pretty heavily involved - and I mean, involved - in being number one assistant to Sonny. So he needed some coaching help.

Rollie, a moon-faced, innocent-looking, ex-guard who was sharp as a tack and could operate with the best of them despite his deceptive facade, came aboard for a brief year and was a good man. He was a good on-the-field coach, an effective recruiter, a good speaker for the post-season banquets. Just a good all-around man. Rollie enjoyed life and he believed in taking the time to smell the flowers. I like that in a man. Rollie, of course, stepped onto the CU scene just as the championship and the collapse of the program were coming to a head, almost simultaneously. He didn't get his roots in very deep, not that he could have had he wanted to. But he did his job efficiently then got the hell out of Boulder as fast as he could when the season ended, joining Dan Devine's Missouri staff before the explosion. Rollie served well there, too, then became head coach and athletic director at Northern Michigan and then joined Devine on the Green Bay staff in 1971.

16. ED FARHAT

Probably the man who got the worst deal in the Sonny Grandelius firing was Ed Farhat, a short, dark, little guy who had been a great prep coach at Muskegon Catholic high in Michigan and who Sonny had tried to hire at least twice previously. But Ed had a real good situation at Muskegon and was reluctant to move west until he could see that the situation was stable for Sonny at Colorado. When the Buffaloes stormed through the 1961 Big Eight schedule undefeated with a young team which would return an extremely sound nucleus for 1962, Ed was convinced that the time was right and accepted the job as Rollie Dotsch's replacement. Ed's timing was worse than that of Dan Stavely and Jocko Nelson in 1958. He got fired in two months! Before he'd even been to a CU practice. But Ed didn't go down with the rest of the staff. Because he just had to be innocent and because he was a good coach with a fine background, he was retained on the staff by incoming Bud Davis. Ed, however, had come out of that tough Michigan State school of football - he had done his graduate work at East Lansing - and he was always an outsider on Bud's staff which was heavily oriented toward the forward pass. So Ed, along with Dal Ward who had been re-activated by Bud, stood on the outside and watched the 1962 season develop, if that's what you could call it, a pair of hard-nosed, ram-it-down-their-throats-on-the-ground coaches from the old school. Completely out of tune with what was happening on the CU football scene. Frustrated. Unhappy. And, basically, unproductive.

Mercifully, the season ended and everybody got fired again and everybody went back to where they came from, including Ed Farhat, who was welcomed back to Muskegon Catholic high where he had been, and was to be again, so productive. The 1962 season soon became a blurred memory. But the memory of Ed Farhat stands out with me. He deserved a better chance. Because he was a good man.

17-18-19-20-21. *DAL WARD, DON STIMACK, BOB BECKETT, PHIL CANTWELL, JIM SMITH*

I'm lumping the rest of Bud Davis' staff together because they weren't around long enough, or didn't accomplish enough, for me to learn very much about them.

Dal Ward, of course, had been gutted by his treatment during the preceding three years when he was relegated to the humiliating position of a physical education instructor. Besides, he had been a head coach too long and was now too old to be a good, aggressive, energy-filled, unquestioning assistant as he had once been under Bernie Bierman.

Don Stimack, was a tough, good high school coach at Delta, who also had been hired by Sonny, like Ed Farhat, and been retained by Bud as freshman coach. As frosh coach, Don wasn't really involved too much with what was going on with the varsity so 1962 can't be blamed on him. Don didn't have too much of a chance to prove himself as a freshman coach, either, because he didn't have much of a freshman squad. Just a bunch of passed-over preps and general rejects, and not even very many of these although there were a few youngsters who were destined to develop into pretty fair varsity hands for Eddie Crowder in the next three years. Men like Steve Sidwell, Larry Ferraro, Ray LeMasters, Frank Rogers, Dick Taylor and Frank Van Valkenburg. But not many and so Don Stimack came and went, like Farhat, a good coach who just never had a chance.

Bob Beckett, who coached the line for Bud Davis, had been a head coach at Loveland where Bud, who was from that city, had served as his assistant in 1954. Bob had coached such a recent CU star as Eddie Dove and had been a good end in his playing days in the tough program of Bowden Wyatt at Wyoming so he knew football. But CU's offense in 1962 quickly deteriorated into a pure pass attack and Bob's linemen never really got toughened to the demanding tempo of a running game. And pass blocking quickly becomes a pro-type technique of grabbing and jerking and tripping and clawing and strictly a defensive device rather than an offensive attack. And you don't get very tough grabbing and jerking and tripping and clawing and all that pass-blocking kind of stuff that drop-back teams do.

If there was a take-charge guy on the whole CU staff in 1962 it was Phil Cantwell, the end coach and a former end at Notre Dame on some of Frank Leahy's great teams. Like I said earlier, I've never seen many end coaches who didn't preach the benefits of an all-out passing offense. They get judged on how many catches their men made and it's hard to be an impressive receiver when you only throw on third-and-long. Phil Cantwell was a gregarious, enthusiastic, impressive man who quickly turned the CU offense into basketball-on-grass. You know, lots of passes, quite a few of them completed ones and most of them short ones. With an occasional dribble or two.

One play typifies the 1962 season. We were at Lubbock late in the fall to play an equally-inept Texas Tech team. We were 1-8 going into the game and the Red Raiders were not much, if any, better. It was one of those years for both teams and to compound the crime it even snowed that Saturday in Lubbock so that even the black horse with the red blanket that they use for a mascot down there couldn't even run very good. Not that he had had much chance to on good days because he only circled the field at the start of each half and after Tech touchdowns. So the two teams wallowed around in the mud and we were better wallowers than they were because we were more used to that kind of weather in the late fall. So we were out-wallowing Tech and marching the length of the field and punching it out pretty good on the ground with some pretty fair country runners like Bill Harris, Bill Symons and Leon Mavity knocking it out in good chunks through the muck. At the 7-yard line, quarterback Frank Cesarek decided to cross up Tech on third-and-goal with a flat pass. He threw it with a perfect spiral. Right into the arms of the best receiver on the field, a guy named David Parks who is still playing in the NFL. Only problem at the time was that Parks played for Texas Tech. And he promptly slithered 98 yards straight into the far end zone for a touchdown which broke our backs although the score was a respectable, 21-12, the smallest losing margin for us in that 2-8 season of horrors. In all fairness to Cesarek, I suppose, the movies did reveal that Parks, as Bud Davis liked to joke when all the wounds had healed a couple of million years later, really was the only man open in the pattern. So much for Phil Cantwell, who wherever he is today I'm certain, has got his ends catching a lot of passes.

Jim Smith was another Notre Dame graduate, a former Colorado high school star from Pueblo who was a teammate of Cantwell's at South Bend and who was a Marine Corps buddy of Bud Davis and who was assistant dean of men at CU when Bud hired him to coach the backs. Jim had been a graduate assistant in the early 1950's at both Notre Dame and CU and head coached at a California high school for three years and his father was a good high school coach in Pueblo. But, realistically, Jim wasn't going to be a career football coach or he would have never given it up for an administrative job. He had good running backs at CU but running wasn't our piece of cake that year. The offense was mostly Frank Cesarek throwing to a big good-looking end named John McGuire, who caught 36 passes that year to smash the old record of 26 by single wing quarterback Boyd Dowler in 1957. To show you how accurate - and how short - the CU passing game was, Dowler gained 380 yards with his 26 catches in 1957 while McGuire netted only 376 with his 36. Man, how we could run those three-yard and-out patterns! So Jim went back to administrating, as director of student housing at New Mexico, when the smoke cleared away and the bodies were removed.

And that takes care of the 1962 staff. It was a chaotic season, one which began with a staff turnover just a few days ahead of spring practice which then began with a player rebellion, headed by captain-elect Ken Blair (who was to grab 35 passes himself that fall as part of a do-everything role which included defensive end, linebacker, punting and, occasionally, running from deep punt on fourth down after scooping up or chasing down a bad snap from center.) Blair and the rest of the Buffaloes had campaigned hard for the Bob Ghilotti-Chuck Boerio-Buck Nystrom segment of the Grandelius schism and were loud in their disapproval when everyone was chased and Bud Davis hired from out of the alumni office. Anyway, 1962 was an abortion right from the start and the coaching staff really never got out of the huddle to the line of scrimmage. Fortunately, memory is a considerate part of man's mind and has soothed over the troubled waters of that sorry year of CU's football history. So close the book on 1962 and its men. May the memories rest in peace.

22. RUDY FELDMAN

The chief assistant on the third staff in three years was Rudy Feldman, a ruggedly-handsome, crew cut blond who I'd first met a few years earlier when he was a member of the Iowa State staff under

Jim Myers. Rudy was Eddie Crowder's first lieutenant and there has never been a better one. He was a loyal, disciplined, determined young man of German descent with perfect credentials. Good background: he'd been a tough, smallish single wing guard on some great UCLA teams coached by Red Sanders. After being in the Big Eight that one year at Ames, he was hired at Oklahoma by Bud Wilkinson and it was at Norman that he became a close friend and ally of another young assistant coach, Eddie Crowder. The two men had great respect for each other and they complemented each other beautifully — Crowder the energetic, idea-spewing mind and Feldman a stoic realist who could be depended upon to carry out an order, any order, to its ultimate destination with no questions asked once he'd accepted the assignment. Better than anyone, Rudy knew how to work with Eddie. When to debate a point; how far to pursue the debate; how to keep on a subject, tactfully, until he had made his point.

But Rudy's chief strength was as an on-the-field coach. He handled the defense for Eddie and worked with the defensive line in particular. And like Ray Jenkins and Buck Nystrom and Chuck Boerio, he had that mystic quality which enabled him to be a tough, demanding coach on the practice field yet be accepted by his men. There have been, and will be in the future, exceptions to the rule but I feel strongly that a former linebacker will understand linebackers better as a coach, that a former offensive guard will understand offensive guards best as a coach, and so forth. All of the men I have just mentioned were rough, tough players and very good ones. And, aside from Jenkins who was a fullback at CU but who probably would have been converted into a guard or tackle had he come along today, all these men coached the positions they had played as a collegian.

During the lean days of 1963 and 1964 when the CU program was rebuilding its muscle after near death, Rudy was a rock in the foundation which was being built. Quietly optimistic with a grim strength rippling out of every pore, he gave a feeling of confidence as he helped move the program forward. Tenacious is probably the word which describes Rudy best. He was a bulldog who never let go of his job until it was finished properly. Ironically, Rudy, who was as German as he could be- he could have been by Eric Von Stroheim out of Marlene Dietrich - had a very Jewish-sounding name. To the great delight of Crowder and others, Rudy inevitably got a quick call from the local rabbi whenever he moved into a town. It happened at Norman. And it happened in Boulder. And it probably happened at Albuquerque when he became head coach at New Mexico. But Rudy took this mistake in his religion in relatively good style and continued on his dogged way.

I'll never forget the scene in the Warwick Hotel on the night following our 1967 Bluebonnet Bowl victory over Miami, Rudy's last game on the CU staff. One-by-one, the seniors on the CU defense came by the room where the coaching staff was celebrating to pay their respects to Rudy. And they clustered around Rudy in happy reminiscences of their college careers, which had just ended that afternoon in Rice Stadium. Finally they all sallied forth into the night — the grim German, no longer grim, and his men - comrades all. There were no witnesses except the group itself but it was a night of revelry. Rudy made it to breakfast the next morning, only slightly the worse for the previous evening, and had enough quality to be able to fly to Albuquerque and win the New Mexico head job that same day. And he has become a fine head coach for the Lobos. There was never any doubt in my mind that he wouldn't be. Some guys have "can't miss" labels. Rudy Feldman was one of them. A damned good man.

23. CHET FRANKLIN

Chester Franklin, along with Rudy Feldman, accompanied Eddie Crowder from the Oklahoma staff where he'd been primarily a young aid to Eddie. Chet idolized Crowder and was a loyal, unquestioning aid who came on a little strong at first but who settled down to become a good hand and eventually became the offensive co-ordinator before moving into the pros as an assistant with the San Francisco 49'ers in 1971. Chet was ambitious and eager but somewhat inclined to dismiss anything that had happened at Colorado as below his station in life and, consequently, irritated some of the oldtimers around the program who remembered him as an obscure guard on one of those obscure Utah teams which the Buffaloes, under Ward, used to stomp pretty consistently in the mid-50's . . . after an opening loss to the Redskins in his first encounter with them, Ward went 9-0-1 against Utah in the next 10 years. But Chet gathered up some humility along the way, especially in those early 2-and-8 days when he discovered that it took something more than just being from Wilkinson's Oklahoma staff to build up a program. Chet worked with the ends and backs and generally with the offense and developed well as an on-field coach. But it was as a recruiter that he made his real contribution to the CU comeback. Although he didn't carry the title, Chet was the chief recruiter and he was a very good one who was responsible for the efforts which brought in a great rookie crop in 1964, one which was to catapult the Buffaloes to a 6-2-2 season as sophomores and into the Bluebonnet Bowl as seniors. The crop included such 3-year stalwarts as Dick Anderson, Frank Bosch, Wilmer Cooks, Bill Csikos, John Farler, Charles Greer, William Harris, Bruce Heath, Kerry Mottl, Larry Plantz, Kirk Tracy and Mike

Veeder. The Buffaloes were on their way and there were no secrets to the solution. Go out and get some good men and give them some direction! That's exactly what this young CU staff did and Chester Franklin was the man who most of all helped bring in the bodies. Not that the other coaches didn't work hard at recruiting, too. They did. Everybody on an Eddie Crowder staff works hard - and long - at every phase of his job. But Chet led the way in the vital recruiting department in those early days and even though he gradually concentrated more on coaching and less on recruiting at the close of his 8-year hitch with the Buffaloes, it is from those early days that I value Chet's contribution. Just one more personal memory of Chet Franklin: he had one of the nicest, best-looking wives of any coach that has ever come through our program. And that's a pretty good compliment because football coaches, most of them having been heroes in their undergraduate days, do awfully well, matrimonially. You very seldom see a football coach with a dog for a wife. In fact, I can't recall one. But Ann Franklin ranks right near the top of the list. So, old Chester wasn't a bad recruiter for himself, either!

24. JOE HARPER

For some reason we've had a lot of runty line coaches at CU once that elephantine 1956-57 trio of Marsh Wells, Ray Jenkins and Will Walls went their ways. I guess that might be because little linemen have to learn to live by their wits and not by their brawn so that once they've come through college alive they're in pretty good mental shape to become coaches. And the same rule applies to coaching linemen that does to training dogs. If you're going to be effective as a teacher, you've got to know more than your pupils. Joe Harper was a sharp little guy whose entree to Crowder's newly-formed staff was through Rudy Feldman. Joe had come along at UCLA after Rudy had graduated but was the same type of gritty little guard for two years under the robust leadership of Red Sanders, then when Red checked it in one afternoon in Los Angeles, under Bill Barnes. Joe was a quiet little guy. If I had to compare him to another CU coach, it probably would be Bob Ghilotti. Almost invisible on the practice field and coaching with no noise whatsoever. But coaching well.

The one characteristic of Crowder's early CU teams was that at the start of each season they tried hard but were only fair at moving the ball. But they played tough defense always and, game by game, the offensive line play would get better and better until, by the last half of the season the Buffaloes had developed into a very efficient unit up front and, accordingly, on the ground. Joe Harper was one of the coaches most responsible for this great improvement each season. You don't have to make a lot of noise to be a good coach although it doesn't hurt, especially if you know what you're screaming about. A lot of the sidewalk superintendents who gather along the sidelines at practice daily and gossip and get cold and pontificate but who rarely observe very accurately, though, used to downrate Harper as a coach because they couldn't hear him or even see him very well. But he was a good one. With more to him than a lot of people could see. At the end of the 1967 campaign, Joe decided to get into the head coaching business himself and took a job at California Poly at San Luis Obispo. In case you don't remember, that was the school where the football team got wiped out in a plane crash in the mid-60's. Joe quickly got that program built up and, as of this writing, was doing an excellent job at Cal Poly. You may hear more about him in the future although he may be happy to stay at that level of college football. They're all good levels. Wherever Joe is he'll be a producer. He's that kind of a guy.

25. DON STALWICK

Don Stalwick, another ex-UCLA star and a teammate of Rudy Feldman's there, worked with the backs under Eddie Crowder for two years. Don had been a fine wingback on some outstanding UCLA teams. Again, not a big man by any stretch of the imagination, but a good one. Don was a Bon Vivant, used to the good life. A quiet and respectable swinger, if you like. He really wasn't cut out for the demanding life of an assistant under Eddie Crowder and both men realized it and, to their credit, terminated their working relationship, amicably, after two seasons. Don coached at Claremont College then went into business in California and, I am sure, is doing well for he was a sharp, able man. Let me say this at this point. Being an offensive coach, and in particular, a backfield coach on Eddie Crowder's staff isn't the easiest assignment in the world by a couple of zillion miles. Crowder was a master of offense as a split T quarterback under Bud Wilkinson and, consequently, he is a very knowledgable and very demanding man insofar as the offense is concerned. The same characteristics apply to defense, too. But not quite as intensely as at the offensive end of the field. So exit Stalwick rather quickly and his arrival and departure aren't really significant except that it marked the beginning of a trend. There was, and still is, a lot of coming and going of assistant coaches under Crowder. Like, for example, a parade of 24 assistants in Eddie's first 10 years at the helm. Compared to only 21, spread out over three complete coaching changes, in the preceding 11 years. It's all a matter of individual approach. And I'll say this. I doubt that a coaching staff of Eddie Crowder's ever becomes sedentary.

26. JIM McCONLOGUE

But Don Stalwick wasn't the first to leave. That dubious honor belonged to Jim McConlogue, a big, strapping redhead who came aboard after five years as a head coach, at smallish Lafayette College in Pennsylvania. Jim, who had been involved in playing and coaching at a relative modest level of college football all his life, decided he wanted to see what life was like at the major college level. But it wasn't for him and he was the first to know it and he bailed out after a year, returning to Lafayette and dying, much too young, of a heart attack while on a scouting trip a few years after leaving CU.

Football didn't kill Jim McConlogue, though. For him coaching was a labor of love and he worked at it happily and softly, grinning a lot and thoroughly enjoying his job. He'd been that way all his life and it was a good way. But it wasn't the proper preparation for the stern task which confronted the Eddie Crowder staff back in those grim days of 1963. What killed Jim McConlogue was a series of horrible experiences in the Air Force as a bomber pilot in the ETO in World War II. Jim was one of the sitting ducks in the massive low level air strikes over the Ploesti oil fields and got shot down and spent several torturous months in a Nazi prison camp. That experience took something out of him and, although he appeared to be a healthy, robust giant at 6-5 and 220 pounds, the toll had been taken and the battle wounds were on his insides, invisible to the eye, but there nevertheless with the potence to end his life before his time. I know Jim McConlogue's soul is resting in peace and that he's somewhere right now with a whistle around his neck, helping coach a team at wherever it is that good football coaches go when they leave us.

27. DAN STAVELY

When Eddie Crowder was searching for a good freshman coach, and he knew the importance of that job, a couple of the grizzled and scarred veterans of the CU athletic staff, Dal Ward and Kayo Lam, stumped long and hard for Dan Stavely. Normally, that's the worst way to help a friend. Plug too hard for him to a stranger. But Eddie Crowder wasn't an average young stranger. Perceptive beyond his years, he knew the tremendous value in getting an older and more experienced man to coach and counsel his freshmen. Eddie realized that in a program as demanding as the one he was about to institute, an extremely good man was necessary. Both for the rookies and the older hands. Given a second opportunity to return to his native and beloved Colorado, Dan Stavely didn't waste any time accepting. And if Rudy Feldman was a rock in Eddie Crowder's CU rebuilding foundation, Dan Stavely was a whole quarry. You name it and he was a master. A great recruiter who could charm the heart of the most demanding mother in the world. Or establish a quick rapport with a suspicious father intent on directing his son to the best possible college. And a good on-the-field coach whose frosh teams have compiled an amazing record over those years from 1963. And a great and diligent supervisor of student study sessions who mother-hens his groping greenhorns better than the best mother-hen in the world. And a tremendous man at establishing a healthy relationship with professors, campus administrators and secretaries, maybe as important a contribution as he makes to the CU athletic program.

And, through it all, a devoted working man's Christian who applies sound Christian principles to everything he does. Dan Stavely isn't an angel. He can get down in the pits and drive a team to excellence as good and as tough as any coach. And he knows how to battle and kick and squirm to achieve the victory he sets out after. He isn't a narrow-minded Christian. He enjoys an earthy story as well as the next man, and you'd better enjoy them if you're going to be happy in coaching because you're certainly going to get exposed to a lot of them along the way. When I call Dan Stavely a working man's Christian I mean it as the highest compliment I can give him. In a profession which should, but too often doesn't, produce a beautiful relationship between coach and player, Dan has led a beautiful life and done a beautiful job. His play book and his Bible are equally important in his approach to coaching and life. He is a deeply religious man who once considered very seriously going into the ministry, but went into coaching instead and I am sure he has touched as many lives in a beneficial way in this profession as he might have had he gone on to become a minister. Certainly, he has devoted a good part of his life to studying, and teaching, the Bible. And being a good Christian. His work with the Fellowship of Christian Athletes alone is more than a lot of men accomplish in their lifetimes. And this facet of his life is a relatively small one in comparison to all the other jobs he performs. He has been one of the real leaders in the Colorado movement of the FCA, one of the finest organizations in the world for young people.

If I sound enthusiastic about Dan Stavely it's because I am. I don't think I've ever been around a man quite like him. He's a once-in-a-lifetimer and I'm grateful that I've been one of the people blessed by his friendship.

And, by the way, he's also one of the finest speakers, masters of ceremonies, invocation-or-benediction givers you'll ever find. And he also plays a fair country guitar and sings a loud and melodic hymn or country-western favorite.

But a man has got to have his flaws and Dan Stavely is only human. He's got a big one. He can go to sleep at the drop of a hat. And it makes no matter what he's doing at the time. Down slumps the head and out goes Dan. In a living room chair at the home of a recruit, in a coaches meeting, or at the wheel of his car. In 1963 when the staff was new, Dan and Eddie Crowder were on a recruiting trip on the western slope and returning home through Hot Sulphur Springs where they decided to take the famed health baths. On the rubbing table after almost total immersion in the steaming mineral-laden water and conversing quietly, the two men were at peace with the world when Eddie noticed he was getting no response from Dan. Wiping his eyes and putting on his glasses, Eddie saw that Dan was sound asleep with his arm flopping over the side of the table. This was Eddie's first exposure to this peculiarity of Dan's and he softly grasped his wrist and took his pulse. Maybe, to see if Dan was still alive. The pulse was something like 39. He has a metabolism which can slow down to almost nothing. And undoubtedly prevent a lot of ulcers and heartburn and heart attacks and all those physical afflicttions which can plague a football coach.

My favorite experience with Dan is a recent one which involved us driving to the Denver airport to pick up Milburn and Jane Stone, he of Doc Adams fame in Gunsmoke. Doc flew to Boulder for a game in 1971 and was duly honored by being made the honorary team physician for the Buffaloes. He was just coming off open-heart surgery and hadn't made many public appearances after his recovery but he wanted to come to a CU game because he and Dan had become great friends after being on the program of an athletic banquet together. With me watching him very closely and ready to grab the wheel in case he dropped off en route, Dan got us to Stapleton Field in good shape. It was dark when we left Stapleton so I drove. Dan was riding shotgun and talking to Doc and Jane and I was driving and listening and thoroughly relishing hearing these good friends enjoying each other's company. When suddenly there was a break in the conversation followed by a loud thud. Dan had gone to sleep and his head had flopped over to one side, hitting the window. I'm sure, poor Doc almost had another heart attack thinking that Dan had had one right there in the front seat. But the jolt awoke Dan and, although he dozed briefly the rest of the way, he managed to keep up his end of the conversation.

But, aside from trying to be a good guy to too many people (and that's really not a fault, is it?), that's the only flaw in Dan Stavely that I've ever been able to find. And I've been fairly close to the man for a long time. I guess I love him, too.

28. BILL MONDT

To replace Jim McConlogue, Eddie Crowder reached into the ranks of ex-CU players and came up with one of the line stalwarts on Dal Ward's fine teams of 1956-57-58, Bill Mondt. Bill was an excellent guard on those teams and it was his lead blocks which helped Bob Stransky pick his way for 1097 yards in 1957, second best total in the nation that year. And just as important, insofar as Bill's future was concerned, was his status as a student. Bill attended CU on a Boettcher Scholarship, awarded annually in the state of Colorado to top high school students. At CU, Bill logged better than a B average as he majored in engineering and business. Bill coached just like he played. Quietly. Conscientiously. Intelligently. His primary assignment was with the defensive backfield, though, and I never felt that he was in the right position. A linebacker on defense as a two-way man in college, Bill was more at home working with linemen and, although he did a creditable job, he soon became frustrated. After two years on the CU staff he decided to try the business field and resigned to join the Lego toy division of Samsonite, a new division of that company which had opened a plant in Loveland. But Bill was soon back in coaching as he joined Rudy Feldman as offensive line coach when Rudy became head coach at New Mexico in 1968. Bill has done a good job for Rudy. It's good to have a man of his quality back in coaching. Helping to build young men is much more important, and satisfying, than helping to build toys.

29. PAT CULPEPPER

When Don Stalwick left, Eddie Crowder picked up one of Darrell Royal's brightest young products at Texas, Pat Culpepper, who had been a very fine fullback and linebacker for Darrell. And so inspirational a player, that Royal had kept him on as a full-time special assistant to have him ready when an opening on the regular Longhorn staff developed. But Pat wanted to test his wings somewhere else first so he came to CU as linebacker coach and quickly proved to be an outstanding young teacher and motivator. It was a happy union because the Buffaloes had several bright young linebackers like Kerry Mottl and Steve Graves plus a pair of good veterans in Steve Sidwell and Dennis Drummond and Culpepper, with his enthusiasm and ability to project himself inside of his young men, brought their talents out tremendously well. Culpepper had so much fire, and great credentials as a player - Royal called him one of the most inspirational men who had ever played for him at Texas - that you just had to get after it for him.

This was basically a sophomore team in 1965 and Culpepper's

presence had a great influence on the young men of the defense and the defense led the way in a solid 6-2-2 campaign, yielding only 106 points (compared to 156 the year before, 245 in 1963 and a horrendous 346 the year before Crowder took over.) Only two teams scored more than two touchdowns on the Buffaloes in 1965. The defense was back! And that was the primary task in the re-construction job. Now it was time to get busy with the offense.

Culpepper wasn't destined to stay in the program, though. His roots were in the south and, although Royal didn't call, his former defensive coach at Texas, Jim Pittman, did. Pittman got the head job at Tulane and Pat joined him there. He was to be back at Boulder three years later but it wasn't the same and Culpepper's contribution to the Buffaloes covers 1965 primarily. We hated to see him go, tried to keep him, but he went back to his old coach and you can't fight that.

30. KEN BLAIR

Ken Blair, one of the heroes of the 1961 cliffhanger over Kansas (he caught two of those fourth period touchdown passes) and the captain of the 1962 disaster, returned to his alma mater after a year on the Davidson staff to succeed Culpepper as linebacker coach. Ken, a solid strip of rawhide from Roswell, N.M., had had a fine senior season despite the unhappy circumstances which saturated the entire year. He was a fine offensive end who caught 35 passes, a tough defensive end who was moved to linebacker when deficiencies developed there during the season and also did the punting for the Buffaloes, averaging 39 yards on 45 boots. His personal record was good enough to earn him All-Big Eight selection despite the record of his team. Ken gave Bud Davis all he had despite having been the man who led the protest in the spring against the selection of Bud. When it was obvious that the protest would not have any effect, Ken accepted Bud Davis totally and gave 100 per cent effort throughout the dismal fall.

And when Eddie Crowder took over, Ken stayed on as a graduate assistant and did the job well enough that he was called back quickly when the linebacker job opened. Ken had an excellent ability to communicate to his men and CU's linebackers played well for him and the work of Rick Ogle, Bill Blanchard and Chris Havens formed a solid part of the CU defense in 1969 as the Buffaloes wiped out Alabama in the Liberty Bowl to climax a fine season. And a pair of rookies who were to be big factors in future CU successes, John Stavely and Billy Drake, got their introduction to big league linebacking under Blair.

Kenny's major contribution to the CU program may have been a negative one, however. But it was important in that it taught everyone a lesson in legal pitfalls. Ken, normally an even-tempered man accepted the challenge of a needler in a Boulder restaurant on a Thursday night before an Alumni-Varsity spring game. The two men went into the parking lot to settle their affair and, predictably, Ken worked his opponent over pretty good. Too good, in fact. For although the other man had started the argument and even had taken the first punch, the court ruled that Ken had gone too far in his response. In effect, it's okay to win the fight but don't win it by too much; stop fighting when the battle has been won. Of course, it's a lot easier for a judge to make that ruling than it is for the actual participant to make that judgment during the dual. Anyway, Ken got racked for a good amount of damages and all of us at CU learned what most of us already knew, especially us smallish cowards: he who smiles and walks away, won't get hauled into court another day. And now when any of us begins to blow a fuse at someone, we remember the Ken Blair incident and ease off on the gas. Thanks for the lesson, Ken! I'm sure it's saved a lot of us money and trouble.

And so, after five good years on the CU staff, Ken decided it was time to leave home for other fields and went to UCLA with Pepper Rodgers. I know he's learning new techniques under Pepper. For one thing, Pepper sings in night spots instead of fighting. Kenny, as a former Buffalo, has a special place in my heart. He is a good man. Nearly all old Buffaloes are!

31. LARRY BIELAT

Coming aboard with Blair in 1966 was a personable young high school coach from Chicago, laughing Larry Bielat who had impressed various members of the CU staff who had come across him as they were recruiting the midwest area. Bielat was a Michigan State ex and there were no midwesterners on the CU staff and it was felt that Larry would not only be a good coach, he would strengthen CU's recruiting back in Big Ten country where there were so many good prospects each year. And while Larry didn't exactly burn his name into the CU record book as one of the great recruiters of all time, he did bring in quite a few young men, most of them, unfortunately, relatively untalented insofar as football ability was concerned. But he did add a dimension to the CU staff which was needed at the time — looseness. Larry was a fun-loving guy who could keep things loose and with guys like Rudy Feldman, Chet Franklin, Joe Harper, Bill Mondt and Ken Blair around — none of these men will ever produce many laughs — we needed someone to change a face from grim to grin. And he could do it. And by doing it he brought an important, I feel, quality to the coaching atmosphere. But, generally speaking.

Larry was out-numbered and his humor wasn't always appreciated and he left the first chance he got. Which was to New Mexico with the grimmest German of them all, Rudy Feldman. But Larry didn't stay with Rudy too long and left coaching to launch a chain of soda fountain-type businesses in the Albuquerque area. I know Larry will be a big success . . . I can just see him with that white cap on and that malted milk can in his hand. With a big grin in his face. When they make the movie of his life, Jack Oakie will probably play Bielat. Attaway to go, Larry. You were a good buddy and I liked you! And you weren't too bad a coach, either.

32. BILLY WILLIAMSON

When Bill Mondt checked in his whistle, Eddie Crowder dug into the deep south and came up with a brilliant young defensive backfield coach out of Georgia Tech named Billy Williamson. Billy could have stepped right out of a Confederate officers' club. Dark and handsome with a let-it-all-hang-out attitude, Williamson had been a two-time All-SEC back under one of the south's most respected coaches, Bobby Dodd. Like Culpepper two years earlier, he brought a breath of fresh air — complete with the smell of magnolia blossoms and grits and black-eyed peas — to the CU secondary. Veterans like Dick Anderson, Charles Greer, Mike Bynum, Ike Howard and Steve Tracy reacted to Williamson's directions quickly and the Buffalo back row was brilliant that fall. There is something about football in the south that breeds more enthusiasm into a young man than it seems to do in the north. Or maybe it's just because southerners are warmer, friendlier people who just ooze with southern charm. Anyway, young coaches like Culpepper and Williamson had a charisma you don't find often enough in young coaches. And it really helped them get their points across. For example, Billy Williamson inherited some pretty salty old hands in Anderson, who would make All-American that fall, and Greer and Bynum. You might have assumed that he'd have a tough time winning their respect. Especially when he had just come out of such an impressive place as East Tennessee State. In Johnson City, Tennessee. But it was a case of instant acceptance. You'd have thought the CU veterans were 18-year-old southerners and Williamson had drafted them to save Tara from the Yankees. It was the warmest of weddings and the CU secondary sparkled throughout the fall.

But southern youngsters keep wanting to go back home to the south and when the master calls they go scurrying back to the plantation. So Bobby Dodd beckoned and Billy Williamson went back to Georgia Tech. Again, we tried to keep him but we couldn't compete with that southern cooking. So long, Billy, it was good to have you with us. Even for a short while. And I think you'll find out that it's warmer in the snow when you're winning than it might be in the steaming swamplands of the south when you're losing. But good luck, anyway!

33. DON JAMES

When Eddie Crowder lost his right-hand man, Rudy Feldman, who wore the title of chief assistant, he hired a defensive co-ordinator to take his place. The new man was Don James, a former star quarterback in the Massilon, Ohio football machine coached at that time by Chuck Mather and subsequently a quarterback at Miami (Fla.) and then a fine young defensive backfield coach at Florida State then Michigan who headed up the defensive staff at both those schools. Unimpressive physically - he looked more like a biology professor than a football coach - Don was on the runty side but had a lot of defensive savvy stored away in a fine mind. He came onto the CU scene at a tough time . . . as one of four new assistants, three of them defensive coaches. There was a lot of getting acquainted to be done between new coaches and their players and this time it didn't come off as well as it could have. The Buffalo defense came unglued at midseason and by the end of the season other teams were wearing out the grass in CU's end of the field. The Buffs, who had yielded but 113 points in 11 games in 1967, got punctured for 240 in 10 games and closed out the season with a nightmarish 58-35 loss to Air Force as the Falcons ran wild around and inside the CU flanks.

There was near-panic in the defensive staff room but James and his men bounced back quickly and put some teeth back into the Buffaloes the next fall. The Buffalo defense, after that lapse in 1968 which led to Crowder's first losing season in four years, was sound again and James' shrewd game plans played a big role in the resurgence. Maybe the best, certainly the most effective, defensive plan he ever conceived was the scheme for his final regular season game as a CU coach, the 1970 finale at Air Force. The Falcons were flying high with a tremendous passing attack which featured the catching and running of All-American flanker Ernest Jennings who, as a sophomore two years earlier, had been one of the Bluebirds who had tortured the Buffaloes in that 58-35 rout at Boulder . Air Force had already won a Sugar Bowl berth a week earlier. But the Buffaloes took several spoonsful of sugar out of that bowl with a 49-19 demolition job. James' defensive plan worked beautifully. It involved bump-and-run tactics on Jennings with big, swift sophomore Cullen Bryant whacking away at the Air Force star then one of the safeties, either Pat Murphy or Pete Jacobsen picking him up once he finally escaped Bryant. Jennings was negated completely and James got the game ball. And a new job. Don, a native Ohioan, returned to his home state as head coach at Kent State, getting the job before the Buffaloes met Tulane in the Liberty Bowl in early December. He was a fine addition to the CU staff. A high-class gentleman all the way. One of the more thoughtful thoroughbreds I've come across. A good friend and a good coach.

34. AUGIE TAMMARIELLO

There hadn't been any fellow Italians on the staff since Ghilotti and Boerio got the Lucky Luciano treatment - exile, man! - in 1961 but we got back into a position of power in 1968 and the first one aboard was Augie Tammariello, a tightly-wound little fireball who followed Dan Stavely's trail onto the CU coaching staff as the second Denver University graduate to overcome that disadvantage. Augie, a native Pennsylvanian, had come west in answer to John Roning's call at Denver and had been a fine little fireplug guard and linebacker for the Pioneers. He was an Academic All-American at Denver then did his graduate work and got his first coaching experience there before completing the job at Penn State. Augie was at William & Mary for a year before coming to CU in 1968 as offensive line coach.

He was a noisy Joe Harper. A latin livewire. A good coach. Even though that first year he never quite convinced CU's impending All-American, a huge hessian named Mike Montler, that he knew more about offensive line play than Mike. But he did. It was just that anyone who was 6-5 and 250 and nearly 25 years old didn't need to know a hell of a lot to be an All-American tackle.

Augie's lines in 1969-70-71 were just like a bowl of Rice Krispies: just pour a little milk on them and how they did snap, crackle and pop people! Augie's chief coaching asset is his enthusiasm. It can be on the corny side but it still comes across to those trench-hogs. Put your heart in the end zone and the ball will follow, he likes to scream in his high-pitched voice. With his horn-rimmed glasses bouncing up and down on his nose, he looks like a pudgy little owl, a character straight out of Pogo. But, oh! how he can bring those young offensive lineman along. And how they can carve out those holes for CU's big running backs! For example, the Buffaloes ripped out 2998 rushing yards in 1970 and upped that total to 3099 in 1971.

And through it all, Little Augie keeps crying out for more. He's not mean enough to be Vince Lombardi but he's about the same size as that great man was and he does wear those same tinted glasses. And he does get the same type of results. Keep shouting, Augie! Keep those guards and tackles rolling. We don't wanna get shipped back to Sicily!

35. JIM MORA

Some Italians are loud. Some are short. Most of them, in fact, are both loud and short. Occasionally, you find one who's tall, dark and handsome. And quiet. Like Jim Mora, who acts more like a rich Englishman than a relatively poor Italian. But, then, Jim came out of that famed polishing school of the far west, Stanford. So you could expect him to be pretty well polished. Actually, he's from Occidental. Played there and was head coach there for three years before he went to Stanford as an assistant. Jim and Chet Franklin were Marine Corps buddies and Chet had some Stanford background, too, so Chet helped him get the CU defensive line job in 1968. It took him a little while to get that Occidental and Stanford sleepiness out of his system (maybe it was just his quiet personality) but Jim got his teeth into the bit after a year or so and has done a solid job with the defensive front. You'd think he could communicate with those big, mean-tempered monsters like Herb Orvis and Bill Brundige and Dave Capra and Rich Varriano and Carl Taibi (especially those last three Italians) better if he screamed and waved his arms more but that's not Jim's way. And you've got to admit, his way has worked pretty well.

I have a hunch that Jim is one of those late-blooming coaches who is just beginning to come into his own. If this be true, he has a tremendous future ahead of him because he's already accomplished a lot. An unusual Italian. Calm. Collected. Quiet. No garlic on his breath. Amazing! But we still accept him, don't we, Augie? Because Jim Mora is a great guy.

36. PAT CULPEPPER

Pat Culpepper found life at Tulane just about what we all figured it would be and he got away from Poppa Jim Pittman just as fast as he could when he got the chance to come back to Colorado. But this time it didn't take and Pat could never accept a subservient role on this CU defensive staff. I guess he probably felt that his way was better than Don James' and Pat was a strong-minded young man who had had a lot of success doing it his way. But in 1968 at CU he just drove a wedge into the CU defensive staff. So he was gone almost before Ben Martin's Alpine hat hit the ground following the final Air Force touchdown that November. Gone to that great graveyard in the southwest, Baylor. Probably that's where he belongs. In the southwest, not in a graveyard. You're still a great guy, Hoss! But times and people do change and you changed. See you around.

37. STEVE ORTMAYER

A young man with a dazed-look on his face wandered onto the CU scene as a special graduate assistant in 1967 and quickly proved that looks can be deceiving. Steve Ortmayer turned out to be a very sharp young coach with a persistence not found in many men. He was right out of the Rudy Feldman school. Stolid. Unswerving. A guy who carried out orders to the last little detail. Who never took his nose off the trail until he had gotten what he went after. In short, a fine young coach. And with the qualities which every staff must have in at least one man. Complete dedication to football. It's better if everybody has that quality but it's a little unrealistic to expect it of everyone. Most coaches will give 95-100 percent. But 110 is a little high to expect.

Ortmayer was a center at LaVerne (Calif.) college on a team coached by his uncle. He learned his grid lessons well and I'm sure it was tougher playing for a close relative than it would have been for someone else. He has worked his way around on the CU staff, spending a little time with several groups including both offense and defense and doing a good on-the-field job wherever he's been assigned.

He has been particularly effective as a recruiter, though, and this area is where his tenactiy pays off big. He has worked the Texas and southern areas very diligently and his efforts have been largely responsible for the number of good players who have come to CU from there in recent seasons. I doubt that any other member of the CU staff has logged as many hours on the job as Steve Ortmayer. Eddie Crowder excepted, of course — nobody spends more hours on the job than he does. But, then, he gets paid more.

And underneath that stolid facade lies as good and sharp a sense of humor as I've ever seen. It stays submerged a lot because Steve is a junior member of the firm and he realizes it. But when it surfaces you've got a piece of wit worth waiting for. This is a young man with a bright future. And, ultimately, that dazed look will be taken as an intense look. Maybe that's what it's always been. Italians just don't understand Germans, I guess. But I do understand that Steve Ortmayer is a great young guy and a fine young coach.

38. RICK DUVAL

If Don James came in looking like a biology professor, Rick Duval might have been a mathematics instructor. Dark and handsome, somewhat like Jim Mora only with sharper, colder features. Rick had a certain reservation about him, almost a cold hardness beyond his years. He was only 29 when he volunteered for duty as a special assistant in the fall of 1967 after having served on the Columbia staff for the preceding two seasons. Rick wanted to learn the combination of coaching and administrating under one of the nation's bright young athletic director-head coaches and he selected Eddie Crowder as his model. Rick had gotten the coaching call rather late in his youth; he majored in electrical engineering at Worcester Polytechnic Institute, a school much more noted for its engineering graduates than for its quarterback-safetymen, which Rick was. Rick worked with the defense his first year and is now in charge of the receivers and, as such, coached that formidable fleet of 1971 deep route-runners which included Cliff Branch, Larry Brunson and Marv Whitaker.

But Rick's strength thus far has been as an organization man and in organizing the recruiting in particular. No detail escapes Rick in his recruiting organization. He floods high school seniors, their coaches, their parents, everybody with CU propaganda the year around. Rick is a lot tougher on secretaries and mimeograph machines than any coach I've ever seen. And he ain't too good for a postage machine, either! But if you take care of the little things, the big things take care of themselves. Or something. Whatever, Rick's recruiting program has brought in a lot of powerful prospects since he took over in 1970. And recruiting is still the name of the game. I mean, almost anybody can coach Clifford Branch. The big job is getting him to enroll. And that's what Rick Duval does best. And because of that quality, he is a most important young member of the CU staff. And I also think he's learning what he came here to learn . . . how to be an athletic director-head coach.

39. STEVE SIDWELL

Eddie Crowder didn't go very far to get his next linebacker coach when Pat Culpepper left, naming an ex-CU linebacking star, Steve Sidwell, who had been serving as an administrative aid on Eddie's staff. Big Sid was an All-Big Eight backer for the Buffaloes in 1965, ironically under the direction of Culpepper, the man he succeeded. He had majored in business and was working as the Buff Club liaison man in addition to doing some graduate assisting on the side.

Sid liked what he'd experienced about coaching and decided to go into it fulltime when the chance came. And he quickly became a productive member of the staff, blending in with the rest of the coaches very well and establishing excellent rapport with his players. Sid is a no-nonsense coach who believes in discipline. That's the way he played as an undergraduate when he survived a painful neck injury to become a standout for the Buffaloes. And that's the way he coaches now. All business. But like some of the other good line coaches I've mentioned, with an ability to strike up a good relationship with his men, Sid is a bulldog who overpowers any assignment be it recruiting, finding summer jobs for players or coaching. It's the way which has worked for him and which will continue to work for him in the future as he gets better and better each year. He's a good man with a lot of future ahead of him. He won't let it be any other way.

40. COTTRELL McGOWAN

As more and more black players began making vital contributions to the CU football program, a black assistant coach became necessary and Eddie Crowder hired Cottrell McGowan, a high school coach he'd met and been greatly impressed with while recruiting in the Houston area. Mac has made a valuable contribution to the CU program in what is not the easiest job in the world. But Mac is color blind and does his job which includes working with the offensive backfield and recruiting his native Houston area with easygoing effectiveness. He's a good man who has established an important link of communication to the staff for the black players, many of whom prefer to go to a fellow black for counsel. Mac doesn't pull any punches with either the whites or the blacks. He tells it like it is.

If Mac has a problem as a CU assistant it's one which all Buff backfield coaches have labored under. The boss man, Eddie Crowder, an old backfield man himself, spends a lot of time with the offensive backs and the quarterbacks in particular. So that the other men who work with the offensive backs must yield their place to the boss quite often. Mac has worked with the running backs primarily and he's had several good ones like Jon Keyworth, Charles Davis and John Tarver who really didn't need much except the ball and a couple of steps of daylight. As a recruiter, Mac has produced outstandingly, teaming with Ortmayer to lure such standouts as Davis, J. V. Cain and Bill McDonald out of the Houston area. He's a good guy. We needed him. And I like him.

41. JERRY CLAIBORNE

After the smashing finish to the 1969 campaign which saw the Buffaloes win their last four games, including a particularly satisfying 47-33 triumph over Alabama's gridiron glamour boys in the Liberty Bowl, there was no change in the CU coaching staff. For the only time in Eddie Crowder's first 10 years. But following the 1970 season, three men left: Don James to the Kent State head job, Chet Franklin to the 49'ers and Ken Blair to UCLA. So the almost-annual search for new assistants began again.

The Buffaloes had lost to Tulane in the Liberty Bowl to finish barely over .500 at 6-5 and Eddie Crowder determined to get the best available coach in the nation to head up his defense. His number one choice was Jerry Claiborne, a Bear Bryant disciple who had played for the Bear at Kentucky and coached for him at Kentucky, Texas A&M and Alabama before becoming head coach at Virginia Tech in 1961. Jerry did an amazingly good job at the small, obscure Virginia school, compiling a 61-39-2 record over a decade and taking the Gobblers to two bowl games where his teams gave solidly-favored

Miami and Mississippi teams a full afternoon before bowing. But Jerry suffered the fate which befalls nearly every head coach who wins but doesn't win enough...and you can't hardly win enough for some people and some college presidents who demand a lot more of a football coach than they probably ever produced themselves. So Jerry had a couple of so-so seasons in his ninth and tenth years at Blacksburg and promptly got the ax. Which may have been just about the best thing that ever happened to Jerry because it brought him to Colorado and, after just one season, back into the head coaching profession at Maryland, a major Eastern school which probably wouldn't even schedule Virginia Tech.

Jerry was named assistant head coach by Eddie and took over the defense and he didn't waste any time winning the confidence — and hearts — of everyone in Boulder. He was a thoroughbred and thoroughbreds go right to the front of the class. Jerry was the third southerner to be hired by Eddie and like his predecessors, Pat Culpepper (first term) and Billy Williamson, made an instant hit with both his fellow coaches and the players by his tremendous enthusiasm and knowledge. Jerry was totally dedicated to his profession. He practically lived in his office during those early days on the job as he familiarized himself with his new school. Dropping down to an assistant after being a head coach for 10 years is not an easy thing to do. But Jerry did it with style. You'd never have known he'd been a head coach except for the calm air of class and confidence which he projected. If I had to describe Jerry with one word it would probably be "consistent." He was consistently thorough. Consistently good-natured. Consistently dedicated to the task at hand. Consistently consistent, I guess. As steady as a surgeon's hand. Another word which describes him pretty well is "old-fashioned."

Jerry was right out of the crew-cut school, still wears one. I'd guess if he were still playing, he'd be wearing high-top shoes. Come to think of it, he was just as comfortable as an old pair of shoes. High-top shoes. He believed in the old-fashioned approach. Straightaway. No mincing around. No fancy small talk. Get right to the subject, pardner! Let's not waste each other's time. But he could adjust to the times. He hadn't been on the job much more than two months when a small protest by the black players was fanned into flame by a few discontents. There was some prettty provocative name-calling and the tempest threatened to break out of the teacup. I know the whole situation must have sorely tried Jerry's soul. But this is no longer the day when you can line the protesters up against a figurative wall and execute them summarily. Protests must be heard. Patience must be exerted. And reason must reign ultimately. And it did. Spring practice continued, calm prevailed and the team knit together the next fall to become the first squad in the history of CU to win 10 games. The tenth was a most impressive victory over Houston in its home arena, the Astrodome, in the Astro-Bluebonnet Bowl.

Jerry Claiborne, my private nickname for him was "Coach Calhoun," made as massive a contribution to the season as anyone. His defense played soundly all fall long, weakening only for a brief span in mid-season when several of his line stalwarts were injured. A big part of Jerry's leadership lies in his great faith. In himself. In his program. In his battle plan. But most of all in God. He, like Dan Stavely, is a devoted Christian who isn't ashamed to admit it. We called Dan and Jerry our "resident Christians." Somewhat, but not altogether, facetiously. Deep in our hearts, the rest of us envied their faith. And were all a little the better for it, I'm sure.

Physically, Jerry is built along the lines of Buck Nystrom. And like Buck, he is a pretty good tennis player. He'd lettered in the sport at Kentucky and still trotted over to the campus courts for a game frequently during the one summer he was here. I guess my favorite memory of Jerry, though, is one which involves him during one of his most frustrating coaching moments. He had a big, physically-gifted sophomore linebacker named Charles Battle who had a lot to learn about linebacking but couldn't believe it. So instead of learning he spent most of his time sulking and wondering why he wasn't playing more. He stood about a head taller than Jerry and I can still remember Jerry bellying up to him one afternoon in the early fall — Charles chucked in the towel before late fall — cocking his head to one side and looking up and bawling, "Charles Battle, you're a sorry dawg!" That was as strong a statement as Jerry could make. "Dawg" was the strongest four-letter word I ever heard him use.

And so Jerry got the call from once-mighty Maryland which was tired of suffering through a succession of coaches who couldn't get the job done. Like Eddie Crowder had done a year earlier, they went after the best man who was available. And just like a year before, the best man was Jerry Claiborne. And they got the right man if they're serious about climbing back to the summit they once occupied. If they aren't serious, we've still got a place in our heart for you, Coach Calhoun. Plus a place on our coaching staff. We've always got an opening for a good man at Colorado. Keep hammering away, Coach Calhoun. You're a good man and there's always room at the top for a good man. Especially, for a very, very good man!

42. KAY DALTON

One of the big reasons for the CU turnabout from an on-again, off-again 6-5 team in 1970 to a terrific 10-2, No. 3-in-the-nation outfit in 1971 was the maturity which a pair of older coaches brought to the CU staff. The first was Jerry Claiborne. The second was Kay Dalton, a man who had won at every level — high school, junior college, small college, the pros, and now, at the major college plateau. Kay Dalton broke through an even bigger barrier than had Denver-exes Dan Stavely and Augie Tammariello. He had matriculated up the road from CU at Colorado A&M, now Colorado State University and a one-time fervid foe of the Buffaloes until the two schools went their separate ways in 1959. Dalton built a tremendous record in his first college head coaching assignment at Western State on Colorado's western slope. From 1961-65 his teams there compiled a 33-12-0 record, including 29 straight victories, three conference championships and two post-season bowl appearances.

An outstanding end as a collegian, Kay, predictably, is a staunch believer in the passing game. He came to CU from the wide open game of the Canadian pros, serving as head coach of the Montreal Alouettes for two years and offensive co-ordinator of the British Columbia Lions for two more. Kay's primary duty with the Buffaloes was to pump some new blood into the CU aerial attack. And, like they say in the Prince Albert ads, he had the makings. A corps of fleet deep receivers and a pair of promising rookie arms in quarterbacks Ken Johnson and Joe Duenas. Johnson, in particular, took to Dalton's instruction and was on his way to a super-sophomore season, running the triple option well but also throwing deep as well as any CU passer since Gale Weidner. Unfortunately, Johnson injured his throwing hand in the opening game of the season, missing the next game, then playing the last 10 and playing them well despite a right hand that must have hurt — X-rays taken at the time of the injury looked negative but at the end of the season it appeared clearly that he had suffered a cracked navicular, a bone about the size of a toothpick located at the "V" formed by the thumb and forefinger. Johnson didn't have a tremendously impressive completion record, 64 of 163, but he netted 1126 yards and eight touchdowns through the air. Probably the best record in history by a thrower with a broken bone in his throwing hand.

So Kay Dalton improved the CU aerial game. And he helped stabilize a nervous young staff. He is the complete opposite of Jerry Claiborne. A dark, good-looking guy who appreciates all the good things in life. But, like Jerry Claiborne, he had been to lots of wars and had won a lot of them. There's nothing like winning to build up a man's confidence. Kay Dalton knows his way will win. Anywhere. Including in the Big Eight, when that conference is the mightiest in the land. Attaway to go, Kay, baby. Let's get on with it. Tee it up and let's start swinging! You're a good man.

43. LARRY KENNAN

A lot of Eddie Crowder's assistants have begun their service with him as low-paid volunteer-type assistants, including Larry Kennan, a bright, young high school coach in California who started out by helping Rick Duval recruit that state then moved to Boulder in 1969 and helped out a little with everything. But mostly was a recruiter. He was elevated to full varsity status in 1971 and placed in charge of the tight ends. Larry is a bright little guy who always looks like his eyes are going to pop out of his head. I guess he looks like a wide-eyed innocent. But he ain't. Nobody who has done battle in the recruiting wars can ever be categorized as an innocent. One of Larry's top recruits was quarterback Craig Penrose, one of the finest high school passers on the west coast who promptly developed into the throwing star of the undefeated 1971 CU frosh team.

44. IRV BROWN

Irv Brown, who came to CU as Frank Prentup's successor as baseball coach when Prentup retired from coaching in 1970, was strictly a Jerry Claiborne addition to the football staff and served as a fulltime football man during the 1971 season only. Jerry, like Crowder a shrewd appraiser of men, recognized quickly that Irv Brown had that unique combination of coaching qualities which set him above the crowd. Jerry wanted him on his defensive staff and created a job for Irv as end coach. Irv had coached all sports as a prep coach at Arvada high in the Denver suburban area. And he'd been a good coach. His major college sport as an undergraduate at Colorado State College, now the University of Northern Colorado, was baseball although he played some football as a quarterback. He'd been a successful high school coach in baseball, basketball and football but baseball was his first love and it was that sport which brought him to CU.

Irv did a solid job for Jerry Claiborne. Not because of a deep knowledge of college football techniques but because of the highly contagious enthusiasm he generates and because of his willingness to admit that he had a lot to learn and his ability to work hard and learn it. No one spots a bad coach quicker than his players. Irv Brown was spotted quickly as a good football coach and his men performed excellently for him. That is the ultimate test for a coach: do his men perform for him? Irv Brown's did. In football and in baseball. And will always, I am sure, no matter what the sport or level. He is a very good man. Most of them are.

45. DUKE BENZ

Duke Benz is a peppery little guy who has been hanging around Boulder and CU on-and-off almost forever. He has been a very good small college coach in the east. And also an assistant at Boulder high a few years back. And a volunteer handyman for Dal Ward a good while back. And last fall he finally got aboard as a jack-of-all-trades. Doing some fall recruiting. Working with the punters. Helping with the weight program. Doing everything but mowing the Astroturf. And doing everything with the tremendous energy and enthusiasm which are his trademarks. Duke is a livewire. You sometimes get the impression his last name has been shortened from Benzedrine. Or that his first name ought to be Benny. Duke has done just about everything. Once he went from Boulder to Topeka as an assistant coach at Washburn College and got to Topeka at just about the same time as the worst tornado in the history of that part of Kansas. Both Duke and Topeka survived each other and the tornado. He also doubles as a golf instructor in the Boulder area. Once gave me a free lesson. Unlike most pros who give you one or two pieces of advice for every five dollars worth of lesson, Duke gives about 50. And gives them so fast he looks like a guy trying to kill a hornet with a flyswatter that's got a limp handle. He just bounces around that practice tee. And that's the way he coaches. Buzzes around all the time. I'll say one thing for the little guy — there ain't ever been anybody anywhere more hyperactive than him. And I've got a hunch he might turn out to be a pretty good coach. If he can ever find his niche.

46. DAN RADAKOVICH

How do you go about filling the shoes of a Jerry Claiborne? The same way you got Jerry. By going out and getting the finest man who's on the market. If Eddie Crowder has one outstanding characteristic which makes him unique among the nation's top coaches, it is his ability to find good men. To spot their greatness quickly and hire them. In Dan Radakovich, the latest defensive co-ordinator, he may have come up with a genius. Rad, a quiet, chain-smoking Slovak with clear eyes just like Little Orphan Annie's, isn't the type who impresses at first glance. But start talking football and, in particular, defense, with him and those eyes light up and a spark enters his voice and pretty soon he's laying a lot of good defensive stuff on you. He's a little bit like Jerry Claiborne in his dress. Neither of them will ever get featured in a men's fashion magazine. Jerry was color blind. I don't know what Rad's excuse is. I have a hunch, though, that he figures clothes don't make the man and that they certainly don't make the defense. Most geniuses don't pay much attention to earthy little details like what they wear. They tell me Thomas Edison was one of the sloppiest dressers of all time. Geniuses just sit around and geniusize, I guess. How's that for a new word, Howard Cosell?

Anyway, I've only been around Dan Radakovich for a couple months as I write this. And I'm impressed by him. But, then, I've learned that if Eddie Crowder is impressed by a man I'd damned well better be, too. Because the boss picks them real good. Rad has impressive credentials. A player and long-time assistant at Penn State, one of the most consistent winning programs in the country. And good work recently at Cincinnati and in the pros with Pittsburgh. He's going to be great for us. Attaway to keep spotting them, Eddie! Good to have you with us, Rad! And, by the way, his eyes do have bottoms in them. You just don't notice them at first. Not until the first time you see them light up. When he gets serious about defense.

47. STILL TO COME

This completes the passing parade of assistant coaches. They've all made their contributions. And I'm sure they'll keep coming and going. That's the nature of the game. But they all have one thing in common. They're good guys. At least all the ones I've known have been. I have found there are two things in life which are always good. Assistant coaches and ice cream. I should know! I've had a lot of both.

A GOOD BENCH IS IMPORTANT, TOO

In a college football program, the men on the firing line get most of the attention, the credit and the blame. And this is as it should be. They wage the war on the field. From the pre-battle strategy through the final victory or defeat. There are no higher highs than in victory, and no lower lows than in defeat. There is no emotional middle ground in athletics. Show me a program which doesn't have great emotion in it and I'll show you a program which is fatally afflicted with that greatest killer of coaches, unproductiveness.

But, just as a good team must have a strong bench so must a good program have a strong team of behind-the-scenes performers. In an army it would be the service and supply people. In an athletic program it is the men who do the unglamorous jobs, important jobs but still unglamorous ones, like athletic directors, business managers, ticket managers, trainers, equipment managers, publicity men, etc.

These men are all part of the team and contribute, each in his own way, to the victories and the defeats to the highs and the lows. If you don't think they're important, you just don't understand the situation. Some people regard them as satellites and I suppose, in a way, they are. But they perform important duties and are certainly not parasites although I've run across a few players and coaches, who never got very far up the ladder incidentally, who looked down on them as unimportant little people.

This work would be incomplete if I didn't give a passing mention to several of these people with whom I've worked closely during the past 20 years. Call it a tribute from a fellow satellite, if you like.

1. HARRY CARLSON

I'll start with the man who hired me and who directed the CU athletic department through my first 14 years on the staff, Harry Carlson. He was "The Dean" to most of us and was a respected athletic administrator. Director of CU athletics from 1928-1965, Dean Carlson was good at his job. Not flamboyant. Or fiery. Or dramatic.

But steady. And quiet. Almost obscure. But, in his own way, effective. Bear in mind that little of the important work in the world is done by the screamers, the arm-wavers, the noise-makers. The guys who get the jobs done are the pluggers, the wood-choppers, the quiet workers. They saw away, day after day, year after year. And the never-ending job gets closer to being done even though it can never be finished and the man wears out before the beginning of the end is even in sight. But you've got to keep plugging away. Undramatically, most of the time. But, importantly, nevertheless.

The Dean was this kind of a man. And in the beginning he must have been a more dramatic personality. I saw him only in the final stages of his long career. When the fires of youth had been banked by time. When the fast ball is gone and you depend upon all the tricks you've learned, if you were smart enough to realize that you wouldn't have that fast ball forever to keep you in the game. Dean Carlson was a master of survival. Through storm after storm, he continued calm and serene. Damaged inside sometimes but always cool and collected on the outside. And even though a lot of people felt that maybe he should have pushed all his chips into the pot and survived or died with a particular coach or program that was under fire, there was reason and merit to his program of survival. Someone had to keep coming back home after the funeral and get things going again. And you can't do that when you're dead, too.

So the Dean lived on. Leaving a trail marked by the bodies of the Bunny Oakes, Jim Yeagers, Dal Wards, Sonny Grandeliuses and Bud Davises. But living on to keep the CU program on track even though the mourners of the latest victims didn't appreciate his presence. Most of the time it takes a lot of little things to make something big. This is just as true in college athletics as in anything. So athletic directing is basically doing a lot of little things, keeping somewhere close to even with the jillions of details which must be attended to daily. Listening to the complaints. Of coaches. Of athletes. Of alumni. Of academicians. Of fans. Of everybody. Doing the paperwork which has become time-consuming but so necessary in a university which has grown into a bureaucracy and which, like all bureaucracies, has developed into a huge outhouse in which the paperwork gets more and more time-consuming. . .but is still important if you're going to have a respectable program.

The Dean, when I knew him, had the perfect temperament for all this. And I'm sure he had it in the beginning, too. I can still see him, leaning back against his chair, speaking softly and drawing slowly on his pipe. Almost hypnotizing you into a sense of security and well being. It was almost like lying on a psychiatrist's couch.

Come in, son, and let me help you shed some of your frustrations. Fret not! It isn't that critical. Let the good, gray Dean lay some philosophy on you. It's good therapy! The description of the Dean I'll always remember was created by Harry Farrar, then sports editor of the Denver Post and one of the best writers I've ever been around. It was during the time of the Sonny Grandelius demise and Farrar wrote in his column that Harry Carlson was "an innocent adrift in a sea of sinners." It was an over-simplification, of course. Most good phrases are. The Dean probably wasn't as innocent as the phrase implied. And the sea wasn't all that full of sin and sinners, either.

I think I've appreciated the Dean's work and his role at CU a lot more after I got into the paper-shuffling field myself. It can be a frustrating existence albeit a necessary role. It certainly doesn't have the high highs that coaching does. It's more like groping your way through the fog. Whatever it is, the Dean had a talent for doing it and CU is the better for his having served. He was a good man for his time. No matter what some of you lightweights who might have gotten mesmerized by his pipe might think.

2. KAYO LAM

The full name is William Calvin Lam but he got tagged with the nickname of the feisty, little banty-rooster in the Moon Mullins comic strip early in his life and he's been Kayo ever since. And what a guy! Tempestuous. Impulsive. Reckless. A wildly-pulsating bundle of nervous energy. "Jerky Bill" to his close friends because of his twitching, twisting physical moves. But a great guy. A great friend. And one of the toughest competitors, on or off the field, I've ever known. I won't go into his athletic career since I never saw him compete at anything other than golf or gin rummy, his two major physical activities in his later years and, although he could roll in the longest putts under pressure I've ever seen or knock late in a gin game without batting an eye, these activities couldn't hold a candle to the tigerish accomplishments he made in football, wrestling and track as an undergraduate at CU in the mid-30's.

Kayo stayed right on at CU in a variety of jobs before settling down as the athletic business manager and, as such, the assistant athletic director even though he never carried the title. I'm sure Dean Carlson never felt he was withholding recognition from Kayo but he really should have designated Kayo publicly as his assistant early in their departmental association. Kayo was a product of the old school and the old school was from the days when football was a simple production with plenty of seats always available in the early days of the 26,000-seat natural bowl that was Folsom Stadium. Kayo did a lot of his business-managing, football-wise, out of his hip pocket or out of the cigar box in which he used to keep his tickets and change on road games or even sometimes out of the pillow case in his hotel room where he had been known to hide his valuables before retiring for the night. Kayo and his secretary, Miss Alice Clyncke, kept the operation running about as smoothly as any operation ran in those days and what with him wheeling and dealing out of that cigar box and her coming and going with the egg concession for the department, it wasn't exactly a business operation designed to warm the heart of an auditor, if there is such a thing as an auditor with a heart. But things got done. And this was sufficient in those sleepy days before, and for a few short years after, World War II.

Kayo Lam was probably the most loyal alumnus the University of Colorado ever sent forth into the world. Totally and completely dedicated to his alma mater. Forever. Through thick, thin or whatever other degree of density might be in vogue. His is a loyalty made up of equal parts of intelligent debate or as-tough-as-you-want physical combat. You name it, he'll meet you on your chosen ground, with vocabulary or fist, whichever you prefer. But either way, your meeting will end in a knockout. A kayo, if you prefer. Because he'll take you right to the end of the line. It'll be you or him. And you ought to be prepared to lose.

Most of my major memories of Kayo are funny ones, though, and I don't mean to be disrespectful in telling my favorite one which was also one of my first exposures to the Kayo Lam I got to know so well. It was in 1954 and for the first time we were flying to Missouri for our football game in Columbia. Before that, we'd taken the torturous route of the railroad and there was no more torturous route than the one which finally backed you into Columbia. Instead of a charter, we had bought all the seats on the regular Continental flight to Kansas City (we were even flying with CAL in those days, Mr. Six!) It still wasn't enough seats so Continental had added a second section of the flight, another Convair, for the rest of the players and us satellites and the regular passengers. Some of us went up on the observation deck to watch the first section, which carried our frontline men and coaches, take off. The plane taxied out toward the runway then suddenly stopped. The door opened and out jumped Kayo, hitting the ground about 10 feet below the door at full speed, topcoat flapping in the breeze, one hand holding his hat on his head. He'd discovered he didn't have the tickets. A ground search was hastily organized and we swept through the terminal, eyes glued to the floor. No minesweeper ever searched or swept more intently. Kayo, in the meantime, had slipped into an airport office and called his office in Boulder. Miss Clyncke found the tickets tucked safely away in the

IT'S GREAT TO BE WELL-KNOWN

Kayo Lam and I were the guests of honor at a Denver-based oil company's annual sales meeting in 1956. Their public relations department very thoughtfully sent us this picture to commemorate the occasion. They spelled our names wrong on the cover letters, too.

TWO COACHES AND FRIENDS

Dal Ward and I got our picture taken with some good Buffalo fans at KOA in 1957. From left to right they are sportscaster John Henry, before he got out of the sportscasting business and got hair again, Rocky Head, the football coach at Tincup High who doubled as Darrell Kelly whenever he was in Denver, and Pete Smythe, the mayor of Tincup and proprietor of Pete Symthe's General Store.

safe where Kayo had carefully placed them the day before. The situation was saved! Kayo re-boarded with a sheepish grin on his face and Dal Ward just shrugged his shoulders and the trip went on with the tickets reaching Stapleton in time to make the second section. We used to have a lot of close calls like that in those days. But we always got to where we were going and we always did a pretty fair job after we got there. Not much different, really, than it is today. Except, maybe, that Kayo might have gotten killed by one of the more demanding modern coaches in today's different time and tempo. Kayo was a man of many other talents. All-star quarterback, orchestra leader-drummer, master of the Charleston, one of the all-time great gigglers, back-alley brawler, living room lion, cocktail party colossus. Just about anything he wanted to be. A great guy who is part of a great past. Time may slow him down but it will never stop him. Only the man with the long, white beard and the scythe will ever do that. And even he won't get it done until after he's had a tough struggle. Keep rolling them in, Kayo. You're still the King of the Road!

   3. MISS ALICE CLYNCKE

Keeper of the records, answerer of the phone, counter of the tickets, cleaner-upper of the cash drawer, purveyor of home-laid eggs, sovereign shepherdess of the Colorado Relays, lover of all Buffaloes and most loyal of the loyal. That was Miss Alice Clyncke, who spun her way through life in her Model-A as chief secretary of the athletic department, a hard-working, deadly serious lady who loved her work and who supplied much of the glue which kept the department together, record-wise. She was Kayo Lam's righthand man and nobody ever needed a righthand man more than Kayo who never let a challenge go unanswered even though it might mean 18 holes on the Friday afternoon before a big game. He could make himself available for all those side-duals which spice life even though they may not have been exactly what you were getting paid to do because he had a steady servant like Alice Clyncke always at the ready at the office counter. And Alice didn't swerve from her duty one iota.

I think she secretly envied the wild escapades which her boss was constantly getting in and out of but I know she was content to envy them from a distance, preferring her quiet life in the comfortable confines of her office and the small farm east of Boulder on which she supervised the chickens which provided the eggs, and the egg money, which kept her and her Model A going. Like Dean Carlson, Miss Clyncke was perfectly designed for her times. Friendly and considerate, with no request, no matter how petty or time-consuming, going unanswered by her. In her inconspicuous way, she was probably as important a public relations person as there was in the department.

But time catches up with everyone, even nice ladies, and Miss Clyncke retired, involuntarily, in 1970. And even though she had spent much of her life in the athletic business office, I think she was ready to put the cover on her ancient typewriter. She still had lots of things to do and lots of dances to dance and her job was starting to get a little too confining. It sounds corny to call her a "great old girl." But that's what she was. And I, for one, loved her.

4. LEE AKINS

If you took a vote among all the athletes who have gone through the CU program and asked them who they thought the most of as an undergraduate and who they think the most of today, the winner in a landslide would be Lee Akins. "Silver" to all who knew and loved him and swiped sweat socks and gray CU T-shirts from his equipment room. Silver was everything to everybody. Need anything? Take a dozen. Kayo's got lots of money and we can get more of what you need. Nothing was too good for his beloved Buffaloes. Nothing in the world. Or at least in the equipment room and he kept a lively variety of stock. Silver was equipped to take care of any situation or emergency. If you needed a new set of cleats. Or a chinstrap. Or a new helmet. Or a re-conditioned jock. Or some socks. Or anything. You name it, Silver had it. Or knew where he could get it. Emergencies? Routine for Silver, who had helped Doc Giffin sew up many a wounded warrior. Silver could do anything. And did it for 50 years on the CU campus, going to work in the CU grounds department in 1920, becoming athletic equipment manager in 1936 and retiring in 1970. Silver even kept snake-bite medicine tucked away in his shelves and, although it's never been established that there were ever any vipers on his premises, he had what it took to neutralize their bites, or even the thoughts of them. And what's more, he kept his medicine fresh, replenishing his supply frequently during the course of a year and very frequently during the holiday season when there was always quite a drain on it.

Silver's hair has always been silver, I guess. And his face the color of an out-of-control fire. Snow on the roof and fire in the furnace, best describes him. I never saw a man who could operate so efficiently under the most adverse conditions. In at the crack of dawn and up at the crack of dawn, he always did his job with great precision and care. Silver might be wobbling but his equipment trunks never did and it was always the equipment that got laid out before every game, never Silver.

There are a million stories about Lee, all of them good ones. He enjoyed life, lived it to the hilt, could set a pace which outdistanced the hardiest of after-dark high-steppers, including athletes, and always finished in front. With a grin. And words of admonition for his less hardy sidekicks. Silver had stamina like nobody else, even Kayo Lam, ever had. If most of my Silver stories take place after dark it's because that's when he took place the best. You didn't see much of Silver in the daylight. He came to work at 6:00 a.m. and left as soon as he had the equipment issued for afternoon practice. At nights on the road during football season was when he sparkled. Oh, how he sparkled! He coursed through city streets like a gust of fresh air through the smog. Only, maybe it was the other way around. Silver spread joy wherever he went. A snowy-thatched songbird making people happy with his serenade. Making a few of them who stayed with him too long somewhat sick the next morning, too. But always in the spirit of fun. There were no brawls wherever Silver went. Just a lot of laughs and a lot of good, healthy action.

One of our younger, and less experienced staffmembers, made a trip with us to Tucson in the mid-50's when we were still playing Arizona. This man was old enough to know better but he ignored the advice of those of us who knew Silver best and appointed himself a committee of one to see that Silver kept out of trouble and got back to the hotel okay. Off they went into the night, Silver with a big grin on his face heading for the local Elks Club as a starter and his watchdog with a smug, confident look spread all over his face. About three hours later some of us were winding it up with a steaming cup of Ovaltine and a bowl of fresh fruit ("bowel-sweetener" John Bentley used to call it) at an all-night place on the edge of town when the door flew open and in sailed Silver, his face on fire and his eyes crackling with good cheer. In response to our questions about the whereabouts of his chaperone, Silver grinned and pointed out to the parking lot. There, trying to get out of a car which Silver had driven, was the birddog, almost totally out of it. We drug him out of the car, into the joint, poured a couple cups of hot coffee down him (he was way too far gone for Ovaltine, man!) carted him back to the hotel, propped him up against the door to his room, opened it and watched him fall into it. Silver, meanwhile, had gone his merry way. The next morning, he was on the job, on time and doing his work with a smile. His birddog barely made it to the game and, I am fairly certain, doesn't remember too much about it to this day. That's what kind of a guy Lee Akins was. A man who wanted no shackles. Or needed no chaperones. Just wind him up and he'd set sail into the night and be on the job in a functioning capacity the next day. He had only one slight defect that I can remember. A speech impediment type of thing. He couldn't pronounce "son-of-a-bitch" properly. And it was a fairly important term when he was frustrated or angry or happy or whatever. It always came out, "'some-un-a-bitch." Maybe that's the way he meant it to be.

When Silver retired, we gave him a new white Pontiac, the make of car he'd been driving for several years. We should have given him a fleet of Cadillacs. Silver, we miss you! You were one of a kind and it ain't nearly as much fun without you. Live to be a hundred, old buddy! If one heart-full of love from every player who drew his gear from you is equal to a month of life, you'll live to be a thousand.

5. THE BEST OF THE REST

I've worked with so many nice people as the years have clicked off at CU that it would be nearly impossible to discuss each of them. The four I've mentioned thus far devoted most of their lives to the school and I can't come close to telling how important their contributions have been. They helped bring CU from a young and struggling athletic department into a solid and seasoned one, if you'll pardon the cliches. But there were, and are, many others who have each helped significantly in their own way. Here are some of these people.

Any reminiscing about CU football would be incomplete if Floyd Walters were not included. He was CU's official photographer for many years and shot the football movies through the 1971 season. Floyd was a press box fixture, scurrying softly to and fro from his roost on the photo deck, mother-henning his cameras and equipment into position with the aid of a volunteer or two who took on the heavy work in exchange for a perch in the box, wolfing down an assortment of hot dogs, chicken legs, ham-and-cheese sandwiches or whatever else was available at the free lunch counter and doing a lot of fretting and sighing about whatever happened to meander across his very active mind. And, incidentally, always coming up with a properly exposed, properly framed 1000 feet of game movies.

Like a lot of us, Snappy (not many of us ever called him Floyd) was often reluctant to adapt a modern technique or piece of equipment to his operation. What the hell! If it works and if it's what you prefer, why change? At least, not until you have to replace an old item. Or when a new technique obviously is an improvement. There's an old saying that you ought to "dance with who you brung. . .until she comes up lame or starts leaking badly at the armpits or something" and that was Snappy's philosophy.

It really isn't proper to use that phrase to describe Snappy because he wasn't a dancing man, although I once saw him make some pretty good moves cutting across a dance floor in a Canal Street cabaret in Nogales, Mexico as he was getting away from the hot pursuit of a heavy-legged lady of the afternoon who had been sicked onto Snappy by some of us evils who he had followed during a mid-day excursion into the entertainment section of that border town. But I digress. What I was saying was that Snappy was one of the last of the great masters of the 100-foot reel and watching him change reels, most of the time during a break in the action although he occasionally got trapped into doing it between the time the team broke out of the huddle and snapped the ball, was like watching a crepe maker in a restaurant window or a waiter firing up a shishkebob or one of Tom Wilscam's longest-armed lads whomping up a cup of dutch coffee at his Hungry Dutchman restaurant. You were watching artistry in action, man, when you watched Snappy change reels. The photo deck lost a lot of its color when the 400-foot reels took over but Snappy held out to the very end.

Floyd - let's close out his section on a formal note - retired as CU's photographer in 1970 because of an old knee injury which all the kneeling and bending over and squatting and crouching that a good photographer has to do to get the right angle kept aggravating badly. But he continued to shoot CU football through the 1971 season, winding up his career with the Astro-Bluebonnet Bowl victory over Houston. Upon retirement, Snappy didn't cover his lens and silently fade away, though. Always a busy traveler, he moved right into the tour business and is still scurrying softly to and fro, but now between countries instead of press box levels. And he still does a lot of mother-henning only now it's the novice travelers he has herded together for a tour who he watches over instead of cameras and lenses and 100-foot reels. Younger and more modern equipment-oriented camera men will succeed Snappy. And they'll be good ones. But they'll do well to match Snappy's record of performance. And it's doubtful that any will be as devoted or diligent.

Another fixture on the CU campus scene has been an old friend, Dick Christopher, who has been an accountant somewhere or other ever since I was a student and who served most conscientiously as the athletic ticket manager for more than a decade, from 1967 through 1968, before the nerve-wracking demands of the job finally got to him and caused him to move to a quieter and non-athletic part of the university where he continues to function ably today.

A dapper fellow with a sporty moustache which he has worn ever since I have known him — and that extends well back beyond the time when swatches of hair and beard and sideburn and goatee began cluttering up men's faces like clumps of crab grass in a lawn. Dick worked as hard and long at his job as anyone I've ever seen. And he always got his job done, although sometimes he went right down to the wire with a deadline — as any of us who ever fought a deadline have. If he had one shortcoming, it was that he was too nice a person. Ticket managers get hounded a lot by a lot of people, most of them unreasonable, wanting to get their seats moved upfield or wanting to buy a pair of new seats right next to the four they have on the 40-yard line. Or moving across an aisle or getting away from a drunk who keeps spilling drinks on their fur coats or whatever. A good ticket manager has got to be nice to these customers despite the unreasonableness of their requests. They have to be handled gently. Dick was too gentle and too kind and too often spent too much time placating these people. And, as a result, caused himself too many long, tough hours at night doing the things he might have gotten done during the day. But he was a good man who did a good job and I hated to see him move out of the department although I could understand his desire to get away from that ticket counter. You ought to see it now, Sir Richard!

One of the men who came across our mountain for whom I've had the greatest respect, then and since, was Jack Rockwell who signed on as head trainer in 1953, less than a year after I started to work at CU. We became great buddies immediately, two little guys tucked away in our somewhat obscure corners of the department, each battling furiously to become recognized by our superiors and each totally dedicated to the Buffaloes despite our widely-divergent backgrounds . . . Jack was a Kansas graduate by way of Seattle, Wash. and I was a post-war CU grad out of the cornfields of Iowa.

The Rock was a sharp little guy who dressed like a jockey — very well. He was about the same height as a jockey, too. In fact, we both were and we used to be the subjects of the shower room small talk as to who was the taller. Probably who was the shorter would have been more accurate. There wasn't more than a silly little millimeter's difference in us so the question was never resolved because he got taller haircuts than me and so I wouldn't line up against a measuring wall with him. Besides, Rockwell somewhere along the way, probably during his days as a trainer for a minor league baseball team, had come up with a pair of elevator shoes and he'd sneak them on every once in a while and, consequently, caused a lot of people to think that he really was taller than me. And, although I'd mutter foul whenever I caught him with those high-rise heels on, my major feeling was one of envy — I couldn't afford a pair myself. Actually, on what Dean Carlson was paying me back in those days I could barely afford sneakers and Keds never were designed to add to your physical (or esthetic) stature. But enough about such petty little things as height. We both made a lot of noise as most little men do. And we did convince the powers-that-were rather quickly that we were worth keeping around.

Ray Jenkins called us the "Gold-Dust Twins" and I suppose we did look a little like the pair pictured on that soap box, especially Rock after a couple of months in the summer sun as manager of the Boulder Country Club swimming pool. Never a sun worshipper, and never having a job which got me out of a dark room for very long, I never matched Rock in the complexion category. My eyes used to get as bloodshot as his, on occasion, but that was a hollow consolation.

Anyway, Rock was an outstandingly good trainer, maybe the best in the country after a few years although there were, and still are, a lot of great ones just in the Big Eight. Such as Ken Rawlinson at Oklahoma and Dean Nesmith at Kansas, the guy who Jack learned the ropes under. Like nearly all good men, Jack was a 24-hour-a-day man who lived his job, in or out of his training room. He was a super-active person with an excellent mind who would have been very good at whatever he selected as his field. He quickly became an extremely valued member of the athletic staff because of that great quality a good trainer must have of being able to keep a foot in both camps, as a member of the staff with the complete confidence and respect of the coaches and as a medical minister to the players with the equally-important confidence and respect of them. He worked both sides of the street tremendously well and Dallas Ward loved him. But Dal ran a rather benevolent operation with little of the almost-brutal disregard for players that some programs have and when he got axed and Sonny Grandelius came in with a much more demanding system for the men, Rock found the new approach unsuited to his makeup and went to the St. Louis football Cardinals with Pop Ivy, who he had gotten to know when Pop was coaching in the Canadian pro league.

Jack's career continued to soar upward and I began calling him "Rocket" because he moved up the ladder so quickly and became recognized as one of the best, if not the best, trainer in the NFL. He remained with the Cardinals for over 10 years and recently moved into a management position with Johnson and Johnson, one of the better band-aid companies in the country and an organization he'll serve as faithfully and effectively as he did CU and the St. Louis Cardinals. He's that kind of guy and it was a privilege to be associated with him during our formulative days and to still know him as a very good friend. Keep hustling those ace bandages, Rocko, there ain't nobody knows the business better than you!

Before Rock was Aubrey Allen, a dishpan-faced ex-guard for the Buffaloes who stayed on as trainer after he graduated and was the medicine man when I arrived in 1952. But Aubrey's interest lie in school administration and he moved to California where he got into that field and still is today.

Rock's successor was Lloyd Williams, who had been his student assistant before moving to the Air Force Academy as assistant trainer where he was when Rock left. Willie was a lanky, quiet Coloradoan from the dustlands of Lamar, a well-backgrounded trainer with a degree in physical therapy who served well until he, too, moved into the professional ranks as head trainer for the Denver basketball Rockets in 1967. Willie has flourished with the pros and is still with that organization and doing a good job like he will always do.

Our current tiger of the training room is Monte Smith, a good-looking operator who I first knew as a CU gymnast early in my sports information director days. Monte is still an acrobatic performer whether his performances be on the dance floor, schussing down a ski slope, zipping on and off the field with his first aid kit, or whatever he happens to be doing. He's active and adept. A good man. He didn't come onto the job with the impressive credentials of physical therapists Rockwell and Williams but he grew into the job as well as anyone I've seen and he is an excellent trainer today. His strength lies in his great rapport with the players. He'd have been a great faith healer. Maybe that's what he is. Whatever, he is, he's a good trainer and a good member of our department and almost as good at healing hangovers as Rockwell was although that has gotten to be a lesser and lesser important aspect of the job, insofar as I am concerned, as the years have gone by. But keep that bottle of B-Ones at the ready anyway, Montezuma! The south may rise again.

A somewhat detached, but important, important facet of the athletic scene is the alumni office and I've worked fairly closely with three good directors, Ken Penfold, Bud Davis and Dean Graves.

Ken Penfold was as smooth a smoothie as ever gave a soothing answer to a nervous question by an anxious alumnus; Bud Davis was as bright a man as ever wrote a Coach's Letter (and he very kindly and very ably did that job for Sonny and I in 1961); and Dean Graves is as conscientious and hard-working — and mediocre-golfing — a person as I've ever known. All three are CU graduates who are super-concerned alumni. Good men to have in our ranks.

Ken was a Dal Ward loyalist who didn't appreciate Quigg Newton and resigned a year after Dal was fired and went into the real estate and insurance business in Boulder and made a lot of money and worked hard at it and has subsequently found time to work hard on slowing down his backswing and temper and whiplashes his Kenneth Smith clubs pretty effectively up and down the fairways at the Boulder Country Club as he ages gracefully and handsomely.

Bud Davis, of course, went on to greater things after his innocent and eye-opening interlude as a football coach and was, at this writing, still president of Idaho State University but getting ready to run for the Democratic nomination for United States senator from Idaho. I hope he is successful in his political pursuits. I'd feel a heck of a lot more comfortable knowing there is a man of his ability in Washington. So, get after them, Bud. Kiss those babies. And those Potato Queens. And even those potatoes, if you have too!

Dean Graves is the man on the job today. He's an ex-athlete like both Penfold (baseball) and Davis (football) were, having come out of Longmont with his brother, Dane, at about the same time as Dal Ward took over the CU football program. Dean does a good job and he's athletically-oriented and it's good to have traditionalists like him around who recognize and appreciate the value of a good athletic program to a good university.

Our two football office secretaries must be mentioned at this point. Helen Parquette has been giving loyal and faithful service beyond the line of duty since joining us in the late 1950's as chief secretary to all our athletic directors and head football coaches since. Dan Stavely started calling her "Miss Blue" in 1958 and we've been buzzing her ever since and she constantly amazes me with her efficiency and always-great disposition despite the strain and stress and demands which an always-hectic athletic office creates. The blue in "Miss Blue" stands for true blue.

Her sidekick and chief ally in the football is super-typist Connie Falk, who literally chops out reams of quick work daily as the football secretary. A tiny little lady, Miss Constance grumbles a lot in a cheerful sort of a way, if that's possible, but she performs like a computer. Feed her dictation until she's ready to drop out of her chair, prop her up behind her electric typewriter, then put some cotton in your ears because she'll keep those keys clattering until all your letters are stacked up on your desk by the time she leaves that evening. Her bark is much worse than her bite and you can stand a little yipping during the day from someone who produces as much work as Connie.

There were others who I should have written about, too. Like the late Dr. Giffin, who was our attentive little team physician when I came to CU, Joanie-Woanie Wittenwyler, the best ticket office secretary I've seen (and owner of the longest and shapeliest legs of any secretary we've ever had and wearer of the shortest skirts in the days before everybody started wearing them), and Joyce Crow, who was a super secretary, and Patsy Sue Porter, who was my pretty little student-type part-time secretary for four years and who had those big, beautiful cocker spaniel-type eyes and who I dearly loved but she graduated and got married, like they always do. And a lot of other people, mostly pretty secretaries (who I seem to remember best.) And the current bench-strength on our department team, as bright a crew of young guys as anyone has ever put together, including business manager Ken Farris, ticket manager Jon Burianek, equipment and grounds manager Steve Hatchell, assistant trainer Rich Newton and, occasionally, sports information director Mike Moran. I have to qualify Mike Moran somewhat because he's the lone bachelor on our staff and' as such, leads a precarious physical existence and is always on the brink of extinction, from one source or another, but who has been amazingly resilient heretofore, having survived a constant parade of threats from administrators (like me), athletes whose girl friends he has borrowed, girl friends whose hearts he has stolen and, occasionally, a roiled-up restauranteur. We got a good gang and we got a good thing going! Keep it going, men, we're on our way.

BUFFALOES I'VE WORKED WITH
(PRACTICALLY ALL OF WHOM I'VE LOVED)

So far I've talked about the coaches and other staffmembers and, although they have been extremely important to the CU football program, the real contributors have been the men who strapped on the pads and went to battle every Saturday in the fall. The players are really what a program is all about and, although you never get to know them as well as you'd like, I was fortunate enough to be close enough to them to come up with my own particular set of prejudices about them. And mine are probably as accurate a set as anybody has in his possession at this particular point in history.

You see a lot of outstanding men and average men and unsung men and oversung men and tough men and untough men and almost all kinds of young men go through a program in a quarter of a century but, by and large, most of them are good men and I feel very strongly that they make up as good a group of alumni as a university can produce.

A lot of names come to mind as I move into this section of this book. A lot more don't come to mind and I know that in my typical haste to get this written and in print I'll probably omit some that I'll wish I had included. If you're an old Buffalo and you didn't get mentioned, just assume that you're one of those who I should have remembered but didn't. Then ask me about it the next time I see you and I'll confirm it even if I have to lie.

Any review of the past parade of CU football players ought to begin with a listing of the best ones so that's the route I've chosen. First of all, the best two-way performers and I'll take them by positions. Please note that it was two-way football from 1947-49 then platoon football from 1950-52 then two-way football from 1953 until approximately 1966 and platoon football since. And when the picking gets tough I'll exercise the option of making some exceptions in order to put a player where I feel he deserves to be.

MY ALL TWO-WAY SQUAD FOR THE PAST 25 YEARS

ENDS

We've probably had more outstanding ends at CU in my time than any other position. So many that I could come up with at least three sets which would be a credit to any school's all-star team.

My pick for the top two, though, are Sam Harris (1964-5-6) and Jerry Hillebrand (1959-60-1).

Big Sam, a lethargic-looking but deceptively-active 6-4, 228-pound Hawaiian, was as fine an athlete as I've watched. One of the first blue-chippers recruited by the Eddie Crowder staff in 1963, Sam became a starter immediately as a sophomore in 1964 and, while he was used as a defensive specialist primarily in his last two seasons, he had the speed, agility and hands to become a great tight end and would probably have made it as a pro at that position had he not gotten wiped out by a knee injury early in his senior season. His injury was a tragic thing because the knee never came back properly and it cost him a chance to play professionally. He was as close to a sure thing for the pros as I've ever seen. Sam was strong against the play which came straight at him, agile and powerful at stringing out a sweep and one of the most effective pass rushers I've ever seen. His hands were huge paws and he could jump well, he could have been a good college basketball player, and he could bat down a pass which had already traveled a few feet out of the passer's hand as well as anybody I've ever watched. He was from the island of Oahu and I westernized it to "Wahoo" — he was good-looking enough to have posed for a Marlboro Man ad. Sam should have done better academically than he did but he made the mistake of pinning his hopes almost entirely on a pro career which went out the window with that knee injury.

Sam's running mate on my team, Jerry Hillebrand, was just as big and just as talented and the same type of sleepy-ish athlete as Sam but with the ability to turn it on often enough so that everyone in the stands and in the press box and on the field knew he was the stud end when he wanted to be. His nickname was "Baby Huey" after the cartoon character duck but he was a big, mean man on the football field. At 6-4 and 241 with good speed and mobility, he was a superior athlete and proved it by going on to play for 10 years professionally, most of the time as a linebacker. Jerry could be a frustrating man to watch, though, and you just never felt that he kept his motor turned up to full speed for very long at a time. The game which symbolizes Jerry most to me was at Miami in his senior year, 1961. He had gotten off to a sensational start that year, catching a 40-yard TD pass from Gale Weidner on CU's first possession of the season then in the second quarter of that game against Oklahoma State kicking a 54-yard field goal, the longest in the nation by anyone that year, amateur or pro, and following up a week later with the catch of the winning touchdown in the 20-19 thriller over Kansas. Against Miami, though, Jerry scuffed his only extra point try and went into the fourth period as the potential goat as Miami led, 7-6. But Jerry mashed his footfeed to the floor in an amazing fourth-quarter quick sequence on a punt as he hustled downfield to recover a fumble then, four downs later, booted a perfect placement from the right hashmark at the 27-yard line to win the game, 9-7.

If someone nailed me to the wall and made me list the other two-way ends, in order, I'd sweat a lot then put Wally Merz (1954-5-6) and Lamar Meyer (1954-5) on the second team and Ken Blair (1960-1-2) and Jerry Leahy (1954-5-6) on the third team with Gary Knafelc (1951-2-3) in a special category because, although he played in the two-way days, he didn't fool around much with defense and did practically all of his damage to the other team as a receiver. Knafelc really belongs with the offensive specialists and concentrated on catching the ball during a long and fruitful career with the Green Bay Packers.

Gary was a good looking, 6-4, 210-pounder from Pueblo who had an equally-good looking, big father nicknamed Prince who used to go to a lot of road games and who was one of the few men who could, and would, keep up with Lee Akins after dark. And Gary could keep up with both of them and, occasionally, did. Gary's name probably got mispronounced more than any other CU player's in history and I used to call him "Snowflake," almost out of desperation. He was a fun-loving fellow, always with a grin on his face and a quip on his lips, who could catch the ball as well as any end we've ever had. Gary caught eight touchdown passes as a senior in 1953, still the most ever by a Buffalo in one season.

Wally Merz was a solid, unswerving 6-4, 215-pound end for Dal Ward who could block, tackle and catch the ball whenever they threw it to him, which wasn't very often — he caught 10 passes in three years. He was fortunate in that blocking and playing defense were his strong suits because catching the ball wasn't a very important asset back in those days.

Lamar Meyer returned from the service just in time to win a starting job in 1954 and was a top hand for two seasons. He was on the small side at 6-1 and 195 but he was an exceptionally smart player and an effectively quick receiver. And, most importantly, one of the leaders of the good 1954 and 55 squads.

Ken Blair was another smallish end (6-1, 205) but he was tough and durable, I don't ever remember him missing a minute of play because of an injury, and he could go both ways very well. His two touchdown catches brought the Buffaloes off the deck and on the way to the 20-19 win over Kansas in 1961. A year later, he played, end, linebacker, punter, captain, almost everything, on the Bud Davis team and played well enough to be an All-Big Eight selection.

Jerry Leahy was one of my all-time favorites because he was a living example of the old theory that if you work hard enough and try long enough you can make it somewhere. Jerry didn't make it as a fullback and didn't make it as a linebacker but kept hustling and finally, in his fourth year of school as a red-shirt junior, made it as an end. What do I remember most about him? Just that he was tough. And dependable. And grateful as hell at having finally gotten the opportunity to perform. If every player who checked out his gear as a freshman could have watched the Jerry Leahy story unfold at CU, nobody would ever quit a squad.

So these are the two-way ends. You could put all seven names in a sack and draw out two. No matter who you drew, you'd have as good a pair of ends as you need to be a winner. And these were only the two-way men!

TACKLES

When you move into the interior line you run into an identification problem because this is where the "unknown soldiers" work and it can be very difficult for the casual or unknowledgable observer to make an accurate appraisal of these men. But the good ones always surface, despite the constant clutter of tangled bodies which make up the line of scrimmage after the ball is snapped. And CU has had lots of these infantrymen worthy of inclusion on any all-star list and, overall, as good a group as any which could be put together by any other school in the Big Eight conference.

My first team two-way tackles are Dick Stapp (1954-5-6) and John Wooten (1956-7-8), the former one of the toughest "little" linemen I've ever seen and the latter one of the best big men who ever put on the pads in the Big Eight.

Stapp was 6-0, 207 and tough as nails, a driving blocker who helped clear those big holes in Dal Ward's unbalanced-line single wing attack. On defense, he'd crawl into the middle of Dal's five-man line and do a job normally assigned to one of the biggest linemen on a squad. In a day in which the prototype middle guard was mammoth Les Bingaman of the Detroit Lions, Stapp more than filled the bill for the Buffaloes. Stapp, a baby-faced blue-eyed blond whose looks were completely deceiving, would fight you anywhere, anytime...on the line of scrimmage or in an alley after the game. That was his nature and he never took a backward step in his life, on or off the field. Normally a little tackle goes out of his way not to antagonize his opponent. Stapp went the other direction, setting up the ground rules for the 60-minute battle on the first play of the game. His nickname was "Pinky" but pink wasn't a color you'd ever find on his coat of arms. Black or purple would have been more appropriate. Pinky liked to do something to infuriate his man early in the game. One of the best ways he ever found, and it's easy to understand why it was so effective, was to spit right in his opponent's face, grin and issue the challenge for the day. It was total war from then on and that was the battle condition Pinky liked best. Stapp came from a good, tough family. His younger brother, Bob, came along immediately after Dick and played well for CU. And their father, an Arvada school system employee, must have been the person who instilled the love for combat in his sons. When Ray Jenkins was recruiting Pinky, he was having real trouble convincing him that higher education was the proper path. After listening to his son and the CU coach get nowhere in the debate for the greater part of the evening, the senior Stapp came up with a simple solution, challenging his son to a backyard battle with the winner making the decision as to Dick's future. And he was serious. Dick was so impressed by that display of his dad's desire that he agreed to enroll at CU. He never regretted it as he went on to become a good high school then a college coach at Colorado Mines after his graduation. CU never regretted it, either, getting as fine a lineman, pound-for-pound, as it ever had.

John Wooten (6-2, 228) was considered a giant in his day, and he was. A friendly giant most of the time but a crushing blocker, especially on those trap blocks Marshall Wells taught so well. Today, he'd be considered a runty tackle but he'd still be a good one as a solid 10-year pro career as a starter for the Cleveland Browns, where he became an all-NFL guard, proves. John was one of the team leaders for the Buffaloes during his three years as a regular.

He took over a starting job immediately in his sophomore year and helped lead CU to a fine 7-2-1 regular season then a 27-21 victory over Clemson in the Orange Bowl. The next season the Buffaloes led the nation in rushing offense and big John's path-clearing blocking was one of the major reasons. John actually was labeled as a guard on offense, playing the weak side interior post as the only lineman between the center and the end on that side. Defensively, he was a tackle and a very good one. Big, agile and strong. And a great guy to have on the team because of his great personality and ability to keep everyone loose. John was a happy warrior. His greatest friends were tailback Bob Stransky, who benefited most from John's blocking as he gained over 1000 yards in 1957 and made All-American, and Bob Salerno, a good, tough tackle from Trinidad. I remember Thanksgiving Day in 1957 when the three of them were guests in our home for dinner. My wife, an only child herself and the mother of two small daughters at the time, had never been exposed to the amazing appetites of growing young men. She almost got shin splints lugging the food from the kitchen to the table — the three players could clean off a plate as fast as she could fill it. Fortunately, we have a small house and it isn't a very long haul from the kitchen to the dining area (about three steps, in fact) and she was able to keep pace. Afterwards, the three young men rolled around on the living room floor playing with my little girls, they were nine and six at the time, who still remember that Thanksgiving evening as one of the fun nights in their lives.

John injured a knee early in his senior season and didn't have as good a year as he should have as the leg hampered him considerably through the last part of the fall. But he still played well enough to earn consensus All-American honors although, frankly, his tremendous play as a sophomore and junior contributed as much or more to that recognition as did his play in 1958. But John healed during the winter and earned a starting job as one of the shuttle guards who carried in the plays for Paul Brown's great Cleveland team. John's nickname at CU was ''Sun Devil'', a name he brought with him from his native Carlsbad, New Mexico and he was a witty man and a great person and an outstanding football player and I was, and still am, proud to know him as a good friend.

Picking Stapp and Wooten as the two best, two-way tackles of the past 25 years wasn't as easy as it may seem. There have been lots of good tackles and any of these were good enough to have been on my first team:

Sam Salerno (1953-4-5), a burly brute from Trinidad who required a little waking-up occasionally — he once strolled casually into the opposing team's huddle in his sophomore season, unconsciously not maliciously — but who was a real tiger once he got aroused. Off the field Sam was a gentle giant at 6-1 and 225 but he became a Big Eight heavyweight wrestling champion for Ray Jenkins, gaining mat fame despite a rather limited repertoire of holds. Sam's main move as a wrestler was a "bear hug" in which he simply grabbed his man, squeezed the hell out of him, flopped him to the mat and, most of the time, pinned him. We've gotten a lot of mileage from brother combinations at CU and the Salerno boys, first Sam then Bob, were two of the best of these family twosomes.

Jack Himelwright (1956-7-8) was another fine tackle who was an outstanding wrestler. Show me a good, aggressive tackle and I'll show you a doggoned good heavyweight wrestler — if he has the desire and academic capability to go right from one demanding sport to an even more demanding one. Jack Himelwright was a fine student and a young man who worked hard to become a good football player who actually came to CU as a better wrestler than a gridder but became equally proficient in both sports.

John Denvir (1959-60-1) was another brawny (6-2, 238) but basically gentle person who came in with the wave of giants who were to make the 1961 Big Eight championship squad such a physical one. John, like so many starters on that team, was recruited by Dal Ward — actually he hitchhiked into Boulder on his way west one summer, liked the town and the school and the coaching staff and accepted the scholarship which was offered him sight-unseen insofar as any documented football ability was concerned.

Jim Perkins (1959-60-1) was another big guy (6-5, 230) who was a nice guy on that championship team. He came lumbering out of the mountains of California as one of the rawest, biggest rookies I've ever seen but he improved every year and was a solid contributor to the Colorado championship in 1961. Jim's eyes were set fairly close together and his teammates — and there are no greater caricaturists in the world than teammates — quickly nicknamed Jim "Cyclops."

Bill Frank (1961) was still another giant on that championship team, a 6-4, 232-pounder out of Denver and a lot of other stops along the way including the navy and a California junior college. Bill looked like Buddy Hackett, facially, but the resemblance ended there. Bill was no comedian, a mean, tough tackle who might have made my first team had he stayed around a little longer. But he flunked out before the 1962 season and went right up to Canada where he became a regular in the Canadian Professional league. He continued to expand his reputation as a wild man, on and off the field, up there, incidentally, and, I am sure, has become a legend north of the border by now.

Jerry McClurg (1961-3-4) was another big, green giant (6-4, 230) who could go bear hunting without a gun. Jerry, like so many big men, was on the sleepy side — I guess when you're that big it's just not natural to become ferocious because you might kill somebody unintentionally. Jerry would have been a starter in 1962 but he missed being eligible by a small margin then helped Eddie Crowder's reconstruction program in 1963-4. He, too, went into the Canadian pro ranks and played well up there.

Stan Irvine (1962-3-4) was one of our more agile big tackles, a 6-4, 223-pounder who came to CU as an end and actually played tight end for us as a sophomore. But we had more ends than tackles in those days and Stan, a very fine young man and always a great team man, willingly moved into the interior line and became a good, tough Buffalo there.

These are the top two-way tackles as I remember them. It's tough to bracket them by pairs but, after Stapp and Wooten, I'd do it like this: Sam Salerno and John Denvir, Bill Frank and Jack Himelwright, Jim Perkins and Bob Salerno, and Stan Irvine and Jerry McClurg. Five pretty damned good sets of tackles, any combination of which I wouldn't be afraid to go to war with.

GUARDS

When you talk about CU guards you always begin with Joe Romig (1959-60-1) who is in a class by himself as a competitor, scholar and all-around outstanding human being. Joe did it all: two-time All-American, Academic All-American, captain of his team (the 1961 Big Eight champions), Rhodes Scholar and now a physicist in America's outer space program. Joe is worth a separate chapter in himself and will get it. Right now, I'll just say that he is the number one guard and captain of my all-25-year CU two-way team, one of the toughest, roughest, most-dedicated, meanest-on-the-field, nicest-off-the-field, finest men anyone could ever know. He wasn't very big as great football players go, 5-10 and 199 at the very most, but you can't measure men like Joe Romig with scales and a ruler. Man has never found a way to weigh the mind or the heart or the stomach — three of the most vital component parts in a great man, be he an athlete or a scientist or whatever. If they ever do, Joe Romig would be one of the heaviest men in the history of CU.

Ironically, Joe's teammate on my first team was his backup man. Bob McCullough (1959-60-1) was an injury-plagued 6-2, 221-pound ex-fullback from Montana who had as great a combination of size, speed and strength as I've ever seen. He finally put it altogether in 1961 after being hobbled by neck, ankle and knee injuries through his first three years at CU. Actually Bob started almost as many games as Romig during 1960 and 61 because Joe broke his hand late in 1960 then suffered a pre-season knee injury in 1961 which kept him out of the first game and below top speed for the first month that fall.

I considered Bob our third starting guard on those teams because we had so many good men, especially in the line, that there simply wasn't room on the field at the kickoff for all of them. Big Mac, I know they didn't name the McDonald's special after Bob but they could have with full and proper credit to their product, was a great linebacker, probably the best big one we've ever had. And he was an outstanding offensive lineman, too. He could actually play anywhere in the interior line and play the position well. His injuries were always freakish. I guess he was just accident-prone. In 1960 when he was a junior, he got caught in a tangle and almost got his neck broken. Trainer Lloyd Williams, who watched the incident with horror, said later he'd never seen a neck bend so far the wrong way without breaking. It healed well, though, and he was playing by mid-season then had his fine senior year when he became a regular, then one of the few topflight linemen the early Denver Bronco teams had. But he re-injured the neck and it finally forced his retirement as a player in the late 1960's.

Ranking right behind Romig and McCullough are a trio of quick, tough, smart guards and linebackers, Bill Mondt (1956-7-8), Sherman Pruit (1956-7-8) and Ralph Heck (1960-61). All three were outstanding players, both ways. Mondt was a good-looking, fresh-scrubbed farmboy from Kersey, about the same size as Romig at 5-11, 199, and the same type of person as Joe — extremely intelligent. Smallish men like that need something extra going for them and the best extra they can have is intelligence. Brawn is a fairly good substitute for brains, especially in the middle of a line, but I've never seen many good athletes who weren't sharp, at least on the field, and if they didn't achieve as well in the classroom as they did on the football field it was more because they weren't motivated properly than because of a lack of brainpower. Bill Mondt needed no motivational help on or off the field and was a fine student of football who went on to become a good high school coach then a fine college coach, first right here at CU then at New Mexico.

Sherman Pruit was a red-eyed, rangy slice of raw leather from Roswell, New Mexico who, like Mondt and Romig and McCullough and a lot of other college guards, had been a fine high school fullback. He was a good fullback as a freshman at CU in 1955, doing the spinning and blocking in the single wing very capably but was moved to guard early in his sophomore campaign because of the presence of such gifted fullbacks as John Bayuk then George Adams and Chuck Weiss. Sherman was as tough as rawhide and a great competitor who, like Dick Stapp and Roy Shepherd ahead of him, challenged his always-heavier opponents and battled them right down to the wire. Sherman went on to become a good high school coach, the kind of man who should be leading young men at probably the most impressionable age in their lives. I know he teaches his players to be tough and diligent and fair and you can't give young men a finer beginning in their adult lives.

Sherman Pruit actually finished his college career as a center and the next man on my list, Ralph Heck, began his college play at that position. But both men were outstanding guards and linebackers and, aside from snapping the ball, center isn't that much different from guard so they're guards on my two-way team.

I'm sure you're beginning to get the idea that a good man can play anywhere. My team is full of men who could, and often did, move from one position to another without losing effectiveness. Ralph Heck and Sherman Pruit are two excellent examples; they could make my team at either center or guard. Ralph was only 6-1 and 200 but he looked, and played, bigger. He was a blond, clear-eyed strongboy from Pennsylvania who lost what would have certainly been an all-star senior year when his last season was taken away by the Big Eight conference in its jackal-like, follow-up assault on CU following the NCAA penalties after the 1961 season. Ralph went right into the professional ranks and is still playing today as a starting linebacker for the New York Giants. One of the times I remember about Ralph is meeting his father for the first time. You expect a big, hulking parent to have sired a stallion like Ralph Heck. Instead, his dad was a tiny little butcher from a Pittsburgh suburb who spoke with a decided German accent and who always had a friendly twinkle in his eye. And tremendous pride in his son. It was rightful pride because his son was a fine person and a great football player.

My sixth guard is another smallish man who was one of the senior citizens on Sonny Grandelius' first two teams at CU, Tom Wilscam, who came out of the service to win a starting job for the Buffaloes in 1960 at age 26. Like most smaller linemen (Tom was 5-11 and 188 and is the smallest lineman on my squad) Tom made up for his size deficiencies by being smart and tough and by not ever being intimidated by an opponent, no matter how big or scary he was. Tom got after it pretty good and I've got to admit he was one of my favorites on those 1959 and 1960 teams. It was a real pleasure to sit with him on the flights and I always tried to ride at least one way with him because he was a very mature person who always could give you the temper of the team and a good reading on any current situation. He was shrewd and aggressive and sound as a player and all those characteristics have served him well in his successful business ventures since his graduation. Tom has gotten a lot of mileage from being the "other guard" alongside Joe Romig. He may have been "unknown" but he wasn't unproductive. He's only on my third unit but I know he'd do his job excellently when called upon. That's the way he was in 1959-60 and his steady, though unspectacular work earned him a spot on my team.

These six men, then, make up my guard squad. Romig and McCullough the starters, Heck and Mondt on the backup crew, Pruit and Wilscam on the third unit. This gang would clear out a lot of wide paths for runners to follow and they'd do a lot of whacking and headon-ing and ambushing and blitzing and all those defensive moves which inevitably wind up in a collision at the ball. I'll guarantee you that these are men to match our mountains!

CENTERS

Choosing my two-way centers is just as tough as it is at every other position. You just don't have a good program without a lot of good men and we've had a good program at CU for most of the 25 years I've been following the Buffaloes, first as a student, then as a sportswriter in the Big Eight area and, for the past 20 years, as a member of the athletic department.

My number one center is Walt Klinker, the tough-as-nails hitter from Gunnison who survived some serious shoulder problems to become the All-Big Eight starter on the 1961 champions. His teammates called him "Butch" and nobody was ever more fittingly nicknamed. Butch Klinker was a battler who asked no quarter. He could put it out and he could take it. Life in the middle of the line is a two-way street. You do a lot of handing out and you take a lot of it. Especially when you're down over that ball to snap it and you've got a big middle guard squatting there ready to ring the bell inside your hat the minute you move the ball. Those blows didn't bother Walt but a shoulder which wouldn't stay in place almost drove him to total despair in a frustrating junior season after he had started every game as a sophomore. It was an old high school injury which had been surgically repaired before he enrolled at CU. He re-injured the shoulder in 1960 and had another operation. This one was performed by an up-and-coming young Denver orthopedic specialist and it was one of the most successful bits of surgery ever performed on a Buffalo. Once Butch realized that the shoulder was sound, he got with it again and had a great senior season. The doctor, by the way, was Charlie Brown, and he is still working wonders for the Buffaloes with his knives and sewing kits. You're a good man, Charlie Brown! (And I'm sure you're a rich man from all those surgical fees you've been earning from people like us all these years.) Keep those blades well-honed, Dr. Charlie. We still need you!

We're talking about Walt Klinker, though, and I never think of him without remembering the story of how he decided to come to CU. Walt was a rugged western slope youngster who, automatically, was a little suspicious of a big state university like CU. It somehow didn't seem, at first glance, as the sort of place a cowboy-type like Butch might be happiest at. Other schools in the region have always played this particular point to the hilt when trying to lure a prep great away from CU. They don't succeed most of the time because the real thoroughbreds like Walt Klinker and Bill Mondt and John Bayuk and Bill Symons inevitably make the right decision and attend the college where their educational and athletic potentials get the best opportunities. At any rate, our agricultural and mechanical opponents from up the road at Ft. Collins were in the thick of the psychological warfare battle for Klinker and were about to win it. When Walt told Ray Jenkins, the coach who was recruiting him for CU, he had about made up his mind to attend Colorado A&M (now CSU, although they'll always be the Aggies to CU oldtimers regardless of how many hippies and longhairs and riots and mods and so forth they collect on their campus in their efforts to become a truly all-around university), Jenkins, who hadn't exactly come from a major metropolitan area himself, he had ridden in from Cheraw complete with his cardboard suitcase and laundry bag to win starring roles in football, wrestling and track a couple of decades earlier, went into a rage. If you don't think you can play in the Big Eight and if you don't have the guts to try it, we don't want you and you belong at Aggies, he roared at Klinker. To his credit, Walter picked up the challenge and, forgetting about how was he ever going to learn how to put on a tuxedo and how was he ever going to overcome not having been brought up in a country club atmosphere with gold and silver spoons in his mouth and all that baloney that smaller schools use to combat the big ones in recruiting, he heatedly told Ray Jenkins that he'd show him whether he could play Big Eight football or not and where's your pen and your scholarship form and where do I sign and I'll see you this fall. Period! End of the Walt Klinker recruiting caper. And the beginning of a brilliant Big Eight career which has led since to a fine career as a college coach on Rudy Feldman's most capable New Mexico staff. Ray Jenkins may have looked like a burly bear, you see, but he was a pretty sharp psychologist himself and always at his best when he was competing against the Aggies, on or off the field.

Behind Klinker as the backup center is Larry Ferraro (1963-4-5) a tough little Italian from Trinidad who also had a lot of doubts about enrolling at CU but finally did and, with a lot of hard work and adjustments, like Klinker, made the familiar transition from star high school fullback to star college lineman. Larry's concern in coming to CU was different than Klinker's, though. Larry was rated as one of the best prospects in Colorado in 1962, right when the CU program was at its lowest ebb following the penalties of 1961. So Larry was getting a lot of heat from other area schools and, in particular, from Oklahoma which has always had the scholarships and the recruiting personnel to work extensively outside their primary recruiting area, Texas. Sure the Sooners get a lot of Oklahoma kids on their squads but Bud Wilkinson's real productive territory for recruiting was Texas and it wasn't until one of his ex-quarterbacks, Darrell Royal, returned to the Lone Star state as head coach at Texas that the Longhorns regained their recruiting domination over Oklahoma and an even quicker domination of the series between the two neighboring state universities. But, in 1962, CU had a lot of things going against it, mostly the uncertainties about a situation which included an alumni director suddenly projected into the head coaching job and a lot of undergraduates getting the ax from first the NCAA then the Big Eight and a bright young prospect like Larry Ferraro had to make sure he wasn't heading into an early gridiron grave. But Larry made the right decision and signed with CU and became the starting center as a sophomore and was an All-Big Eight player as a senior. Larry was never a tremendously gifted athlete in any category but he was what coaches call a "woodchopper", always swinging away at the problem of the moment, working furiously to become a better athlete and, inevitably, succeeding. Woodchoppers always topple that tree, no matter how big its diameter or how dull the ax. Larry Ferraro was the kind of an interior lineman that good line coaches, like Buck Nystrom, love because they're always bleeding, or starting to heal, from the bridge of the nose and-or the forehead. Larry Ferraro will never win any Mr. America contests or spring races or a lot of other things. But he managed to get the job done, always. And that's a lot of what it's all about, you know. Pass the chianti, Larry old buddy, you're a good paisano and you can play center on my team anytime!

My third center is a man who was a rugged 6-0, 200-pounder in 1953-4-5. Don Karnoscak came out of the tough territory of Chicago and was one of the few real good men we got out of that part of the country in those days. Dal Ward's staff recruited the Chicago area fairly hard because there were a lot of students at CU from there so it appeared to be a natural thing to do. And also it was a heavily-populated section of the country with a lot of steel mills and coal mines and places like that which spawn a lot of 6-4, 225-pounders. But it was also Big Ten country and that conference was at the height of its power back then so you really didn't get much out of there except a few culls or good-looking players with defects which you couldn't spot from the distance. But Don Karnoscak was a good player, a good offensive center and a fine smart linebacker who was a regular his last two years. His nickname was Duke but he didn't look like a duke. Duke Karnoscak, in fact, would never make honorable mention on an all-good looking team. His face, and especially his nose, got chopped up pretty good somewhere along the way, maybe in some of those tough sections of Chicago. But Duke had a lot of smarts, on and off the gridiron and today is a very successful insurance executive on the west coast. As I recall, Duke went into the marines, got discharged at San Diego and remained there and went into business. One of Duke's finest days as a Buffalo came at Oregon during his junior season. CU, with all kinds of help from a blundering Oregon team finally won the game 13-6 but needed to recover six (of eight) Webfoot fumbles. Karnoscak personally covered four of them for an individual CU record which I doubt will ever be broken. Two of his recoveries were inside the CU 10-yard line and Duke had his hands around the ball on defense that day almost as many times as he did on offense. His first recovery, by the way, came at the Oregon 30 early in the game. The Webfoots got caught up in a little bench confusion then and only sent 10 men on the field to play defense and the Buffaloes promptly broke Homer Jenkins for a 30-yard TD with less than three minutes played and that eventually proved to be the winning margin. That same Oregon team, incidentally, came to Boulder the next year and in the opening game of 1956 humiliated a CU team which was to go on and win the Orange Bowl, 35-0. Two important elements in the 1955 meeting at Eugene were gone the next fall when they opened at Boulder: Duke Karnoscak and eight Oregon fumbles. If Klinker and Ferraro were unable to play, I'd still have good center strength with Karnoscak. And, remember, I'd still have Ralph Heck and Sherman Pruit waiting in the wings.

FULLBACKS

Inasmuch as most of the two-way football that I watched at CU came during the 11 years Dal Ward was head coach, I'm going to select a multiple offense backfield and fill the positions in that alignment which Ward used so effectively in the last three years he coached. This means a fullback who can work the spin series in the single wing, hit in hard on the quick power plays of the T and, most importantly, block. Peculiarly, there are no gridiron goliaths when you check back through the list of two-way men for a fullback. But there have been a lot of excellent all-around performers who make the task of picking the top one as difficult a job as there was in picking this team.

My choice, and all four finalists are bunched very closely together at the finish line, is Loren Schweninger (1959-60-1) the starter on the 1961 champions and, in my opinion, one of the most underrated backs who has played for CU during my time. Schweninger was really built more along the lines of a halfback, he only weighed 179 as a sophomore, but he was a tough, quick, smart fullback who did everything well and who was one of the leaders of that 1961 team, a personable outgoing young man who had a lot of charisma in the days before anyone knew what that word meant. Loren played in Sonny Grandelius' power-oriented Winged-T and really wasn't a workhorse ballcarrier although he did lead the team in carries in 1961 with 122 attempts for 512 yards. But he was a knifing runner with the power to ram out the tough short yardage and, very importantly, he had the speed and maneuverability to go all the way once he got into the secondary. And he was a fine blocker who played as well without the ball as with it, a characteristic a lot of fullbacks don't have to the degree they should. The game in which I remember Loren the best as a runner was a key 22-14 victory over Oklahoma at Norman in 1961. Oklahoma was in the only ''down'' period Bud Wilkinson ever had and I think, had lost four straight games going into this one. But the Sooners were still potentially dangerous — they never lost another game after this one that year—and a modern Colorado team had never won in Norman, and it still isn't an everyday occurrence, so there was a lot of tension going into the game. Schweninger did some great fourth quarter power running to score two touchdowns and bring the Buffaloes from behind. One of my vivid memories of that game is the scene in our coaches' spotting booth in the press box after Loren's second TD. We were now ahead by eight points and an extra point kick would give us the point which would put the game beyond reach. I was in the coaches' booth sweating it out with Buck Nystrom and Chuck Boerio and Bob Ghilotti and we had just started to relax when we saw the Buffaloes lining up for a 2-point try. All three men began screaming into the phone at the same time and there was bedlam in the booth as they realized we were gambling when we didn't need to. But they couldn't get their point across to the coach at the other end of the line and we tried for two and failed to make it and had to sweat out the possibility of a tie right down to the final play. Buck Nystrom was so furious and frustrated that he picked up the phone and threw it against the plate glass window of the closed-in booth so hard that I still don't know why it didn't shatter the window and go plummeting down into the crowd. But, instead, it bounced straight back and nearly hit me in the face. Life in a coaches' booth isn't exactly always calm and serene and, in this instance, it was downright dangerous. An upset line coach like Buck Nystrom in a small booth can make a bull in a china shop look like a pillow fight in a girls' dorm. And I once saw an irate coach from Kansas State smash a door right off its hinges and down the stairwell into the next level with one swipe of his mighty paw. He was an old line coach, too, and hell hath no fury like a frustrated line coach. One of Harry Carlson's favorite sayings was that, "Hell hath no fury like a non-combatant." He was talking about alumni and Monday morning quarterbacks and those types and his saying has lots of merit. But I still have to go along with an upset line coach as the most dangerous form of aroused human.

Getting back to Loren Schweninger, though, he was also a fine defensive back. His speed and quickness and mental agility helped him tremendously here and set him just a cut above the average fullback, most of whom were big strong linebacker-types. Schweninger's defensive play, incidentally, provided one of the few bright spots in the Buffs' Orange Bowl appearance against LSU that winter. He slid over into the deep flat and intercepted an LSU pass and sped 59 yards down the sideline for CU's only score of the game.

My number two fullback, and he was the same type of player as Loren Schweninger, is Emerson Wilson (1953-4-5), a fine all-around performer who stepped into an injury-created vacuum as a rookie and promptly led the Buffaloes in rushing in 1953 with a 591-yard season. Emerson got his chance when both returning lettermen, Bill Horton and Don Shelley, were injured in pre-season practice. They never got the job away from him as he ran, faked, blocked and tackled in superb style even though he was a rookie. Emerson opened his career with a brilliant 87-yard performance to lead CU to a 21-20 upset over Washington at Seattle and his 41-yard burst up the middle on a picture-play scored the winning touchdown. Emerson was a fine linebacker, too, very adept at diagnosing a play and getting there in a hurry. Emerson never was better than in his sophomore season as an elbow injury knocked him out of the first two games as a junior and he really never got into high gear after that. As a senior he was moved to wingback in an attempt to fill the void created by the loss of

3-year regular Frank Bernardi and also to make room for he and John Bayuk in the same backfield. But the switch never came off well and the whole season ended on a disappointing note. But the Emerson Wilson who played fullback for CU in 1953 and when he was healthy in 1954 was good enough to be the backup man on my all-star team and there would be no noticeable change in quality when either he or Schweninger was on the field. The quality which put these two men at the head of the list is intelligence. There's nothing like a few extra ergs of brainpower working for you and these two men had an oversupply. Consequently, they were always in the game, sharp in their approach to any situation be it an offensive or defensive one.

My third fullback is Chuck Weiss (1958-9-60), a hard-hitting 6-1, 210-pounder who was also an excellent linebacker. Weiss was probably a stronger runner than Schweninger or Wilson but he wasn't as quick or fast and, although, he was good defensively he wasn't as good as either man. But how Weiss could barrel up the middle on those single wing trap plays that open up a hole so wide you sometimes wondered if there weren't a snowplow leading the way. As a runner, though, Weiss was overshadowed as a sophomore by tailback Howard Cook and wingback Eddie Dove. Then in his last two years he was used mostly as a blocker, and he was a good one, in Sonny's offense which never rolled up the ground yardage that Ward's did. For example, Weiss gained 452 yards as a sophomore but was third on the team, nearly 200 yards behind both Cook and Dove. As a senior in 1960, he gained only 391 yards but led the team by nearly 150 yards over the second man, Jerry Steffen. Weiss' biggest moment came as a senior when he mashed into the end zone to score the only touchdown in what for a decade had figured to be the most magnificent moment in all of CU football history, the first modern win over Oklahoma. It came on that touchdown, 7-0 in 1960, but, ironically, the glamour was gone. Gone for two reasons: (1) Dal Ward, who had brought the Buffaloes to the brink of that victory so many times, was gone and (2) the Sooners of 1960 weren't the Sooners of 1950-59. So Weiss wedged his way into the end zone for what should have been the most famous touchdown in CU history only to find that his achievement produced only a dull thud, not much louder than the noise he made landing in the end zone. Chuck Weiss was also partially-responsible for another episode which comes popping out of a cobwebby corner of my memory when I think of 1958. Chuck's high school coach, Norm Galloway, hung up his high school hat after several years at Fergus Falls, Minn. and joined the CU operation as a rather grizzled and scarred graduate-type assistant.

Norm was a good old boy good for a lot of laughs and a lot of fun and we sometimes wondered if he hadn't spent too much time as a player backing up a weak line but he worked hard that fall and got here just in time to get in on the firing and he was gone with the first mid-winter Chinook that came roaring down through Boulder Canyon. In winding down the unpredictable paths of such a mysterious thing as memory you run across vignettes involving some basically forgettable characters who you somehow remember. Like Norm Galloway.

My fourth fullback, and we went to a lot of battles and won most of them with him, is John Bayuk, "The Beast" of 1954-5-6 fame, a 6-1, 223-pound baby tank who could move with amazing quickness and speed and had tremendous power — from the ankles up. John was almost a perfect single wing fullback...an excellent, surehanded ballhandler who executed his assignments well, never fumbled (he went through his entire senior season without a fumble to earn the undying admiration of Dal Ward who saw his 1958 team fumble 13 times, losing seven, against Air Force in Dal's final game as head coach at CU), and ran with tremendous power up the middle on those trap plays. When I say that John had great power from the ankles up I mean that it was almost impossible to get him down quickly if you tackled him high. But you had a chance if you got him down around the ankles because he ran so hard and he was so big that he had a tendency to be a little topheavy. But he could bull his way upfield with more tacklers riding him than any other back I've ever seen. John looked like an overloaded stagecoach on some of his trips up the middle.

Any mention of John Bayuk has got to include how he got his nickname, "The Beast." I always got the credit (or the blame in the case of some of his friends from Salida who felt that the nickname was not altogether flattering to their favorite fullback.) But good nicknames often are not flattering. Rather, they are nearly always accurate in describing someone in a caricaturing sort of a way. And it's very difficult for anyone to manufacture them. The best ones come by accident, generally from a teammate and almost never from the hard-trying mind of an ambitious publicity man. When John was a sophomore we played our first road game, after two easy home breathers (61-0 over Drake and 46-0 over Colorado A&M), at Kansas and it was a typically sweltering early fall day in Lawrence. CU was a solid favorite but the score was 0-0 at the half as neither team could function well in heat and humidity. But Frank Bernardi, who had forgotten to get off the train during its early morning stop in Lawrence and who was hurriedly traced and found in Kansas City wondering what had happened to the rest of the team, made a couple of sensational catches in the third quarter to break it open and CU led 21-0 going into the fourth and everyone was pretty well pooped and we were ahead so we could afford to send in our sophomores like John. But Kansas was still trying to pull it out and kept their weary regulars in and John Bayuk bloody well ran roughshod over them, hauling hordes of them with him as he mauled his way for 71 yards and a final touchdown in the last 15 minutes and looking just awesome in doing it. We always caught a late-night train for Denver so we'd go back to the hotel and have dinner and wait around the lobby until it was time to go to the depot. About an hour after we had gotten back to the hotel the team was milling around the lobby killing time and some of the faithful followers who had come to Lawrence, also on the train, were downstairs clustered around a piano at which one of the greatest, and most talented, CU laylists of them all, Pete Smythe, was plunking off some of his well-known Rocky Mountain classics such as "Wolfe of Wolf Creek Pass" and "You Pulled the Plug from My Bathtub of Dreams and Our Love Went Down the Drain" when a little old lady, obviously not one of our alumni group (she was sober, for one thing) came in with a lost look on her face. She asked if there was anyone present who knew the Colorado players and I was pushed toward her and greeted with this question, "Where is that beast who wears No. 30? I want to see what he looks like up close!" And there it was. Instant-nickname. I pointed out John, who was grinning up against a post in the picturesque old lobby of the Eldridge Hotel — also called the Bright Kentucky by KU's resident humorist and sports information director, the late (and great) Don Pierce — and John spoke nicely to the lady and assured her that he really was a normal, everyday, nice guy but one hell of a mean fullback and that those Jayhawkers would have been wiser to have just gotten clear out of his way. She was properly impressed and went back home and belted down a couple of cups of peppermint tea or Ovaltine or hot water and lemon juice or whatever and listened to the Grand Old Opery and went to sleep and had bad dreams, I'm sure, of that beast who wore No. 30 and who was so mean to her precious, but not too talented, Jayhawkers.

It's too bad John didn't make it as my number one fullback because he's gonna end up with more space than the other three put together. But he was a colorful character as well as a fine fullback and I just can't get past him without remembering a lot of things. For one thing, John impressed people on first contact as a big, dumb kid from the mountains. He sort of looked like a big old bear who had just come out of his cave after a winter's sleep. But he was a pretty shrewd young man. Not a Rhodes Scholar, mind you, but a soundly intelligent person who could think more than adequately beneath his deceptive facade. We had a lot of trouble getting John onto the campus, too, just like we did Walt Klinker, and the same coach, Ray Jenkins, was in charge of the project. John was a big, friendly puppydog of a high school senior who wanted to make everybody happy and who had a lot of coaches chasing him with their tongues hanging out after his prep career which included being a conference champion hurdler in addition to his gridiron exploits. A small western slope school (Western State, I think) talked John into visiting their campus while they were having pre-season workouts. When he didn't show up in Boulder, Jenkins got busy and found out where he was and went after him. There was some reluctance at the school to let Ray make off with their fine young potential fullback but he marched right into the dormitory where the athletes were quartered, jammed John's belongings into his suitcase and led Bayuk through the door, followed by a nervous cluster of athletes who had been ordered to keep John in hand but who didn't quite know how to get him away from that scowling giant of a Ray Jenkins who had him so firmly, and so ferociously, in tow.

They got out of town okay, surviving a few muttered threats to tip over Ray's car. Jenkins, you must realize, wasn't about to let anyone he had worked so hard to get away. For example, during one particularly trying period in the recruitment of John, Ray had spent a long evening in the Bayuk living room on a hot, dry summer night singing the praises of CU to John and his family. After you sing the praises so long on a hot, dry mountain night your throat gets awful dry and you really need some soothing liquid to cool your throat and set your nerves at ease. Like a water glass of good, cool wine — John had a lot of Italian blood in him on his mother's side and you just knew there was a barrel of cool, sparkling dago red somewhere on the premises. And, sure enough, after what seemed like an eon to Jenkins, Mrs. Bayuk announced that it was time to knock off the small talk and have something to drink and Ray's eyes lit up and his tongue started unswelling. Whereupon Mrs. Bayuk got up and marched into the kitchen and came back with a pitcher of Kool-Aid. To his credit, Jenks sipped it down just as though it were something better then zipped out as fast as he could and washed the taste of that Kool-Aid out of his mouth with a couple of steins of that stuff that the Coors family makes out of mountain water and hops and barley. Recruiting ain't all roses and candy, you know! Every now and then you run into those long, hot summer nights and Kool-Aid. But not very often.

No story of John Bayuk would be complete without mentioning one of his, and CU's, most memorable moments...in Columbia in 1956 when CU needed only a tie with Missouri to win the Big Eight spot, as runnerup to Oklahoma, in the Orange Bowl. But it was one of those afternoons when everything was going wrong. Right from the start when CU figured it would confuse the Tiger defense by running from a left formation single wing and totally screwed up the first two plays to get off to a start from which they never would have recovered had it not been for Bayuk. Missouri was in front 14-0 late in the third quarter and the Buffaloes were getting very nervous and were in a sort of desperate situation at fourth-and-three on about the Missouri 35. We had to go for it and when you were in trouble on short yardage situations in the old single wing days, you gave it to your fullback. It wasn't any secret because good offensive coaches like Dal Ward didn't worry whether you knew what he was going to do or not because if he did it right it would work and most of his teams did it right. But not this day. Bayuk was swarmed over at the line of scrimmage. Buried, I mean! There was a collective groan and a sigh then more groans in the Colorado section of the Missouri pressbox. When all of a sudden we saw referee Cliff Ogden run up to the pile and fling down his flag and march off a 15-yard penalty against the Tigers. It was Easter Sunday for the Buffaloes and they came charging up out of that tomb and scored and eventually tied the Tigers and went to the Orange Bowl and beat Clemson there. We didn't get the full story until after the game. The Missouri player who drew the penalty had punched John, screaming that John had bitten him in the forearm. Lots of funny things happen under those pileups and the guy did have some tooth marks on his forearm. But, to his everlasting credit, Cliff Ogden said he didn't see any biting going on and you could have bitten yourself, son, and let's just walk off 15 yards to keep you from punching anybody in the face again. On the plane back, John took the fifth amendment when asked whether he had bitten the Missouri guard but when one of his teammates got him off to one side on the plane going home and asked him, confidentially, how did Tiger meat taste, John grinned his big grin and replied, "Salty, man!"

End of the John Bayuk section. Except that in the Orange Bowl that January, he was right there when he was needed as he bulled his way in from the 8-yard line to score the touchdown which brought the Buffaloes from behind to win the game, 27-21. John Bayuk was always there when he was needed and that's what fullbacking is all about. Being there when you're needed.

And so we have four fullbacks. A pair of lean all-arounders in Schweninger and Wilson and a pair of strong jackhammer types in Weiss and Bayuk. Not a bad foursome and, although there will be much more glamourous names on my team, the fullbacking is in totally dependable hands.

QUARTERBACKS

In this multiple offense backfield a quarterback must be able to play blocking back and while he blocks most of the time he must also handle the ball in the buck-lateral series and is a primary short receiver on pass plays plus being able to handle the ball in the T and dropback pass or rollout and run or pass. This is a most demanding set of assignments and Boyd Dowler (1956-7-8) is easily the man with the greatest variety of talents to fill this role.

Boyd was a single wing tailback in high school at Cheyenne, Wyo. and played that position as a freshman at CU but was moved to quarterback as a sophomore in 1956 when Dal Ward finally went to a multiple offense. Dowler was the major reason he finally put some T into his offensive plan, the first quarterback he'd had who wasn't an old high school fullback or, in some cases even, an old high school guard. Quarterbacking in the single wing required brawn mostly. You had to be a good blocker. If you could do anything else it was simply a bonus. Dowler, however, was a tremendously gifted athlete who did continue his track career in college as a fine high hurdler and who could have been a very good basketball player. At 6-4 and 200 he was a brilliant sophomore prospect and quickly got his chance, starting the second half of the first game of the season after the Buffaloes, with veteran Dick Hyson unable to move the team in a horrible first half against Oregon, and never relinquishing the job thereafter.

Dowler's direction got the Buffaloes untracked and, though they failed to score in that second half of that 35-0 loss to Oregon, Boyd's interception and return inside the Webfoot 10 set up CU's most serious threat of the day. After that stumbling start the Buffaloes went on to a 7-2-1 record, losing again only to Oklahoma (after leading in that game, 20-6 at the half) and going on to win the Orange Bowl. Boyd was a fine ballhandler off the T and a good dropback passer although the Buffaloes didn't put the ball in the air a whole lot. But he threw two touchdown passes to Frank Clarke in that rally which produced the 14-14 tie with Missouri that year to get the Buffaloes into the Orange Bowl. He was an adequate blocker, not exactly a scythe out there cutting down potential enemy tacklers but he could tangle them up pretty good by throwing that long body in their paths. He was a pretty good runner who could cover a lot of ground with his long strides and who had pretty decent power although that wasn't his strong suit. Boyd could roll out and run or throw off the T. But it was as a receiver from the blocking back position in the single wing that he really stood out. And that talent was what got him drafted high by the Green Bay Packers and led to a brilliant pro career as one of the stalwarts in the Vince Lombardi legend. Dowler looked like a big turkey ambling into the short flats and pulling down wobbling throws from a crew of mediocre passing tailbacks like Bob Stransky who could barely throw a spiral but who completed 18 of 32 as a senior in 1957, most of them short end-over-enders to Dowler, who caught 26 for 380 yards that fall as a junior. In addition to his excellent height, Boyd had two of the greatest hands I've ever seen and he had such a good touch that he used to dribble a football around on the practice field, keeping it bouncing just as though it were round. Boyd was also a fine punter. He took a little time getting off his punts but he could really boom them down the field. He never really developed his kicking accuracy, though, and never mastered the art of kicking it out of bounds deep in enemy territory. I can still see Boyd taking the snap on about his own 50 yard line and zinging that ball way over the goal posts for a 15-yard net punt. In those days a punter lost 20 yards off his distance on a touchback but Boyd still averaged over 42 yards in his career punting. The coaches called him "Skinny" for a while but that nickname died a welcome death early and then some of us called him "Boyd the Broomstick" but names like that weren't too nice for a guy who was making as valuable a contribution as he was so we just called him Boyd and, more importantly, called on him often to do a lot of key playing for us during the three years he was here.

Behind Boyd Dowler, I'd have to put his backup man on those 1956-7-8 teams, Ralph Herbst, who also came to CU as a tailback and who turned out to be a fine multiple offense quarterback, alternating with Dowler throughout his career under the substition rules of the day which did not permit a player to re-enter a game once he left it during the remainder of the quarter unless he had started the quarter and, in that case, he could re-enter once.

Ralph was smart and talented and tough. Had Boyd Dowler not been on the squad, he'd have been an outstanding regular, I'm sure.

But he never could bump Boyd out of the starting job. To his credit, though, he accepted his role as the No. 2 man with class and style and always performed well when he got the chance. Ralph was probably a better runner than Boyd and maybe technically a better blocker. And although he wasn't as impressive an athlete as Boyd he was a good one and having two good quarterbacks on a team is very important and CU had two good ones in 1956-7-8 and so do I on my all-star team.

I really had to think a long while before coming up with a third quarterback on this team. There were lots of men who would have qualified had they played two-way football. Men like Bobby Anderson, Bernie McCall, Hale Irwin, Frank Montera, Gale Weidner. But although all except Anderson played at least one year of two-way (sort-of) football, they all ended up as specialists. I think I'd probably pick McCall for my man because he was big enough and strong enough to be a fine multiple offense quarterback. I really think he could have been a great single wing tailback, too, because he could run and throw with equal effectiveness. Bernie was the workhorse quarterback, "Iron Man" I called him in those tough days of the rebuilding program when Eddie Crowder was new on the job and the Buffaloes were bounding back from misfortune.

Dowler, Herbst and McCall. Not a bad trio. I'd take them anytime!

TAILBACKS

One thing about Dallas Ward as a coach: he always had a lot of good tailbacks around. They were the key men in his single wing offense and you couldn't have too many of them. Just like quarterbacks today. The tailbacks were the do-everything men. You needed a genuine triple-threater in that position. And he had to be a good defensive back, too, because he was generally the safetyman or, in some cases, a halfback and, in all cases, a man who had to be able to defend against the deep pass or make the open field tackle or come up quickly to support against the power play.

My number one tailback is Carroll Hardy (1951-2-3-4), probably the greatest athlete who has ever come through the program while I've been around and I'll match him against anybody in the history of the school, including the legendary Byron "Whizzer" White who I never had the privilege of seeing but who couldn't have had any more physical equipment than Carroll although he undoubtedly was more durable and maybe was a tougher competitor. I think that a lot of us are guilty of the same wrong to a great athlete like Carroll Hardy: we expect too much of them and want them to do something great on every play. I suppose that's the burden a great athlete must bear: over-anticipation from his followers. I know this: Carroll Hardy could send more sparks of excitement through Folsom Stadium's stands by just coming out of the huddle than a lot of good men produced in their careers. What an athlete! He was 6-0, 185, could run a :09.8 hundred, had a good arm (although this was probably the least impressive weapon in his arsenal), could punt, placekick, play defense, return kickoffs and punts. Everything! And do all these things electrifyingly well. The only other player I've seen at CU who could generate the same kind of excitement by just touching the ball was Clifford Branch. And the only other player I've ever seen who fits into this category was the Bobby Reynolds of Nebraska's 1950 season. These three men just made you drool with anticipation. But I never really did drool too much about Reynolds, never having been, I'm somewhat proud to admit, a Nebraska fan, stemming from my childhood in Iowa when my beloved Hawkeyes and Cyclones used to get whomped regularly by the Cornhuskers in the 1930's.

We used to get after Carroll a lot because he was so overprotective of his great body. He preached about the importance of physical conditioning and body care so much, in fact, that his teammates, including one of his best friends, Don Branby, that nail-eating, spike-chewing defensive All-American in 1952, nicknamed him "Preacher." Carroll wasn't the most enthusiastic practice player in the world and he was good enough to be able to get away without doing a whole lot of scrimmaging during the week. I remember some of us back in those days used to try to figure out what kind of a statue we'd erect in Carroll's memory once he was graduated and the best one we could come up with was a statue of a player in a snow-white practice uniform. But that was unfair because Preacher did practice a lot and he did perform with pain when he had to. I can remember when he was a junior, in the 1953 opener at Seattle, he got tackled hard and landed on the ball with a couple of Washington players jammed right on top of him and he wound up with some torn rib muscles, one of the most painful injuries you can have.

Carroll was helped to the bench, very probably out for the rest of the game and maybe longer. CU nursed its 21-20 lead early in the fourth quarter but Washington was moving into excellent field position, slowly but relentlessly. So Carroll got off the bench midway through the quarter to make a long punt return which moved the ball beyond midfield and put the game out of danger. He kept aggravating the injury and couldn't help us much during the early part of that season but at Oklahoma, in our usual stemwinder late that October, Carroll came back and we nearly got an upset tie (whatever that is) as he sprinted right up the middle for a 35-yard touchdown toward the end of an 83-yard (in only nine carries) afternoon. He was so weak, from not having been able to play himself into good condition, that he collapsed in the end zone at the end of his TD burst and was unable to play again and his replacement, an overly-confident-for-no-reason-junior who I deign not to name, cost us a 20-20 tie by not deflecting Merrill Green out of bounds as he sped down the sideline inside our man who could have reached out and pushed him over the sideline but who instead froze and didn't move as Green scored the winning touchdown with less than a minute to play.

So Preach played in pain and played well in pain. I've tried not to use statistics too much in making his presentation. Statistics are basically cold, unemotional things and I want this book to be warm and somewhat emotional if possible. But in Carroll Hardy's case I think you need to look at the figures of his senior year to appreciate his contribution to the team. He was the team's top scorer (nine touchdowns and 14 of 19 extra points for 68 points), top kickoff returner (five for 157 yards), top punt returner (11 for 138 yards), top punter (26 for a 41.6 average), top interceptor (three for 90 yards), top passer (12 of 25 for 189 yards) and third-leading rusher (70 carries for 642 yards) but his per-carry average of 9.2 yards was the best in the Big Eight that fall. On top of all that, Carroll was an outstanding defensive back, a sure tackler with the great speed to run down almost anyone unless they had too overwhelming a lead on him. In the 1953 game against Missouri, I saw him gain 10 yards on a Tiger halfback and catch him at the CU 20 after a 50-yard gain. But the game I remember Carroll Hardy best in was his farewell performance in a Colorado football uniform, the final game of the 1954 season, one which had started out so promisingly but was torpedoed by Nebraska and Oklahoma in mid-season. The Buffaloes were out of the Orange Bowl chase but all Kansas State had to do was win this game and they were in. Hardy and his teammates ruined the Wildcat season quickly. In the most amazing display of running I've ever seen, anywhere by anybody, Carroll gained 238 yards in 10 carries, a Big Eight and CU record which stood for several years and was broken only by workhorse backs like Dwight Nichols and Bob Anderson and Charlie Davis who needed a whole lot more than 10 carries to beat that mark. Not that these men weren't great. But how do you top a 24-yard per carry average? For the first touchdown of the game. Carroll circled his right end on a simple single wing sweep. He broke open but the K-State left halfback and safetyman were converging on him with an angle. Preach simply turned on his supercharger and reached the meeting place, and was gone, before they arrived, even though they had the shortest route to get there.

The two K-Staters, finding only air instead of Hardy, crashed into each other and when they turned around saw Carroll downing the ball in the end zone. And late in the game with the crowd screaming for Carroll to run just one more time and everybody knowing he'd run if he possibly could, even on a pass play (he always preferred to run instead of pass), Preach swung wide on a running pass, reversed his field twice and when he had everybody spread out, streaked 46 yards inside the 15, got piled on with the penalty moving the ball to the one and scored on the final CU offensive play of the game, a 38-14 victory. It was a fitting finish to a great 4-year career which had also seen Carroll hit, field and run brilliantly as the baseball team's regular centerfielder during that span and also set the school record in the broad jump despite competing only in the indoor season. Carroll continued his great performances into the pros, making it big as a wide receiver for the San Francisco 49'ers but giving up pro football after a year to play baseball in a career which saw him play five years, first for Cleveland then for Boston in the American League. But Preach's best sport, a lot of us felt, was football and his baseball career was very ordinary as he failed to hit well enough to be a big league regular. Most of his baseball fame came as a late-inning defensive replacement for the great Ted Williams and his one claim to fame was that he became the only man to ever pinch hit for Williams, the occasion arising when Williams was injured when he hit himself in the instep with a foul ball and had to leave the game. It was in the first inning against Baltimore and Carroll, who had just been traded to Boston where he became known as Ted's "caddy" because of his late-inning takeovers, was sent to the plate to finish Williams' turn. How did Preach handle his moment in baseball history? He promptly bounced into a doubleplay to end the inning. Had the sport been football, and a similar situation arisen, I'm sure Preach would have run for a touchdown. But that's life!

Even though Hardy was such a great athlete, picking him over a fellow South Dakotan, Bob Stransky (who came to CU from Yankton while Carroll came by way of Sturgis), wasn't exactly easy. Carroll was bigger, faster, stronger, a better passer, almost a better anything than Stransky. But Stransky had two important advantages over Hardy: he was more durable and he followed his interference better on those devastating single wing sweeps. Carroll was hurt a lot and below top speed a lot, consequently. And his only fault as a runner was that he was too fast and too many times got to where the hole was supposed to be before his blockers got there. So there wouldn't be too much of a hole and, accordingly, not too much of a gain. Stransky, however, was a master at staying with his friends. He was always in the middle of his blockers, waiting for them to do their work then making his move into the daylight. Bob wasn't a strong runner and didn't have the brilliant speed of Hardy although he had good speed. He was fast enough to be a fine hurdler in high school, though, and certainly fast enough so that no one ever caught him from behind. But his chief characteristic as a runner was his ability to change speeds and directions and see when and where to do it with his great peripheral vision. We nicknamed him "Stop-and-Go" Stransky, Colorado's traffic light tailback and the words were more descriptive than appealing. Unlike Hardy, Bob had a terrible time getting his college career going and was down on himself, as were several of the coaches, early in his sophomore year but came on strong when he finally put it together. I guess the best description for Bob as a runner would be "sneaky." He wasn't very impressive slithering through a secondary but he could always find the daylight. One thing I always liked about Bob was that he was a smart runner who recognized his limitations. He wasn't big and strong like a Bob Anderson (he was 6-0 and 180 as a senior) and knew he wouldn't be too effective at bulling over a tackler like a bigger man could. So instead of trying a lot of straight-ahead power, he was always looking for the daylight to either side. When he was tackled there was never any great impact. A tackler couldn't pull the trigger on him because he had to make sure he had him. And Stransky, instead of slamming into a pointless collision (like tough little Homer Jenkins used to do), would just sort of settle softly to the ground. Discretion is the better part of valor. Especially for a smallish tailback. And Stransky managed to total 1097 yards rushing as a senior, the second best mark in the nation that year. He also totalled 1387 yards of total offense to rank fourth, nationally, in that category. And he was an All-American halfback that year. As a junior Bob was a key man on the Orange Bowl championship team. Early in the year, he slipped around the Kansas end for 80 yards and the touchdown which changed a 20-25 deficit into a 26-25 victory in a crucial early season game for the Buffaloes. And when the Buffs reached Miami and finally came from behind after blowing a big halftime lead to try to protect a precarious 27-21 lead late in the game, it was Stransky who came up with his second interception of the day to kill a Clemson threat which had gotten very seriously deep into CU territory. I'd have to call Bob Stransky the most effective tailback I've seen. Not the best athlete but the guy who got the most out of his ability. A good man to have on the field. And a player I'm proud to have on my team.

Hardy and Stransky stand out as the two best tailbacks I've seen at CU but there have been a lot of other good ones who wouldn't exactly disgrace an all-star team like mine. Roughly in order, I'd list them like this:

Bill Symons, a big, strong fast runner from Nucla who had everything going for him except coaching stability. Bill was recruited by the Sonny Grandelius staff which fought off the collegiate world to keep him in Colorado. Bill had three different head coaches in his first three years at CU and although he did get to play his last two years under the same coach, Eddie Crowder, he never reached the consistency he undoubtedly would have attained had he not been bounced from system to system. Bill reached that level after he finished at CU, earning stardom at Toronto in the Canadian pro ranks where he was one of the top backs in the league for several years. Bill was drafted by the Green Bay Packers originally and almost made that team right back there in the middle of that Lombardi dynasty. But he had some leg problems and got cut and finally made it in Canada. I was glad for Bill because he was always one of my favorites, a happy-go-lucky guy who always had a smile on his face despite a frustrating college football career. He ended it in style, though, returning an Air Force kickoff 91 yards in his last game to insure a satisfying 28-25 upset of the Falcons. Bill always had a lot of trouble keeping his footing whenever he cut sharply or reversed his direction quickly as a Buffalo. At Green Bay when he reported for rookie camp, they measured him for his equipment and discovered that he was wearing shoes which were two sizes too big for him. Bill didn't realize it and Lee Akins' policy at CU, as it probably was anywhere else but isn't at CU anymore, was to just ask a player what size shoes he wore and give that size to him. Who knows how much more mileage we might have gotten out of Bill if we'd have measured his feet instead of taking his word? But I have a hunch it was all those changes in coaches which kept him down more than the size of the shoes he wore.

Bill Harris. The first Bill Harris we had. Back in 1961-2-3. A big (6-2, 198) strong back with excellent speed, Buffalo Bill was a dependable workhorse who could carry the ball all afternoon if he had to. And I can remember one afternoon when he did, against Kansas State in 1962 when he carried 35 times for 156 yards in a 6-0 victory. It was the busiest game of the year by any runner in the nation that fall and Bill was a weary Buffalo when the gun sounded. But he never flinched at hard work and was always more than ready to do his share or more. He was a fine sophomore on the 1961 champions and I can remember the Kansas State game that year at Manhattan which we were supposed to win easily but had to sweat to get it and finally got it put away 13-0 when Bill came on in the last half to make his college debut by bolting 12 yards to move the ball into scoring position then getting the touchdown on a 6-yard burst. Ironically, Bill hadn't even played in the first three games that season and wasn't even on the traveling squad for the first trip of the season to Miami a week earlier. Chuck Boerio nicknamed him the ''Water Buffalo'' because on one of the first times he'd come up to the varsity practice field for a scrimmage as a freshman, it had rained and Bill slogged through the mud just like a big water buffalo. I remember that Bill wore one of the biggest headgears I've ever seen. Something like a size eight. But he could run with authority and was always a pleasant person to work with. A good man.

Harry Narcisian (1947-8-9) was a fine little tailback for both Jim Yeager and Dal Ward. I can remember what probably was his greatest game, against Utah State in Boulder as a junior in 1948 when he literally exploded in the fourth quarter to lead the Buffaloes to three touchdowns in a 28-14 win two weeks after driving Kansas State crazy with four touchdowns in a 51-7 Homecoming win over the Wildcats in a game which was rated dead even at the start. Harry was a :09.9 sprinter and a good baseball player but he banged up a leg and didn't have as good a senior season as he should have. But he was an exciting little man at 5-10 and 170 and how he could zip through that broken field traffic! He was a good passer, too. And a fine kick returner. He'd carry his weight on any all-star team.

Leon Mavity (1961-62-63) was another of those good athletes who got innocently caught in the coaching shuffle which saw him play under a different leader in each of his varsity seasons. Leon was a compact, tough, versatile back who was equally effective on either offense or defense. He was a hard runner and a smart one who peeled off one of the niftiest punt returns in Folsom Field history the first time he ever fielded a kick in college, twisting 60 yards for a touchdown in a magnificent display of broken field running. Leon was a regular as a sophomore on the Big Eight champions, the only rookie to earn that honor and he and junior Ken Blair were the only two underclassmen in the starting lineup. Leon was one of the heroes of the 34-10 upset of Air Force in the final game of 1962 as he intercepted a Falcon pass and skipped nine easy yards into the end zone when Air Force had fought back to 14-10 after trailing 14-0 early in the game. Mavity's TD broke the back of the Falcon comeback. Leon was also a fine baseball outfielder with excellent power at the plate. I remember him best, though, as a truly nice human being with a peculiar style of speech which made him sound like a tough from the sidewalks of New York when actually he was a very neat young man from Illinois.

Homer Jenkins (1953-4-5) was as good a little man as I've ever seen but he was always trying to smash down someone bigger and always coming away wounded and he really never put an entire season together. We called him "Hot Rod" and he could do as many things with a football as anybody I've ever seen. Nobody ever made a more impressive debut as a sophomore than did Homer at Seattle in 1953 when he took over after Carroll Hardy was injured early in the game and promptly workhorsed for 38 yards in 17 carries, threw two touchdown passes, intercepted a pass and returned it 19 yards, returned a punt 16 yards and a kickoff for 45 yards and punted four times for a 42-yard average. But Homer got a broken leg three weeks later when he tried to run a fumbled kickoff out of the end zone against Kansas instead of downing it for a touchback (Homer never did know when to give up) to wipe out the last half of his sophomore season. As a junior, he was playing brilliantly at, of all places, single wing fullback (at 5-10, 175) when tore a hamstring very badly and eventually had to have it repaired surgically following the season.

He had a good senior season but that year, 1955, was a disappointing one for the Buffaloes and nobody really was scintillating as the Buffs lost four of their last six games to finish 6-4. Homer was a bright little guy who had classroom claustrophobia — sitting in one made him nervous and he didn't do it unless he absolutely had to — and he was also a stubborn little guy who had to learn everything for himself. I can remember that we played a mid-season game at Arizona when he was a sophomore and it was a Saturday night affair in Tucson and we stayed over and took the team to Nogales, Mexico and the one thing we always did before these trips over the border was warn the players that whatever you do don't eat any fresh fruits or vegetables. Hot Rod wasn't in Nogales a half-hour before he found an attractive restaurant that he just knew served good food and, especially, salad so he had himself a meal and re-joined the group. By the time we got on the plane to fly back to Denver that Sunday evening, Homer was known as "Hot Rod Homer with the Torrid Tailpipe" and I think he lost about 10 pounds before he got sealed and I'm sure that he never tried the salad again in Nogales but most people never try it the first time. But Homer did. I guess he was just accident-prone. But when you got him all glued together he could make things happen on a football field and I've got a place for him anytime.

So those are my tailbacks and I know I've left out some good ones. But you have to draw the line somewhere and I've got a lot of good men on my side of the line. We'll move that ball!

WINGBACKS

I've deliberately saved wingback for last because two of my all-time favorites are locked in a dead heat for the number one job and there's no way I can break the tie. Not only were they two of my favorite players, they still are two of my favorite friends and they have a lot of other things in common, too, besides my friendship and complete admiration. They are Frank Bernardi (1952-3-4) and Eddie Dove (1956-7-8), two of the toughest, best little backs anyone ever had at one school. Both were tremendous competitors. Just tremendous. I think that was the one thing which made them stand so tall on or off a football field. Their total degree of intensity. They got with it. Oh, how they got with it! Their relatively small bodies (Bernardi was 5-9, 175 and Dove was a stringy 6-2, 177, officially, but he used to hide weights in his armpits for the official weigh-ins and I doubt that he ever weighed more than 165 when he played for us) almost couldn't contain the huge motors each had.

I'll take them the coward's way, chronologically and alphabetically, and start with Bernardi, a squatty, swarthy little Italian out of Elmhurst, Illinois who had originally enrolled at Indiana then pulled out and headed for Arizona only to stop off at Denver for a quick look at CU before continuing to Tucson. He never left Boulder and had his bags sent back from Tucson and, if you think that was a mixed-up way to launch his college career, just wait until you hear how he began as a football player at CU. Frank was ineligible as a freshman, even though freshman were eligible in 1951, because he was considered a transfer having actually been enrolled at Indiana. He got off brilliantly at CU, winning the 1952 season opener against an upset-bent San Jose State team with a 63-yard punt return. Two weeks later he took a short Zack Jordan pass and fled 87 yards against Kansas for CU's longest play of the season. But then he injured a knee and it was going in and out on him like a yo-yo by the time I arrived on the job that fall. I can remember one of the first things I ever did as sports information director was to attend a practice and get drafted to help trainer Aubrey Allen carry Frank off the field and into the dressing room after it had gone out on him during a Tuesday scrimmage. Frank was really down in the dumps and near tears as Aubrey and I tried to cheer him up with a lot of platitudes. What he was looking at was an operation and the thought of it wasn't too cheerful. Frank had the operation and it was a major success. The knee never bothered him again and he came back strong with two brilliant seasons in both football and baseball and actually played professionally in each sport after graduation. Frank could do it all as a wingback. He was a strong runner with outstanding balance and the ability to push himself back on balance with his free hand when he got tripped up. We used to call him ''Tripod'' because it seemed like he was always running on two

EDDIE DOVE

A group of his teammates was admiring the nose of Eddie Dove, which got broken when he got kicked in the face during the 1956 Oklahoma game. In the back row were Howard Vest, Wally Merz and Gerry Leahy. On the left side of the front row was Bob Stransky, on the right Jim Uhlir. The guy with the band-aid on his nose is Dove.

FRANK BERNARDI

Trainer Jack Rockwell (right) and Dick Freund (52) help Frank Bernardi off the field at Columbia after he got his face bashed in while blocking an extra point against Missouri in 1954.

legs and one hand. He was also one of the swiftest men, laterally, I've ever seen and this was very important in running the deep reverse in the single wing. He could really come zinging back across that backfield to take the handoff. And he was a lefthander which made his wingback reverse passing even more accurate. I think the reverse pass when Frank was playing was probably the most effective single play Dal Ward ever had. It didn't get used much but it worked almost every time we tried it. Frank also had good power. He was built awful close to the ground and was stocky despite not being very heavy.

    He was very good in a broken field and I can remember a punt return against Nebraska at Lincoln in 1953 when he twisted back and forth across the field, making big figure "S's" for what seemed like five minutes. When he was finally run down he was so exhausted that he fumbled away the ball. It was a 14-10 victory and somewhat of an upset and Frank played a major role in it, throwing a reverse pass to Gary Knafelc for the winning touchdown then making a big third down tackle at the goal line to stop Nebraska's good running back, Bob Smith, when it looked as though Smith had clear sailing into the end zone. Smith was behind his big fullback, Ray Novak, with only Bernardi having a chance to stop him. I don't know how he did it — I have a hunch Novak helped by not getting too excited about his block — but Frank went right through Novak and stopped Smith for no gain and the entire Buff line held on the next play. That's as good a game to remember Frank by as any but I can remember that in that 238-yard performance by Carroll Hardy in their last game, Frank got 113 himself. He was always doing things like that and getting overshadowed by somebody else like Carroll Hardy or John Bayuk or Homer Jenkins. He and Hardy were known as the "Touchdown Twins," a very original designation which I, as a novice sports information director, had nothing to do with coining. They also were the All-Big Eight halfbacks that year, one of the few times that a single school has produced both in one year. But you can't talk about Frank Bernardi without mentioning one of the most poignant moments in modern CU football history. At Missouri in a "nothing" game in 1954. Neither team was going anywhere except to the end of the schedule. CU was ahead 19-13 in the fourth period but Missouri tied it with a touchdown and lined up for what would have been the winning extra point. Bernardi lined up outside his own left end and took off at the snap as though the conference championship depended on his blocking the kick. He dove and got a hand on the ball, deflecting it. As he was crashing to the ground, end Wally Merz, coming in a split second later from the other side kicked Frank in the face, breaking his nose and messing up his face real good. Still groggy from the knockout after the game in the dressing room, Frank was asked if he thought he'd be ready to play by the following Saturday. "I don't run with my nose," he growled. "I'll be ready Monday." And, sure enough, he was the first man out to practice on Monday...to try out a special birdcage mask on his helmet to make sure he could see okay through it. That's the kind of guy he was. A thoroughbred. One of a kind.

But along came almost an exact carbon copy of him two years later when skinny Eddie Dove checked out a wingback's gear for the 1956 season.

I doubt that Eddie weighed 160 when he came to CU from Loveland as a freshman end. Like Bernardi, he had been an outstanding high school hurdler as well as a fine football player. And, like Bernardi, Dove became a brilliant 2-sport star at CU, continuing in the hurdles and consistently ranking with the Big Eight's best in the lows.

Actually, it was through the desperate last-minute work of track coach Frank Potts that Eddie got his scholarship to CU. The football staff had made its overtures to Eddie but hadn't followed up because he was sort of a puny looking youngster, certainly not a gilt-edged, blue-chip, can't-miss football prospect. He was in track, though, and when Potts got the word that another state school was ready to make a big deal of offering Eddie a fancily-packaged scholarship scroll at the Loveland awards assembly, Frank got busy, probably on his beat-up old typewriter, and got some kind of a paper symbolizing a CU scholarship and rushed to Loveland and presented it to Eddie who was dying to come to CU but thought they'd never ask. So Potts, who had done a couple of hitches as CU's temporary football coach and done them well, got himself a whale of a hurdler and Dal Ward a whale of a wingback. Despite his slender build, Dove was tremendously durable on the football field and actually had more trouble in track as a heel injury kept him hobbled through much of his junior track season. He was one of the rookies who moved into the starting backfield at the half of the opening game of the 1956 season and helped spark the Buffaloes to the Orange Bowl where his wingback reverses picked up key yardage throughout that game. In the Oklahoma game that fall, Eddie got kicked in the face by Sooner All-American Tommy McDonald, not too bad a little competitor himself. Oklahoma liked to run those quick plays and CU's men had orders to keep the ballcarrier on the ground as long as possible to give the defense as much time as possible to get ready for the next play. Eddie got Tommy down in the second quarter and McDonald, who was a wild man anyway, was kicking and screaming at Eddie and, accidentally I'm sure, caught him in the face with a heel, breaking Eddie's nose. Jack Rockwell came out and stuck a band-aid across it and Eddie played that way the rest of the game. Eddie could run that deep reverse excellently, too, and he could pop through on the quick handoffs from the T-formation which the Buffaloes were using for the first time in his sophomore season. Eddie was also an adequate passer off that reverse action, completing 10 of 17 during his career (Bernardi was 20 for 45.) I think that of all the great runs I watched Eddie make, his 90-yard touchdown against Kansas as a junior in 1957 was one of the prettiest I've ever seen. We were going north and Eddie swung wide around his left end, a sweep off the T as I remember. Like Bob Stransky and Bernardi he could put on the brakes to take advantage of his blockers and he timed his moves perfectly as he set up five great blocks which helped him go all the way. On defense, Eddie was a slashing tackler who had no fear of headon collisions with bigger men. Ironically, he went three years as a defensive regular without intercepting a pass. I say "ironically" because he was drafted by San Francisco and promptly made that team as a defensive halfback and was a regular for the 49'ers then the New York Giants for more than 10 seasons. Eddie may have made the 49'ers draft list with his fine performance in the Shrine East-West game at San Francisco after his senior season. He intercepted a pass and had an excellent punt return in that all-star game to serve notice that he could hold his own in any kind of company. Which reminds me of another Frank Bernardi story. Frank also was selected to play in the Shrine East-West game after his senior year but had one concern that Dove didn't. Bernardi was going to play offensive halfback in the game and the West was going to use the T-formation, something which Frank hadn't run since his high school days. When he was asked whether he was worried about taking the handoffs from a T-quarterback, Frank merely grinned and guessed that anyone who had been taking the ball on spinners from John Bayuk ought to be able to handle just about anything. But he did slip into the CU fieldhouse a few times before going to San Francisco to work on taking some straight handoffs.

Bernardi and Dove. What a pair of wingbacks! And what a pair of men! I've got a private little niche in my memory which only a special kind of person can get into. Bernardi and Dove were the first two into it and it's still a pretty exclusive little club because only Joe Romig and Bob Anderson have made it since. You can have your Four Horseman or your Million Dollar Infield or whatever other special group you choose to come up with. I'll take these four men and match them against any other four men in the world. There might be a few schools who might match my four aces but nobody could top them. And I'm not so sure that anyone could equal them. After all, it's pretty tough to match four aces.

THE COACH

Now that I've picked an all-two way team, I've got to name a coaching staff. Five-man staffs were popular in those times when two-way football was in vogue and it's easy for me to pick five men.

First of all, my line coach would be Jim Yeager and he'd also be in charge of putting in the screen passes because he always got a lot of mileage out of them. My chief offensive coach would be Dal Ward, whose team could move the ball as well as any teams I've ever seen. My coach in charge of public relations would be Bud Davis, as personable man as I've ever known. He'd also be in charge of writing the Coach's Letter because he wrote the best ones I've ever seen...in 1961 and he wasn't even a coach then. My coach in charge of fundraising would be Sonny Grandelius, who was the best man at finding a Buffalo buck I've ever known. Sonny could handle the defense, too, because his teams were mean in that phase of the game. My head coach would be Eddie Crowder, the best all-around administrator I've ever known and a man without a peer at keeping a staff and a program moving forward. Eddie would also be responsible for the quarterbacks.

My coaching staff would match my football squad. And the publicity man? I'd do it for nothing. In fact, I'd almost pay for the privilege of being around a group of men like this squad and staff which I've selected. Just blow that whistle, or ring that bell, me and my gang, would sure give 'em hell!

MY THREE-DEEP

Here, in lineup form, is my 3-deep:
LE: Sam Harris, Wally Merz, Ken Blair.
LT: John Wooten, John Denvir, Bill Frank.
LG: Bob McCullough, Ralph Heck, Tom Wilscam.
C: Walt Klinker, Larry Ferraro, Don Karnoscak.
RG: Joe Romig, Bill Mondt, Sherman Pruit.
RT: Dick Stapp, Sam Salerno, Jack Himelwright.
RE: Jerry Hillebrand, Lamar Meyer, Jerry Leahy.
QB: Boyd Dowler, Ralph Herbst, Bernie McCall.
LH: Carroll Hardy, Bob Stransky, Bill Symons.
RH: Frank Bernardi and Eddie Dove.
FB: Loren Schweninger, Emerson Wilson, Chuck Weiss.

MY ALL-25 YEAR PLATOON TEAMS

Platoon football was legislated out of existence just after I returned to CU, as sports information director, in mid-season of 1952 so that my first full season on the job, in 1953, marked the return of two-way football to college. There are arguments for both substitution systems. Two-way football demands an athlete who is a more complete football player, one who has the best combination of offensive and defensive skills. But not necessarily outstanding skills either way. Platoon football, on the other hand, lets a coach put men on the field who are particularly skilled at the particular phase of the game they play. The result is undoubtedly a better game. More skilled players mean more skilled performances. But football is a great game either way and you can't really foul it up with a substitution rule. Some of the most thrilling games I've seen were played in the two-way days. And the great athletes can play both ways skillfully so you hate to see a Bobby Anderson not taking a shot at defense where he'd have been just as great as he was on offense or a Dick Anderson not getting a chance to carry the ball as a fullback — he was as good a high school runner as I've seen and displayed his fine running ability every time he intercepted a pass, the latest piece of evidence being his sensational touchdown return to break the backs of the Baltimore Colts in the game which catapulted his Miami Dolphins into the 1972 Super Bowl. I must admit, though, that platoon football enables players to polish their specialties better and lets more men play and makes for fresher men on the field. But it's also a more expensive game with larger squads and larger coaching staffs and I doubt that it ever gets legislated out of existence again. But if we did return to two-way football I certainly wouldn't slash my wrists because it would still be an entertaining game. The sight of a Carroll Hardy running down a ballcarrier in the secondary or a Bob Stransky picking his way through a broken field with an interception was just as thrilling as watching them run from scrimmage. And had platoon football been in effect in

1953 and 54 I'd have been denied the opportunity to watch a master of pass defense like Frank Bernardi keep nudging his man off balance with deft digs to the ribs as they were moving downfield in the pattern. Or even, and the memory of this sight is more humorous than was the actual observing it as it occurred, a John Bayuk, pawing and snorting in the secondary, looking, most of the time in vain, for the ball. And does anyone remember that the great passer in CU history, Gale Weidner, scored his first touchdown with a 94-yard interception return for CU's first TD of the 1959 season?

In selecting my offensive and defensive platoons for the past 25 years, I note one thing. Most of the men who I name would have been good, solid two-way performers. A good football player is a good football player. Wherever you position him. What a game we'd have if we could take the first offensive and defensive platoons and match them against the first and second two-way teams! I don't know who would win. But I do know that there'd be 44 fine football players in the game. Herewith, are those platoons.

THE OFFENSIVE PLATOON
ENDS

My offensive alignment will include a split and tight end, two running halfbacks and a power fullback who can block and pick up the tough short yardage. My split end is the most exciting receiver I've ever watched, Clifford Branch, the smallish (5-11, 165) 9.2 flyer of 1970-71. Clifford was that rare speedster, a sprinter with balance. Most sprinters run with so much forward lean that they crash and burn at the slightest impact. And they don't have the balance to work their way through a broken field. But Cliff Branch could turn it on and off and change direction as well as that past master, Bob Stransky, ever could. He made some of the most exciting runs I've ever seen. Literally, breathtaking. I've never seen a player who could bring the entire Colorado cheering section to its feet by just fielding a punt. Cliff got, I think, a bad rap about having bad hands because he did drop several kicks and passes during his two years at CU. But he also made a lot of tough catches in the heavy traffic of pursuing pass defenders or in the face of the charge of punt coverages. I've seen him make diving catches and hang onto the ball. Catch the hook simultaneously with the arrival of a defensive halfback into the small of his back. And, sometimes foolhardily, catching a punt without signaling a fair catch and immediately getting bent over backwards without coughing up the ball. Clifford may have had quick eyes which sometimes left the flight of the ball before it arrived. But I never felt that he had bad hands. And how he could fly!

Clifford's presence on my offensive platoon as a wide receiver brings five different ways to produce the bomb: by taking a short pass and using his great speed to go all the way, by beating the secondary deep, by coming back on the end-around, by returning a punt or by returning a kickoff. This little guy could kill you more ways than an armed posse. And he never left any traces, except an occasional burned spot on the turf where his wheels spun when he turned on full throttle.

My tight end is a contemporary of Clifford's who, like most tight ends, never got a lot of publicity but always did his job superbly whether it was blocking at the line of scrimmage, throwing a key second block downfield, catching the tough inside pass for the first down or going deep to haul down a gamebreaker. My man is Bob Masten (1969-70-1), as tough a competitor as I ever saw and a man who came up with as many key plays as any I've ever watched. Bob wasn't very big (6-2, 195) but he was another tough-as-nails competitor who had the ability to make the big play in the clutch. Ironically, he scored only one touchdown in three years as a regular — and that one in the 32nd game of his career. But he really pulled the Buffaloes off the deck on consecutive Saturdays as a sophomore in 1969. He grabbed a Paul Arendt pass for a big gain in the closing minutes against Kansas when the Buffs trailed 14-10. His catch and run set up a Bob Anderson touchdown and a 17-14 victory. A week later, with CU trailing by the same score in the final two minutes against Oklahoma State, Bob went high into the air at the 3-yard line to outfight two Cowboy defenders for a desperation pass from Jimmy Bratten.

In three years, I can remember Bob dropping only one pass he should have caught. And he must have caught at least a dozen he had no business getting. I can remember, especially, a leaping, twisting catch which he made in the first half of the Ohio State game as he went crashing over the sideline after coming down with the ball. It, as much as any one play, set the tone for the Buffs' performance that September, 1971 afternoon in Columbus when CU proved to the world that it belonged among the nation's elite. I can also remember a play against Alabama in the 1969 Liberty Bowl game when Bob scooped up a bouncing kickoff which threatened to screw up CU's pet reverse. But he alertly grabbed the ball, however, and got it over to Steve Engel then got in the blocking pattern and helped clear the way for Steve's 91-yard touchdown. Bob had several spectacular offensive plays in his career but I think that his work as a blocker, play after play, unspectacular block after unspectacular block, was his greatest

VIVA LA VICTORY

This was taken with two of my brothers, Cliff Branch (left) and Larry Brunson, two exciting little guys who made a lot of great things happen for the Buffaloes in 1970 and '71. We had just landed in Denver after beating Ohio State in 1971 and we all had new hats to celebrate the victory.

contribution to the Colorado team.

Behind my No. 1 combination of Branch and Masten, come Frank Clarke and J. V. Cain then Monte Huber and Mike Pruett.

Clarke (1955-56), like Branch, was a junior college transfer. But, unlike Branch, he was strong and big (6-0, 210). He had fine speed, could run the 100 in under 10 seconds and had great hands and was also an excellent placekicker. One of Frank's greatest days came against Utah in 1955 when he caught 63 and 37-yard touchdown passes. But the most important day he ever had was at Missouri in 1956 when he caught 17 and 18-yard TD passes from Boyd Dowler to bring the Buffaloes from a 14-0 deficit to a 14-14 tie which gave them the Big Eight berth in the Orange Bowl that season. Frank's great ability earned him a long professional career, the best years coming at Dallas where he was an important man in that new franchise's building program.

My number two tight end is a young man who could well move ahead of Bob Masten in the next two years. He is J. V. Cain, who has just finished his sophomore season as this was written. If he stays healthy in his junior and senior seasons, he should be an All-American because he has everything — size (6-5, 220 and still growing), excellent speed, great hands and super strength as a runner. What a great future he faces!

My third unit ends, Monte Huber and Mike Pruett were the starters in 1967-8-9 and were among the class which became the first at CU to play in bowls two of their three years. Both men were quarterbacks in high school, Huber at Ft. Collins Poudre and Pruett at Delta. Little (5-11, 185) Huber became the most prolific receiver in CU history, catching 118 in three seasons for 1499 yards. His ability included excellent hands and excellent broken field running ability and he was a good man in the clutch. Lanky (6-3, 220) Pruett, like Masten, was not a frequent target in the CU patterns but he could catch the ball in a crowd and was an effective blocker who made a contribution on almost every play.

Still another excellent receiver for the Buffaloes was Chuck Mosher who caught 36 passes for 668 yards in 1949-50-1, a career record which stood until Huber came along. Mosher was a big receiver, built along the lines of Frank Clarke at 6-3, 200, and he could step onto this team without causing any reduction of quality.

TACKLES

My offensive tackles are monstrous Mike Montler (1966-7-8) and Jack Jorgenson (1949-50-1). Montler, a hulking 6-4, 235-pounder came to CU out of the Marine Corps to become the most impressive tackle in CU history. Mike had excellent agility to go along with his size and played very well for three years although his class finished on a sour note, losing four straight games to close out the 1968 season. Despite that tailspinning finish, though, Mike still had enough performance in his record to earn consensus All-American honors and has gone on to become a regular with the New England Patriots. Oddly enough, Montler wasn't impressive enough as a prep to impress the people at Ohio State. He was from Columbus, right there in Woody Hayes country. But, like so many young men do, he grew up in the Marines and was a most desirable prospective college gridder when he was discharged. Fortunately, CU had an ex-Marine on its staff in Chet Franklin, whose great diligence as a recruiter, brought Montler to Boulder.

Jorgenson was a jolly 6-4, 235-pound giant who combined a happy-go-lucky off-field personality with an aggressive all-business approach once he strapped on his pads. He was one of the first bluechip players Dal Ward recruited for the Buffaloes and his presence in the offensive line played a big role in CU's quick rise under Dal. The Buffaloes were 7-3 in Jorgy's senior season. Unfortunately, Jack was cut down by polio a few years following his graduation from Colorado. But the same hard work and perserverance which made him a great player enabled him to overcome much of the crippling effects of the disease which never did cut down the size of his ever-present grin. Jack and Montler were as good a pair of oak trees as you could ever build an offensive line around. They'd stand out on anybody's lineup.

Behind these two come one of the current tousle-haired tigers, Jake Zumbach, a 6-2, 240-pound JC transfer who quickly became a regular on the 1971 team, and Kile Morgan (1966-7-8), who needed a redshirt year to get his personal program cranked up then became an extremely steady regular midway through his junior season. Kile was a sleeping giant for much of his first two years as he was tried at linebacker, then defensive middle guard, then offensive guard before finally becoming a good, tough tackle as a junior. Zumbach, who often looks like a fugitive from Muscles Beach with his lion's mane of hair and wide assortment of tattered clothing, made a spectacular debut in a CU uniform, almost decapitating ex-All American Dick Anderson with a vicious forearm in the 1971 Alumni-Varsity spring game. That was an omen of things to come as Zumbach stiffened a lot of people that fall, many of them unsuspecting secondary defenders who got caught looking the other way by big Jake as he roared downfield on second efforts.

My next choices are a pair of men who didn't get a lot of publicity but who, like Kile Morgan, were solid, effective tackles. Bill Csikos (1965-6-7) came to CU after originally being headed for Air Force Academy — he actually attended Air Force Academy prep school for one year — and became a 2-year regular for the Buffaloes, playing well as a member of CU's 1967 Bluebonnet Bowl champions despite a nagging illness which pulled his weight down from 227 to barely more than 200 by season's end. Jim Phillips (1968-9-70), was a moody 6-3, 240-pounder who served his sophomore apprenticeship behind Montler then took over as a very sound regular for the next two years. Jim was an extremely intelligent person, in the classroom as well as on the playing field, and his combination of brains and brawn set him above the crowd.

GUARDS

Dennis Havig (1968-9-70) and Roger Hunt (1951-2-3), a pair of men with different kinds of backfield history in their records, are my picks for the starting offensive guards. Havig (6-3, 240) was a former high school fullback star at Powell, Wyo. who gained 30 pounds at CU and became an outstanding offensive guard after moving into a starting job midway through his sophomore season. Dennis had excellent speed and mobility to go along with his size and the extra weight he added in college didn't slow him down a bit. Havig was a real man. Man enough to absorb the initial disappointment of being moved from the spotlight of the backfield into the darkness of the interior offensive line and keep improving until he became one of the Big Eight's best as a senior.

Hunt (6-0, 195) went the opposite route, earning his reputation as a quick, deadly-blocking guard for two years then moving into the backfield as a blocking back in 1953 when he was deemed the best man for that job by Ward. Roger was a picturebook performer as a guard with excellent speed and agility which made him an outstanding lead blocker and a very effective openfield blocker. He was also one of the quickest offensive linemen downfield under punts I've ever seen, ranking with Don Popplewell in that category. Roger was an outstanding student, too, and eventually graduated from CU law school. His intelligence, as much as his physical ability, was what led Ward to move him into the backfield as a senior. And, even though a blocking back in Dal's single wing was basically a guard who didn't have to start from a squat, moving to that position still required considerable adjustment on Roger's part. He also became one of the team's placekickers that season and won the opening game at Washington with the extra point in a 21-20 victory. I remember it vividly because Roger took the biggest divot I've ever seen on that kick. It looked like Jack Nicklaus hitting a wedge off a soft fairway. It was my first full season as CU's publicity man and my first week-long advance of a game and I had spent an extremely active week in Seattle, working night and day but, in particular, the nights, and my vision was a little shaky by gametime and the Washington press box hangs out from very high cantilevered stands with the results that you're looking almost straight down on the game so that viewing conditions aren't exactly ideal, particularly for a man with tired eyes which were weak to start with.

When Roger kicked the ball, out of Homer Jenkins' hold, I think, two things sailed up in the air. One barely looped over the line of scrimmage while the other barely flopped over the crossbar. Fortunately, the ball went further than the divot. Unlike a lot of my golf shots. I remember another rather bizarre play involving Roger later that fall. It came on a fourth-down from the Oklahoma 26-yard line with the Sooners hard-pressed to hold a 20-13 lead going into the final few minutes. CU called a buck lateral, one of Ward's favorite clutch plays in those early days of his CU career, with Roger taking the ball from fullback Emerson Wilson and pitching it out to tailback Ronnie Johnson. But an Oklahoma tackle anticipated the play perfectly and was standing between Roger and Ron, waiting to intercept the lateral. So Roger calmly pulled the ball in like a yo-yo, spun back to the weak side and headed for the flag. The Oklahoma secondary had been waiting for the buck lateral, too, and they were all headed for their left side where the play was going before Roger peeled back naked. Nobody caught him and suddenly CU had a 20-20 tie which promptly evaporated when linebacker Ken Huffer got nailed for 15 yards on a holding penalty to give the Sooners new life after they had apparently failed to make a first down with time running out. Merrill Green then zipped 51 yards down the sideline on a counter to score with only 36 seconds left to bring on the annual heartburn and heartbreak for the Buffaloes. But even the pain of the defeat couldn't blunt the brilliance of Roger's improvisation which brought the touchdown. To give you an idea of how often a CU quarterback carried the ball in those days, Roger finished the season with four carries for 33 yards, 26 of them on that one play in Norman. But two of his carries were for touchdowns and he added 14 of 15 extra point tries for 26 points and returned eight punts for 160 yards and even punted twice for a 33-yard average so you can see he was a pretty handy man to have around.

Backing up Havig and Hunt on my team are Kirk Tracy (1965-6-7) and Dick Knowlton (1951-2-3). Kirk was an average-sized 200-pound guard when he came to CU but through an intensive weight program built himself to a barrel-chested 225 pounds by his senior year. Kirk was another intelligent lineman who got maximum mileage out of his ability which did not include great quickness. But he knew all the moves and knew the quickest routes to where he was supposed to go and was a very important member of a good offensive line. He was one of the men who was injured in CU's fifth straight victory of 1967, at Nebraska, which lifted the Buffaloes into third place in the nation. With Kirk and several other offensive starters on the shelf for the next two weeks, the Buffs bowed on consecutive Saturdays to Oklahoma State and Oklahoma but then, as the wounded began to return, finished strongly and whopped Miami in the Bluebonnet Bowl. Kirk came back quicker from a rather severe knee sprain than a man that big normally would and was an instrumental factor in the Buffaloes' stretch drive which saw them win their last four games that season.

Dick Knowlton was a lean, rangy (6-2, 195) regular in 1951-2-3, one of the best pulling guards Dal Ward ever had — and Dal Ward always had a lot of good pulling guards and tailbacks on his squads. Dick was an offensive starter in his first two seasons and a very good one. When two-way football came back in his senior year, he quickly adjusted to become an excellent defensive lineman. He was a running mate of Roger Hunt's and, like Roger, he was a very personable and highly-intelligent young man. They were as fine a pair of men as ever graced any CU squad and they both have solid positions on my squad.

My third set of guards is a pair of relatively unsung players who both played very consistently and earned impressive honors as seniors. John Beard (1965-6) was a junior college transfer whose status on the CU squad was recognized by his teammates who elected him co-captain in 1966. Beard was a country-westernish 6-0, 206-pounder from Bakersfield, Calif. who was coached there by former CU star Paul Briggs. John is a highly-successful rancher back in the Bakersfield area today and I'm sure he still likes to relax by putting on a stack of Ray Price records on his stereo and listening to the mellow tones of the Cherokee Cowboy. On the football field, he was a highly-efficient blocker and an excellent leader whose running mate as co-captain was Hale Irwin. The other guard is Dick Melin (1967-8-9) who was a reserve linebacker in 1967 then took over as a starting offensive guard as a junior and earned All-Big Eight honors as a senior. Melin was an exceptionally good student. Most of my guard selections were, proving that you've got to have more than meat and muscle to be an outstanding interior offensive lineman. Dick was a quiet, darkly-handsome 6-0, 217-pounder whose strong suit was consistency. You could always depend on him for a solid performance and men like him have been critically important in the building of the fine offensive lines which have featured CU's football teams in recent seasons under first Joe Harper then Augie Tammariello.

CENTER

Don Popplewell (1968-9-70) earns the starting center position on my team, mainly on the strength of a great junior season in which he did it all — blocked, hustled downfield under punts and helped lead the team as one of the squad's personality boys. Don (6-2, 240) came to CU from right under the shadow of Missouri as a defensive end and looked to be an excellent prospect at that position as a freshman. But a need for the development of a good center arose that spring and the dashing Don got the opportunity. He didn't waste any time taking over as the number one man and became a 3-year standout for the Buffaloes. He was the best center I've ever seen at covering a punt and was a deadly tackler when he got to the ball. Don tapered off slightly as a senior but not so much that it was noticeable; he was the consensus All-American that year.

Behind Don is another personality boy, bubbling Bruce Heath (1965-6-7), the anchor of the middle of the CU offensive line in 1966-67 and one of the mainstays of the Bluebonnet Bowl champions as a senior. Bruce really made the rounds of the lineup searching for a spot. A tackle in high school, he was tried at end, guard, linebacker, defensive halfback and middle guard before finally settling down at center as a junior. Bruce was another of those near-A students, like so many of the other interior linemen on this team, and he was just as bright on the football field, a real hustler and one of the most vocal Buffaloes I've ever known. You always knew when Bruce was around because he did a lot of talking. But he did a lot of talking with his performances on the field, too, unlike a lot of men who merely do a lot of talking. Bruce was a man you liked to have around, on and off the field. A lot of class.

The number three center is Dave Hill (1951-2-3), a relatively obscure lineman back in those days but a good one, nevertheless. Dave started most of the time as a sophomore, alternated with Ken Huffer in 1952 as a junior then won the starting job back the next year when he also doubled as a pretty tough linebacker. Dave had good speed and quickness and was a very effective blocker on those double-teams from the unbalanced line which opened so many big holes for the fullback blasting up the middle. Hill also was a ranking student and is now a professor in the CU geography department.

QUARTERBACK

Gale Weidner (1959-60-1) gets first call at quarterback because of a fine career in which his strong right arm was practically the entire CU offense when he was a sophomore. By the time he was a senior he had developed into a solid all-around quarterback who could throw very effectively, although he now had a running attack to work with so didn't have to throw as much as he did as a rookie. Gale could run very well on the bootlegs when that call came up and, most of all, he was the stabilizing playmaker of a championship team. Even though he became a solid star at the helm of Sonny Grandelius' winged-T (and, shotgun, as a sophomore) attack, I would have loved to have seen Gale operate as the quarterback-tailback in Dal Ward's multiple offense. He came to CU as a top running back out of Troy, Montana in 1958. What a fine tailback he'd have made. A strong, swift runner with an excellent arm. I have a hunch he'd have ranked right up there with Carroll Hardy in the all-time category. But he also flourished under Sonny, who gave him his unqualified support right from the start, labeling him as CU's number one quarterback in the spring of his freshman year and building up Gale's confidence so that he was able to come through with a sparkling rookie campaign. Gale could really zing that ball to his target. We called him "Whip" because he threw so hard. He had great receivers in Jerry Hillebrand, Gary Henson, Bill Elkins, Chuck McBride and Ken Blair and he owned practically every CU passing record by the time he graduated, throwing for 1200 yards as a sophomore and finishing with 3033 career yards on 219 completions. One of Gale's greatest days came early in his career, in the first victory he ever engineered for the Buffaloes, a 20-17 nervewracker at Kansas State in 1959.

In that one, Gale passed for 180 yards and ran for 67 more and finally won the game with a 20-yard TD strike to Henson. He accounted for 247 of CU's 324 yards that afternoon to play a key role in the first Sonny Grandelius victory at CU, one which snapped a 3-game losing streak which had threatened to turn 1959 into a disaster. The victory, however, got the Buffaloes on track and they finished 5-5 and came within a cold, icy afternoon at Lincoln of going all the way to the Orange Bowl. The most remembered Weidner performance, of course, was his three touchdown passes in the fourth quarter against Kansas in 1961 as he finally got the Buffaloes warmed up to wipe out what had appeared to be a winning performance by such Kansas stars as John Hadl and Curtis McClinton. Weidner ran often as a sophomore, carrying the ball 51 times for 105 net yards, a total which is more impressive when you realize that it included a lot of yards lost trying to pass. But Sonny limited his running rather sharply over the next two years, preferring to protect him from that wear and tear to save his strong right arm which was a much more important part of the CU attack. Gale was a likeable, personable young man. He was quite proud of his ability and got prouder of it year by year. But he had a right to be. Because he was a fine football player. A champion.

My backup quarterback is Ken Johnson, the sophomore playmaker of the 1971 Astro-Bluebonnet Bowl champions. Like Weidner, Johnson can do it all. Handle the ball, run and pass. But, most of all, come up with the big play to lift a team. No rookie quarterback ever faced a tougher baptism as Kenny took the field for the first time on the Buffaloes' first possession of 1971, at their own 3-yard line in that most rabid of gridiron arenas, Louisiana State's 67,000-seat Tiger Stadium. Ken calmly steered the Buffaloes out of that hole, eventually hit Willie Nichols for a perfectly-thrown cross-field TD pass and followed up with a perfectly-timed lateral which freed Charlie Davis for another touchdown to shock the proud and seldom-defeated-at-home Tigers. Two weeks later at Ohio State, Ken calmly ducked inside his own right end and broke back against the grain to gallop 39 yards for the deciding touchdown in an even bigger upset than the one he'd directed at Louisiana State. To be a good quarterback and a good leader, you've got to have class and character and cool and a lot of good things. Johnson has them all, including a lot of courage — he played almost the entire season in 1971 with a broken bone in his right wrist. Before the injury, which came early in the opening game against LSU, he had been throwing the long pass spectacularly. The injury hampered his throwing somewhat but he still threw the ball very well when he had to. Only the possibility of the right hand failing to knit properly stands between Kenny and a brilliant 3-year career, one which could very possibly establish him as the finest quarterback in CU history. He can be that good.

My third man is one of the most exciting little guys who ever pulled on a CU uniform, diminutive (5-10, 173), dapper Danny Kelly (1965-6-7), one of the quickest, squirmiest, most effective scrambling quarterbacks I've been privileged to cheer. Dan was on the brittle side, he broke something practically every year, and only this physical flaw kept him from being higher on my list. As a sophomore, he broke an arm making a tackle in the opening game of the season at Southern California. Before he graduated, he had amassed another broken arm, a broken foot, a broken hand...and a partridge in a pear tree. But, oh, how the little guy could squirt out around that end on a bootleg. He was quick as a cat and as bright as a button and could peel back and forth across the field, changing direction on a dime to leave pursuers clawing at the air, and, on occasion, using a desperately scrambling referee as a screen. Dan could throw the ball adequately, too. But it was his quickness to the outside as a runner which was his most effective move. He could punt fairly well, too, although he never booted for a great average over the course of a season. Probably his finest performance as a Buffalo came when he was a junior in 1966 at Iowa State as he befuddled the Cyclone defenses with 156 yards rushing for three touchdowns and added 86 more through the air to lead a 41-21 rout. A week later against Nebraska in Boulder, he was on the verge of doing the same thing, scrambling and twisting and turning on a play late in the first half to finally spot Larry Plantz all alone in the end zone and hit him with a perfect 29-yard pass to give the Buffaloes a 19-7 halftime lead. But Dan suffered a broken bone in his right hand early in the third quarter and the Buffalo offense lost much of its spark with its sparkplug injured and Nebraska nipped CU at the wire, 21-19. The Cornhuskers stayed alive in the fourth quarter when CU's ace defensive end, Bill Fairband, couldn't hang onto an interception which would have given him a cinch touchdown and put the game out of reach. Danny Kelly was one of my favorite "Irishmen" of all time. He set off as many fireworks in Folsom Stadium as Franny Reich ever did on any Fourth of July. I have a special place for him in my heart, too, because he unintentionally got me a seat on the only baseball trip I ever made outside of an occasional excursion to Golden to play Colorado Mines. In 1968 Dan was due to be the regular shortstop for CU, and a good one, and the Buffaloes were scheduled for a spring vacation junket to Honolulu to play a series of service teams there. Coach Frank Prentup only had 18 men on his squad and the traveling party, the expenses of which were to be borne by the U.S. Navy, was limited to 20 (18 players and two coaches.) But Dan ran aground on a scholastic reef, as my old friend, Don Pierce, used to say, and became ineligible at mid-year. There was an empty paid-for space and guess who got to go? Lay that lei on me, you swivel-hipped lovely! Thanks for the exciting moments you gave us on the football and baseball field, Irishman. And also for the trip to Hawaii. You were my kind of a guy. There was never a dull moment when you were on the field. Next time around, though, get better bones, will you, little buddy?

HALFBACKS

The best two halfbacks I've seen on the offensive platoons at CU have been Bob Anderson (1967-8-9) and Charlie Davis, the brilliant sophomore star of the 1971 team. These two men didn't have tremendous speed. You wouldn't pick them if you were putting together a sprint relay team. But blinding speed isn't the most important asset in running with a football. A good running back has got to have heart. And strength. And durability. And maneuverability. And a workhorse nature, the willingness to work hard and take a lot of punishment. And be a good blocker. If a back has great speed to go along with all this, he's a once-in-a-lifetime man. Once in a lifetime is a pretty demanding criterion and I guess that that back still hasn't come along in mine. Great speed, ironically, is one of the most frequently-appearing qualities a lot of unsuccessful candidates for this once-in-a-lifetime role have had. The other component parts are the toughest to come by, though, and that is why Anderson and Davis were so great. They were tough and durable and competitive and highly effective, each in his own way. If they had had sub 10-second speed, they might have been declared unfair by the rules committee.

Anderson, like Joe Romig, stands out in my book as a truly unique human being. You don't get to know many young men of his quality in a lifetime and I guess I'm lucky to have known he and Joe. Joe is captain of my two-way team and Bobby is captain of my platoon team. He and Joe are the subjects of a following chapter so I won't go into great detail about him here other than his qualifications as a running back. Bobby, of course, was a do-everything quarterback under Emerson Wilson at Boulder High and filled the same role for CU in his first two varsity seasons. When injuries depleted CU's corps of running backs early in 1969, the coaching staff, in a tremendous mid-week gamble before the third game of the fall, against Indiana, moved Bobby to running back. The Buffaloes had talented young quarterbacks working behind Bob in junior Jimmy Bratten and sophomore Paul Arendt and Bob had the mental and physical capacity to move to running back and make the CU backfield a multiple-threat offensive group again instead of the almost totally-quarterback-oriented attack which it had become with only Anderson an effective runner after a pre-season knee injury had sidelined Steve Engel and his replacements had come up short. The move was amazingly successful due, almost totally, to the tremendously positive attitude of Anderson who, even though he was being taken out of the limelight and the total offense situation of quarterback, told Crowder that he'd play tackle if it helped the team. Anderson's greatest asset as a player was his tremendous desire. A desire which made him a total winner, a man who radiated success to the rest of the squad. You just knew good things were going to happen when Bob Anderson was on the team and they nearly always did and he was generally responsible, with his running or his blocking or his faking, for making them happen. Bob was a truly inspirational player and a good team must have at least one person on it like Bob who can produce the spiritual lift that is necessary to make a good team great or a great team even greater.

Charlie Davis, my other halfback, can give a team a lot of lift, too. But he does it with his flashing feet and powerful legs and tremendous maneuverability. I have never seen a back of his size and strength who can move like Charlie. He has the quickest feet I've ever seen. He doesn't have the straightaway speed of Gale Sayers although, frankly, Sayers never really realized his potential until after he had left Kansas and matured and was used more effectively by the Chicago Bears. But Charlie can jump around like Sayers except that Gale really seemed to bound through the air, like a deer, while Davis seems to glide, almost slither, back and forth. Davis might have more straightaway power than Sayers. He's certainly in Gale's class insofar as his moves and his effectiveness and had a much more sensational sophomore season than Gale who, it must be admitted, was used quite a bit as a flanker and only topped 1000 yards in one of his three years at Kansas. The other back who Davis reminds me of is Hugh McIlhenny, that big, mobile broken field beauty who played so sensationally at Washington then with the San Francisco 49'ers. And Charlie, of course, reminds all of us CU veterans of little Woody Shelton, that wiggly little wingback for Dal Ward in 1950-51-52. Except that Shelton was only 5-6 and 146 and, if you can believe it, wasn't as fast as Charlie. Woody was as tough to trap in the open field as a scared mouse in a family room. But when he broke into the open and leveled off for the goal line, a lot of people were capable of catching him. And he certainly didn't pack the power of Davis although he was a rugged little bantamweight whose heart was as big as anyone's. Davis, of course, had just finished his sophomore season as this team was selected so it must be assumed that he has two tremendous years ahead. He has all the component parts mentioned at the beginning of this section: power, heart, desire, toughness, agility and durability. If he stays healthy and, in particular, those great wheels stay sound, he could wind up his career as the greatest back in the history of the Big Eight. I know that that is covering quite a bit of territory and is sure to bring up a rumble of protest from every camp in the conference. But this is my team and these are my opinions and it's my book and I stand behind my statement, extreme as it may sound. Certainly, Charlie - and it's a shame he didn't come from that colorfully-named Texas town of Cut And Shoot that a prizefighter named Roy Harris came out of a few years ago to get kayoed by Floyd Patterson in a heavyweight championship match because Cut And Shoot describes Charlie's football running ability a lot better than it did Harris' fighting ability because he just cut and folded up. Charlie Davis, on the other hand, is a beautiful sight as he cuts inside or outside of a groping tackler then shoots downfield to repeat his move at the next confrontation. Sports fans, and in particular, football fans, tend to be greedy. When they have a man with the moves of a Charlie Davis they would like for him to have Clifford Branch's speed, too. And wouldn't that be something! But, then again, if Charlie had that kind of speed maybe he wouldn't have those moves. I'll take him like he is because I really didn't notice too many defensive backs catching him from behind last fall. Football is a game of short sprints and both Charlie Davis and Bobby Anderson had enough speed to get to where they were going most of the times they got into the open. Namely, the end zone. Andy probably dragged more tacklers into the end zone than any other halfback or quarterback in Big Eight history. And more than most fullbacks, who earn their scholarships by dragging opponents over the goal line. Charlie knows how to get into that six-point sod, too. Against Houston in the 1971 Astro-Bluebonnet Bowl he scored his first touchdown with a straight-right-to-the-head stiff-arm at the three followed by a cartwheel over the goal line. His second one of the night came on a high-stepping hurdle over the last man in his way. Men like Anderson and Davis know what the name of the game is for a halfback and the name of the game is touchdown. Andy scored 40 TDs in three seasons while Charlie got 10 in his first. The name of the game for a halfback is also net yards. Andy netted 2728 for a CU career record which was immediately challenged by Charlie in a scintillating sophomore season which saw him thread his way for 1386 yards. Andy's greatest afternoon came against Alabama in the Liberty Bowl, his final game in a CU uniform. He ran over, around, through, past - any way you can think of - the proud Crimson Tide defenders for 254 yards (in 35 carries) and three touchdowns. For good measure, he completed three of four passes for 41 more yards and a 23-yard kickoff return. After three years as a CU star it seemed, going into that final game, that there was nothing Bobby could do to improve on his previous performances. But Bobby was always up to an occasion and you'd have to admit he bowed out with a performance to end all performances. Charlie Davis, on the other hand, set a single game standard as a rookie which even as great a back as he might never be able to top, netting 342 yards in 34 carries against Oklahoma State in the tenth game of his college career. And if you don't think that feat isn't going to be tough to top, consider this. There has been only one other single-game performance in the first 102 years of college football better than that!

Maybe my starting halfbacks don't have blinding speed. But they've got everything else and you can load your backfield with racehorses, I'll take my two stallions anytime.

You'd expect a considerable drop in quality once you get beyond Anderson and Davis but my second pair of halfbacks doesn't drop off too much. They are Zack Jordan (1950-1-2) and William Harris (1965-6-7). Jordan was one of the last of the genuine triple-threaters, a single wing tailback who was a good passer and runner and a great punter and quick kicker. He was Dal Ward's first really great tailback and Ward got maximum mileage out of Zack's talents. Zack was a moody man who could get down on himself harder than any coach ever could but the CU staff and, in particular, backfield coach Frank Prentup, who handled Jordan in both football and baseball (he was an excellent shortstop), kept Zack's spirits sufficiently high to enable him to put together three outstanding seasons for the Buffaloes. Zack finished with 3035 yards in total offense, a record which stood until Gale Weidner eclipsed it with a 3195 total which was in turn shattered by Anderson's 5017. Zack wasn't exactly a picturebook performer. He was sneaky fast, just sort of slipped along behind all those blockers on those single wing sweeps and off tackle plays and threw with almost a sidearm motion and boosted his punting average with some great quick kicks which seemed to bounce higher and farther and farther once they cleared the safetyman's head. As a sophomore, Zack set an NCAA punting record of 48.2 yards, a fantastic average no matter how many quick kicks you included. Quick kicking, after all, was an art, too, and Zack was as good at this as anyone I've ever seen. He was a beautiful punter, too, arching the ball high and always in a perfect spiral. I think the kick most people remember Zack for was his quick kick from the CU end zone against Oklahoma in that 21-21 tie at Boulder in 1952. With the Buffaloes in deep trouble at third down near their own goal line, Zack calmly took the snap from center rocked back and quick kicked the ball 77 yards to turn the situation completely around. In Ward's closing years as head coach, the fickle fans booed whenever the Buffs quick kicked. Nobody booed that day in 1952, though, and even though the quick kick has practically faded out of football at all levels, it was still one of the prettiest, and one of the best, plays in the game when executed by a master like Jordan. But Zack wasn't just a kicker, as those 3035 total yards attest. His best game, statistically, came as a sophomore when he rushed for 167 yards and passed for 109, to almost singlehandedly lead the Buffaloes to a near-upset of Missouri in a game in which the Buffaloes fell short by two extra points, 21-19. But his greatest performance, I think, was in that 21-21 tie with those Eddie Crowder-quarterbacked Sooners in 1952 when the Buffaloes became the first conference team in five years to escape defeat by Oklahoma. Actually, the Sooners had to climb off the deck late in the game with a flawless 78-yard drive which began with Crowder sending Billy Vessels around end for 18 yards on a fourth-and-two situation at the Sooner 30 and ended with the Heisman Trophy winner crashing over from the one on the 13th play of the drive, the touchdown coming with but 1:51 left in the game. Jordan promptly sparked the Buffaloes in a desperate closing counterattack which saw the Buffaloes cover 62 yards in five plays only to have time run out on them as they tried frantically to get one more play off. The Buffaloes had a first down at the Oklahoma 21 when the gun sounded. In that game, Zack zipped for 14 rushing yards, completed six of 11 passes for 66 yards, caught two passes for 31 yards and punted seven times for a 56-yard average. He scored all three CU touchdowns that day, on runs of 10 and six yards and a catch of a 16-yard Lee Venzke pass. Not too shabby an afternoon against one of the nation's top teams for a 5-11, 180-pound sidearmer with sneaky fast speed and questionable power. In football you pay off on performance not form. And Zack Jordan produced a lot of good days for the Buffaloes and Dal Ward.

Jordan's running mate on my second unit, William Harris, was a compact 6-0, 184-pounder who wasn't big for a running back in a power-oriented offense but he took as much punishment without flinching as any player I've ever been around. I think William Harris was as tough a back as we've had, one who could play with pain and play well despite it. Bill could have been a fine defensive back, too, and was, in fact, a defensive regular as a freshman. But, given a trial at running back in pre-season practice of his sophomore season he won the starting job with a 3-touchdown performance in the first intra-squad scrimmage of the fall and was the starter for the next three years with the exception of the late part of his senior year when a knee which had been giving him trouble finally gave in on him and required surgery causing him to miss the last two games plus the Bluebonnet Bowl victory over Miami. Bill was more of a slashing power runner than a breakaway threat although he had excellent speed and was clocked in :09.8 in the 100 as a member of the Buffalo track squad as a junior. But the knee injury which he suffered originally as a sophomore kept bothering him and that, plus pulled muscle problems, caused him to bypass track as a senior. Bill was sophomore back of the year in the Big Eight in 1965 when his power bursts off tackle helped him to an impressive 680 yards in 142 carries, the most spectacular one a 76-yard explosion against Oklahoma State. Bill was also an effective blocker and did some punting and quick kicking for the Buffaloes, too. He was an outstanding member of the teams which brought CU back to gridiron respectability, lifting the Buffaloes from the gloom of three straight 2-8 seasons as Harris and his mates recorded 6-2-2, 7-3 and 9-2 campaigns, capping their career with the 31-21 triumph over Miami in Houston's Bluebonnet Bowl on December 23, 1967.

William Harris was one of the most important figures, and the man the Buffaloes gave the ball to in the tough situations, in the reconstruction period. He was a man ready for his time and his time involved building the Buffaloes, slowly but surely, into a position of national prominence, on the way to the heights the school finally achieved with its third place in 1971's national rankings. Although the 1971 Buffaloes were the highest-finishing CU team in history, they weren't the first to reach as high as third in the nation. Harris and his 1967 teammates occupied that lofty spot briefly in 1967 after winning their first five games.

My third set of halfbacks is Ted Woods (1959-60-1) and Jon Keyworth, a star in 1970 as a sophomore but shelved with a broken leg in 1971 and still with two seasons of eligibility left. Woods was a powerful sprinter with Olympic-class speed in the 440 and he made the 1960 U.S. Olympic team as a member of the mile relay team after a brilliant sophomore track season in which he won the NCAA 400 meters with a meet record tying :45.7. Despite that blinding speed, Teddy was more of a power runner than a fancy flier in Sonny Grandelius' winged-T attack. Like a lot of sprinters, Ted was basically a straightaway runner and lacked the moves which would have made him a fantastic runner. In all fairness to Teddy, his running talents were relatively unused until he came to CU — he was a guard much of the time in high school in his native Pittsburgh, Pa. although he was used some at fullback there. At CU he was an end as a freshman, a fullback in the spring of his first year on campus and was finally moved to halfback as a sophomore. His initial varsity season was relatively undistinguished as he carried only 13 times for 47 yards and failed to letter. He missed nearly half of the pre-season practice sessions as a junior because of his presence on the Olympic team at Rome late in the summer and only netted 244 yards in 64 carries that fall. In 1961, though, he came into his own and led the Big Eight champions in rushing with 525 yards in 107 carries for an excellent 4.9-yard average. Teddy broke an 81-yard punt return in the opening game of the season, against Oklahoma State, for the longest gainer of his career. But, like William Harris, he was a tough, straightahead power runner rather than a will-o-the-wisp. Teddy was a regular in the days when black athletes were just beginning to come into prominence in college football. The familiar old prejudices were draped all over all black backs in those days and one of the greatest of the bad raps was that the blacks didn't like the rough action and weren't mentally tough. A totally untrue knock on them and Teddy Woods proved the untruth of that piece of prejudice with a constantly courageous series of performances for the Buffaloes. He was the first fine black back the Buffaloes have had and has been followed by an impressive line of tough-as-they-come men such as slender Eddie Coleman, who was one class behind Teddy, Bill Harris, William Harris, Charles Greer, John Tarver and Charles Davis. Each of these men played every game to the hilt and asked no quarter. The black athlete's role has been firmly established, both quality and quantity-wise, in football during the past 15 years.

Serving as the workhorse running back for the Alumni team in three consecutive spring games. I called him "Top Cat" after a television series of that era because he was a big cat on the football field and the top cat out there. Teddy was a great friend, still is and he can have a suit on my football team any time. You just can't have too many top cats around and Teddy was the number one cat of them all.

Keyworth came bursting onto the CU scene in a delayed start in much the same style as the first Bill Harris in 1962 and Estes Banks (a swift halfback in 1964-5-6 who was passed over at picture day as a sophomore but started the opening game three weeks later). Jon didn't even make the first trip of the 1970 season to Indiana then finished the fall as the Buffaloes' second leading rusher with 667 yards, only 12 behind leader Ward Walsh. Keyworth's nine touchdowns led the Buffaloes in that department. He was the biggest halfback in CU history, a hulking 6-5, 224-pounder with savage power which he was just beginning to realize he had by the end of the season. Jon was an awesome sight taking beautifully-timed pitchouts from Jimmy Bratten and storming into the secondary like a runaway truck. Misfortune put a temporary interruption in his career a year later, though, as he suffered a broken leg after catching a flat pass in the first quarter of the opening game of the season at Louisiana State. Keyworth, stretched out and almost at a standstill, to catch the slightly-underthrown pass near the line of scrimmage was hit hard but broke away from the first two tacklers and was staggering back to balance when he was finally flattened by LSU's All-American tackle Ron Estay and crashed out of control, breaking his leg. But Keyworth was back in action the following spring and looked good as a wingback where he should become a very good receiver and potent runner after his catches and on reverses and sweeps from his new position. He's a gifted young man with the talent to play several positions, was a tight end and a quarterback as a freshman and actually was the backup quarterback for the Buffaloes in the 1970 Liberty Bowl, having been hurriedly groomed for the role after Bratten re-injured a knee at the opening practice in Memphis leaving the team with only Paul Arendt. Keep your eyes on Keyworth in 1972 and 73. He'll be making some big plays for the Buffaloes. He made enough of them in his sophomore season to earn a spot on my 3-deep.

FULLBACK

In my book, fullbacks are awarded their scholarships on the strength of being able to block and to pick up the critical first downs on third-and-three-type situations. My choice, accordingly, is big Wilmer Cooks (1965-6-7), who filled that bill perfectly and gets my nod despite a career that was clouded continually by shoulder and leg injuries. Wilmer had operations on both shoulders following his sophomore and junior seasons and had leg trouble as a senior but he put it all together in a great junior season which was relatively free of injuries. He had tremendous strength and could bend a line as good as any fullback who ever lived. Wilmer had pretty fair speed for a 6-2, 224-pounder but he drove forward so hard when he ran that he lost his balance easily when he broke into the open, which wasn't often because he got the ball on those tough yardage situations when the defenses were packed in tight around the line of scrimmage to stop the fullback charge they knew was coming. Wilmer would go ramming into those stacked up defenses and wedge into the mass of bodies. Slowly but surely the mass would move back as Wilmer drove forward. In what to me is one of the most amazing, and revealing, statistics of that 1966 season, Wilmer was called on 30 times in the critical third and fourth down situations and came through with either the first down or a touchdown 25 times. He was a good blocker, too, and just as importantly served as a screen behind which darting Danny Kelly would hide, bursting out from behind Wilmer's protective hulk when the time was opportune. If Wilmer had a weakness it was that he had a low pain tolerance. Which is perfectly normal. Most people do. But, occasionally you get a person who can play with pain. And play well. Like a William Harris. Or a Rocky Martin. Or a John Stearns. Or a Frank Bernardi. But that kind of man is an exception. Most men have got to heal before they can perform effectively. When you have a big, strong man like Wilmer you assume he is indestructable or, at the least, immune to pain. He wasn't and he needed time to recover just like most people. It was unfortunate that he was injured through much of his three years on the varsity. My first vivid memory of Wilmer Cooks was in his freshman year when he annihilated the Wyoming and Air Force freshman teams with a total of 301 yards in those two games and, at Air Force that fall, literally running roughshod over hopelessly-overmatched opponents. Wilmer looked like a giant running through a field of midgets in that game. He closed out his varsity career with a solid performance, too, gaining 74 yards in 17 carries, 63 of those yards coming in the second half, and scoring the clinching touchdown in the 31-21 win over Miami in the Bluebonnet Bowl. It was a great way to finish and Wilmer finished with a flourish before a large number of his friends and family in his native Texas.

My backup man behind Cooks is Ward Walsh, an excellent all-around fullback in 1968-9-70 who really never got the credit he deserved. Ward was as good a blocking fullback as I have ever seen (and fullbacks do a lot of blocking in Eddie Crowder's offense) and an excellent runner with probably the best breakaway threat of any fullback we've had since Loren Schweninger. Ward had the speed to go all the way and did several times, his longest TD gallop being for 47 yards against Kansas in 1970 on a run in which he changed direction twice in a halfback-like exhibition of open field running. Ward almost broke a 60-yarder in that game but made one move too many and cut back into the arms of a pursuer. He got 87 yards in just six carries that day and finished his regular season career with a 101-yard day against Air Force. Probably his most satisfying day, though, was as a junior in the Liberty Bowl victory over Alabama. Ward had not scored a touchdown during the regular season after having gotten six TDs as a rookie the year before. But he broke wide open with the quick handoff on the triple option to bolt 13 then 15 yards to score. But, even though Ward was an extremely good runner, I remember the bigger-than-he-appeared 6-0, 220-pounder just as much as a blocker as he led the way for Jimmy Bratten who cut inside or outside his blocks to pick up consistent yardage and occasionally flipped the ball to either Jon Keyworth or John Tarver who trailed Bratten on the option. Walsh was also an effective target on a screen pass and had the maneuverability to pick up big yardage when he took the ball out in the flat behind a blocking convoy. Both Walsh and Cooks could have played defense, too, had they been competing under two-way rules.

My number three fullback is John Tarver (1969-70-1) who edges out Merv Hodel (1949-50-1) on the strength of being a better blocker. Hodel was one of the best ball carrying fullbacks CU has ever had, gaining 2102 yards during his career for what at that time was a school record. Merv and Bobby Anderson were the two greatest Buffaloes at smelling that end zone. When either of those men got the ball inside the 10-yard line it was a touchdown almost every time. Tarver, though, was a much better blocker and had as much speed although he may not have been quite as agile as Merv, who doubled in track as a Big Eight champion hurdler. Hodel was a better pass receiver than Tarver, too, and his 23 catches in 1950 for 244 yards, most of them on screens, is still the most ever caught by a CU fullback and he caught a total of 48 passes during his career, more than most CU ends. But I'll take Tarver because he had the power to knock back an enemy line, the speed to break for a long gain and the strength to throw a most efficient block. John actually was a halfback, and a very good one, alternating as the starter in 1970 with Jon Keyworth and finishing a close third in rushing with 623 yards that fall. When Charles Davis came on so impressively in spring practice in 1971, John was moved to fullback so that both men could appear in the same backfield. John responded to a switch which could have dampened his enthusiasm but didn't by coming up with a fine season and playing a very instrumental role in Colorado's 10-2 record. I gained great admiration for John Tarver in a season which began unpleasantly, with a potentially-disruptive player uprising halfway through spring practice. The blacks on the team were nervous about their roles and, for the most part, it was understandable nervousness. John, as an upcoming senior who had been a co-starter during the previous fall, was one of the black leaders on the squad, a leader of both black and white players. John asked the questions he felt he needed to ask but, once he got his answers, pushed the incident aside and performed with enthusiasm in the fall with his blocks being constant and important factors in the great sophomore season of Charles Davis. I felt that John Tarver was one of the biggest individual factors in the 1971 team's surprising surge to a 10-2 record, the first team in the history of CU to win that many games, and a third-place national ranking. John was the second leading rusher on the team with 677 yards and his 5.6 rushing average was second only to Davis' 6.3 among the team's regular runners. John was an impressive sight blasting through the line, with or without the ball. He looked much bigger than his 6-2 and 208. I think he was probably closer to 225 when the season ended and he has the frame to carry that kind of weight and I hope he gets a fair trial with the pros because I think he has the stuff to be a good one.

This completes my offensive squad. And what a great one it would be. I have brilliant receivers with wide men who can fly, tight ends who can catch the ball in traffic, huge tackles, quick strong guards, big fast centers, quarterbacks who can throw or run, powerful halfbacks and sprinter types and passing threats, and big, bruising, blocking, bucking fullbacks. Hey, you Nebraskas and Oklahomas and Alabamas and Notre Dames and Southern Californias and Longhorns and Razorbacks and Buckeyes and all you consistently high-ranked national powers! Line up your best defenders of the past 25 years and let me and my Buffaloes at you. We'd show you that Colorado belongs in your class, too!

THE OFFENSIVE THREE-DEEP

SE — Cliff Branch, Frank Clarke, Monte Huber.
TE — Bob Masten, J.V. Cain, Mike Pruett.
T — Mike Montler, Jake Zumbach, Bill Csikos.
T — Jack Jorgenson, Kile Morgan, Jim Phillips.
G — Dennis Havig, Kirk Tracy, Dick Melin.
G — Roger Hunt, Dick Knowlton, John Beard.
C — Don Popplewell, Bruce Heath, Dave Hill.
QB — Gale Weidner, Ken Johnson, Dan Kelly.
HB — Bob Anderson, William Harris, Ted Woods.
HB — Charles Davis, Zack Jordan, Jon Keyworth.
FB — Wilmer Cooks, Ward Walsh, John Tarver.

THE DEFENSIVE PLATOON
THE ENDS

When you put together a defensive team you look for tough, mean men who like to hit people and hit them hard. And when you assemble the front line you're really not interested in finesse, although subtle moves and techniques can be a big help to a defensive lineman. But, basically, what you want is a rough, tough man with good speed and mobility but, most of all, a burning desire to get to the ball and cause an accident there. My starting defensive ends both had these qualities. And had them in abundance. They are Herb Orvis (1969-70-1) and Bill Fairband (1964-5-6), two of the toughest, quickest, meanest terminals you'd ever find, at any school.

Orvis was a handsome 6-5, 235-pounder with a face which combined the good looks of a matinee idol with the innocence of a choir boy. But his temper was practically always very ill. Herb was an angry young man. Angry all the time on the football field. And angry most of the time off it. He wasn't necessarily the most pleasant person to be around when he wasn't in uniform. And he was never pleasant to be around on the field, unless things were going his team's way completely, and that wasn't the case very often because Herb was a most demanding young man, a ferocious competitor who was happy with nothing less than total victory. He was a good man to have on your side. As strong as he was mean, he was the type of player who instilled fear in opposing backs and, in particular, quarterbacks. He was good against a play coming right at him and he was strong and adept at handling a sweep. But his forte was rushing the passer. When an opposing quarterback set up in the pocket, Herb pulled out all the stops. When he got rid of his blockers he could put on a tremendous burst of speed and he nearly always went for the head. In truth, if he had a flaw it was being a headhunter and sometimes flying over the top of a quarterback if that quarterback had the presence of mind to duck under Herb's charge. But if he missed an occasional tackle because of this, he more than made up for it by really creaming his man when he did make connections - and that was most of the time.

Herb could be a gentle, almost placid, man off the gridiron. But most of my memories of him involve toughness. When he suffered a fairly severe ankle sprain at Ohio State in his senior year, he was almost furious at the thought of being disabled. He, in fact, made a dramatic re-appearance one week later, going in the fourth quarter of a tense battle with Kansas State, a team which was close to getting its second straight upset over the Buffaloes after a big CU win. The Wildcats had shocked the Buffs 21-20 the preceding year, a week after CU had punished Penn State, 41-13, to snap the Nittany Lions' 31-game undefeated string, longest in the nation at the time. And they were giving the Buffaloes fits this October, 1971 afternoon in Boulder. Colorado had lost the services of regular tackle Stu Aldrich, who had been carried off the field earlier with a knee injury which required surgery the following Monday. And end Rick Kay had followed Orvis to the disabled list a week previously at Ohio State, breaking his arm late in that game. So the entire left side of the CU defensive line was wiped out and Kansas State was exploiting that gap in the Buffalo defense. But just when the Wildcats appeared to be getting the upper hand and that the Buffaloes were becoming disheartened, Orvis put himself in the game and his appearance had a dramatic effect on his teammates who stiffened and held the Wildcats to help turn the game around and into a 31-21 CU victory. A man like Orvis, who makes the big play, has the ability to give a lift to his team just by his presence. Orvis didn't make any big plays against Kansas State in his brief appearance in the game. But the fact that he was on the field rallied the CU defense and that quality is one of the great assets of an outstanding competitor. Orvis had trouble with the ankle for most of the rest of the season but never missed a game even though he could have hurt his chances to make All-American by playing when he was below par. He was not necessarily compassionate with those of us in the publicity department, either. I know that I almost tasted his forearm or straight right or something one afternoon in the training room when he accosted me, livid because a Denver sportswriter had listed him as a doubtful performer for that week's game. We had given an accurate report that he would play but would not be at full speed. It was the writer who expanded that report into a "can't-play" statement, not us. But that was a fairly feeble defense in the training room with Herb bearing down on my unprotected, and tender, throat. Fortunately, Herb veered off and decided to set the record straight himself and did make several phone calls to members of the media that night, informing them that, contrary to any published or unpublished reports, he would be ready to play, and ready to play well, that Saturday. Herb had come to CU out of the army and the story of how he ended up at Boulder is worth mentioning. Missouri coach Dan Devine was scheduled to make a month-long tour of U.S. army bases in western Europe in the summer of 1967 but had to cancel out because of a last-minute schedule conflict. He recommended that Eddie Crowder take his place and Crowder accepted the invitation. One of Eddie's appearances was at Weisbaden, Germany where Herb was stationed. Herb's coach gave him glowing recommendations and Eddie assigned Chet Franklin to the case upon his return and Chet kept in contact with Herb and got him to enroll at CU after his discharge from the army a year later. So Dan Devine got an assist on the play and CU got an All-American end and a man who played a big role in leading the Buffaloes to three straight bowl games. Herb and the members of his class became the first CU players in history to appear in three bowl games.

Bill Fairband (6-2, 221) wasn't as big or ill-tempered as Orvis but he had better speed and quickness and was just as good at shedding blockers. Speed was a big thing in Bill's life. He was a :09.8 sprinter in high school and, although he didn't participate in track in college, he continued his association with speed by a love for fast motorcycles and quick women. Bill was a dashing sight, roaring around Boulder on his big Harley-Davidson and he and his whirling wheels gave a lot of thrills to a lot of pretty young ladies who got some of the rides of their young lives on his machine. But this is a book about football and Fairband earned his starting job on this team with his action on the field not off it. Bill actually began his college career as an offensive end and was the backup slot end as a sophomore and might have won a starting offensive job in 1965 had he been able to hang onto the ball better. But he dropped too many passes to be a surefire receiver so he was moved to defense early in his junior year when tough Ray LeMasters was knocked out for the season by a knee injury. It was a master move because Bill quickly became an outstanding defensive end. He had excellent hands on defense and never dropped a ballcarrier in two seasons. Bill's fine play helped the Buffaloes to 6-2-2 and 7-3 records in his last two seasons. One of the plays, however, he'll never forget is an unpleasant memory. In 1966 at Boulder, the Buffaloes had mighty Nebraska on the ropes, leading, 19-7, with less than 13 minutes left to play. The Cornhuskers were passing desperately and quarterback Bob Churchich threw one into his left flat. The line of scrimmage was about the Nebraska 30 and Fairband covered his short zone perfectly and the ball came straight to him and all he had to do was catch it and breeze 35 unmolested yards into the end zone to wrap up the victory. But the ball slipped through his arms and Nebraska went on to win the game in the closing minute, 21-19. No one felt worse about the play then Bill but he produced a lot more pleasant memories for CU football than he did unpleasant ones. Bill went on to make it in the pros with the Oakland Raiders where one of his coaches was a former member of Sonny Grandelius' CU staff, John Polonchek. But a knee injury cut short his career just when he was moving into play-for-pay stardom. Bill returned to Boulder in 1972 to play with the Alumni in the annual spring game. He showed quickly he still knew what defense was all about, making several good plays and stopping what appeared to be a sure Varsity touchdown drive as he covered a fumble in the Alumni end zone for a touchback.

Even though Orvis and Fairband were tremendous defensive ends, you can get a lot of arguments that my next pair have just as much claim to the starting jobs on this team. The number two tandem is Mike Schnitker (1966-7-8) and Don Branby (1950-1-2), a pair of brawling Buffaloes who asked no quarter when they waded into battle. Schnitker was a good-natured 6-2, 230-pounder from ex-CU star Tom Hancock's outstanding Lakewood high school program. Mike and his sidekick, linebacker Rocky Martin, were a happy-go-lucky team, happiest when they were dealing out punishment to enemy backs. Mike got a tough break when he received a bad knee injury in the final game of his junior season in 1967 and had to have immediate surgery and missed the Bluebonnet Bowl game that December. He recovered fully, though, and earned All-Big Eight honors as a senior even though the team, which he helped captain, faded at the finish and didn't give him a second chance at a bowl. Mike was a resilient young man with the mental and physical ability to bounce back from a knee operation. His ability to adjust served him well as a professional, too, as he moved into the offensive line and became a starting guard for the Denver Broncos in 1971. Big Mike was one of my favorites. A fine fellow as well as a fine end.

His running mate, Don Branby, packed a double dose of toughness into a relatively small body. Don was almost a midget by today's standards, at 6-1 and 195. But he had the same on-field disposition as Orvis. Just plain mean. And very persistent. It's possible to make All-American on the impetus of one outstanding performance if it comes early in the season in a nationally-prominent game. Don did it by gaining instant notoriety because of his role in the CU defensive plan in the 21-21 tie with Oklahoma in 1952. Don's assignment was to harass the Oklahoma quarterback who was named Eddie Crowder and who was one of the most adroit ballhandlers in the history of college football. Crowder was like a wizard in the Sooner backfield, slipping the ball to powerful runners like Billy Vessels and Buck McPhail then carrying out a masterful fake, or hiding it on his hip and keeping or passing, or sneaking it to his other halfback, Buddy Leake. It was one of the finest-functioning offensive units which had ever been assembled and Crowder's skill at the controls was a major factor in the Sooners' ability to move the ball. Branby's job was to shadow Crowder, belt him around, dog him, upset his timing, just plain give him a bad time. Branby carried out his assignment with so much enthusiasm and effectiveness that Bud Wilkinson wanted to have him banned from football for the rest of the season for being too rough. But you'd have to say that Branby carried out his assignment efficiently. You'd also have to admit that he may have done it just a little bit too enthusiastically because there were times when Crowder handed off right away on a dive play and retreated away from the line of scrimmage only to straighten up just in time to get knocked down by the ever-attentive Branby. At any rate, the Buffaloes almost came away with an upset and, even though Oklahoma tied the score in the final two minutes, it was the first time in five years they failed to defeat a Big Eight opponent. And, to Crowder's credit, even though he took a pretty rough physical working over that afternoon, he still had enough left at the finish to take the Sooners into the end zone for the tying points. Of course, it didn't hurt to have stallions like Vessels, who would go on to win the Heisman Trophy that year, McPhail and Leake to hand the ball to. It was one of the three greatest backfields I've ever seen in the Big Eight and all of them were Oklahoma units. The next one was the Jimmy Harris-Tommy McDonald-Clendon Thomas-Billy Pricer foursome in 1956. And the greatest of all, I think, was the 1971 Sooner assortment which included Jack Mildren, Greg Pruitt, Joe Wylie and Leon Crosswhite. Harris and Mildren were gutty, good quarterbacks and I'm sure they could have survived the assault of a Don Branby. But only Crowder had to face that challenge. Branby, incidentally, wasn't just a football bully. He was an outstanding 3-sport athlete and earned nine letters at CU. He was a power-hitting firstbaseman in baseball for Frank Prentup and a mauling menace in basketball where he saw action as a reserve for Bebe Lee. Branby hit the boards in basketball with the same zest with which he hit quarterbacks in football. He played in the days when it was good tactics to deliberately foul an opponent late in the game. Branby was the best man on the squad in this department. Nobody could escape his contact. Jack Froistad still holds the CU record for fouling out of a game in the shortest time. Branby might have gotten this record had he played more. But, for sure, he got the most mileage out of his fouls. They were never gentle. Gentleness wasn't Don's strong suit. And that was one of the big reasons he was such a fine football player.

My third set of ends is Mike Veeder (1965-6-7) and Ray LeMasters (1963-4-5). Mike was a late-blooming, 6-4, 218-pounder who came to life as a senior when he became an outstanding defensive end. Mike had excellent agility for a big man. He didn't have the type of mean streak which Orvis and Branby had but he was an alert, opportunistic end. He played a very important part in the 21-16 upset of Nebraska in 1967, a victory which lifted the Buffaloes to third place in the national rankings. Mike's biggest moment as a Buffalo came near the end of the first half of that game in Lincoln when he took a lateral from Dick Anderson after Andy had intercepted a Frank Patrick pass and galloped the last 50 yards of a 70-yard CU touchdown play. The defense, with unknown substitute halfback Jeff Raymond returning another interception 76 yards, won that game and Veeder, who also recovered a Patrick fumble to stop a fourth-quarter Nebraska penetration, was one of the key contributors.

LeMasters was a rugged redhead who got as much out of his ability as anyone who ever started for CU. He was on the smallish side, beginning college life as a 185-pound fullback, moving to slot end and going both ways as a junior then earning a starting defensive job after building his weight up to 200 entering his senior season. Ray was having a good senior year when he tore up a knee as he landed wrong on it after leaping over a blocker while making a typically reckless all-out effort. Ray was a great competitor, as fiery as the color of his hair and he was the reddest redhead who ever pulled on a CU uniform.

TACKLES

The six tackles on my squad are big enough and strong enough to pull a stagecoach or spell the Budweiser horses. A good tackle ought to be big enough to tower over the rest of his side of the line like a big, old oak tree. And, even though you get an exception like Dick Stapp, once in a while, for the most part you've got to have big, hulking brutes if you're going to have an outstanding team. My half-dozen horses are, in order, Bill Sabatino (1964-5-6) and Bill Brundige (1967-8-9), Frank Bosch (1965-6-7) and Carl Taibi (1969-70-1), and Dave Capra (1968-9-70) and Jim Stander (1951-2-3). Stander, at 6-4 and 224, is the runt of the litter. But in his day he was a giant: there weren't too many mastodons at that time, the 240-pounder was an exception rather than the rule and 225 was a big man.

Sabatino (6-3, 233) was the first bluechip lineman recruited by the Eddie Crowder staff and he was a beefy boulder in the CU defensive line for three years. Not exceptionally quick for a tackle, he played his position well and could lunge as effectively as any down lineman we've ever had. Sab was as strong as a bull and had an especially solid foundation. In fact, had his teammates been as incisive with a nickname as those swashbucklers who played for Sonny Grandelius, Bill might have taken over Jerry Hillebrand's old handle, Baby Huey. If you'll recall, Baby Huey's outstanding physical characteristic was a huge derriere. Nobody ever had a huger one than Sab, if you'll pardon the expression. Sab was durable and tough and tenacious. He was one of the men who helped bring back respectability to the CU defense. Opponents didn't fool around much trying to run at Bill when he was on the field. An easygoing, likable person out of uniform, he was a formidable barrier at the line of scrimmage. He was what the Buffaloes needed most of all in those comeback years of post-1962.

Bill Brundige (6-5, 235) was the quickest big man we've ever had. Off the field he looked like a giant owl with completely misleading looks. Bill had reddish hair and wore big horned-rim glasses and was a scholar who stayed at a B-level all the way through college. From the tiny northern Colorado community of Haxtun, he was a most unlikely All-American, bursting into full stardom suddenly as a senior after relatively unspectacular seasons in his first two varsity years. Bill was a late-season starter at end on the Bluebonnet Bowl championship team of 1967 but he had been a reserve tackle most of the fall, coming on in relief of Frank Bosch or Ron Scott after those two had worn down the men across the line of scrimmage. Brundige was a fine pass rusher who has continued to sparkle in that department in a professional career with the Washington Redskins. As a senior, he played end and teamed with sophomore Herb Orvis to give the Buffaloes an awesome pass rush. Bill made All-American, along with Bobby Anderson, that year and he proved to the nation he was a legitimate star as he made several crushing tackles behind the line of scrimmage in the Liberty Bowl victory over Alabama. Bill was a bright young man with a very inquisitive mind. He has expanded his talents as a pro in Washington where he also has his own radio show in the off season. At CU, though, Bill did most of his talking with his aggressive actions on the football field. And he was a convincing figure.

Frank Bosch (6-4, 240) came to CU as a good but not necessarily great prospect out of Idaho where he had been an excellent gridder and wrestler at Boise after a big scare midway through his prep career when surgery was required to remove some infected lymph glands. I called him "Bosco" which was the name of a chocolate syrup which I used to eat a lot of when I was a growing boy. Bosco had pretty much stopped growing when he came to CU, although he later swelled up to 260 during a pro career with Baltimore and Washington, but he still ate up a lot of ball carriers as a regular for the Buffaloes in each of his three seasons. Frank was a solid student of the game and continued to serve CU well as a graduate assistant and as a player-coach in the annual Alumni-Varsity spring game.

Carl Taibi (6-4, 239) was one of the most valuable, and least heralded, members of the 1971 Buffaloes, a strong, willing giant in the middle of the defensive line who had tremendous desire, a desire which enabled him to recover almost miraculously quick after a midseason knee injury threatened to close his career too soon. Off the field you might think Carl was one of those "gentle giants" better suited for a role on a tug-of-war team than on a nationally-ranked football squad. A pair of sleepy, almond-shaped eyes resting a few inches above an ever-present grin belied his aggressive nature on the gridiron. Compounding this deceptive appearance was his role as one of the guitar-playing members of Dan Stavely's musical group, called the "Shower Room Five," which made frequent appearances at meetings of the Fellowship of Christian Athletes and other youth gatherings. End Willie Nichols, who had come to CU along with Carl from Pueblo, nicknamed him, "Luke," for a reason which only Willie knew. It wasn't after St. Luke, although Carl was a good Christian and worthy of that name. Gentle off the field, he was quick and aggressive on it. He gave the impression of being a lumbering, slowish lineman. But he made a lot of tackles behind the line of scrimmage and you don't do that unless you can move. Big Luke could move with the best of them. And he wasn't too bad on that guitar, either!

Stander was one of the stalwarts on the first fine teams put together by Dal Ward. He developed quickly and won a starting defensive job in his sophomore season, 1951, and was one of the anchors of the defensive line three years during which the Buffaloes logged a 19-9-2 record. They called him "The Tree" and he was one of the solid timbers in those CU lines. Nobody ever chopped him down, either.

Dave Capra (6-3, 240), like Taibi, was another sleepy-looking Italian who came to life whenever he moved onto the football field. Dave was a man of few words who let his actions speak for him. His idea of a speech was to grunt a couple of times and he never overwhelmed anybody with personality. But he was a solid, very conscientious athlete who overcame knee and shoulder injuries to work his way into the starting lineup during his junior season. Dave, who had been a high school fullback, spent a lot of hours in the weight room and became tremendously strong. He always made sure there was plenty of fuel in his system to feed those muscles. If they ever named an all-time CU eating team, he might be the captain and coach. When Dave lowered his head over his plate, things began disappearing and you often worried that he might devour the plate, and maybe a section of the table, when he started shoveling in the rations. But Dave never ate himself into a stupor. In fact, he always played like he was hungry. And hungry football players are the best ones.

GUARD

Exercising my option as the assembler of this all-star team, I am using a five-man defensive line with three linebackers, two cornerbacks and a safety man. My number one middle guard is one of only two rookies in my starting lineup and, by rookie, I mean a player who had not completed his college eligibility when this team was put together. He is Bud Magrum, the most recent of an impressive array of service veterans to enroll at CU following their discharge. Mike Montler and Herb Orvis, who preceded Magrum in this route to Boulder, made All-American. Magrum will, too, and could conceivably beat the time schedules of the other two who earned their national honors as seniors. Magrum got a good leg up with a tremendous sophomore season which was further enhanced by his team's 10-2 record topped by the impressive win over Houston in the Astro-Bluebonnet Bowl and even further spotlighted by CU's final third place national ranking following the bowl games. Two factors are vital in a player's making All-American and only one involves his ability and playing record. Equally important is the team he plays on. It must be a good or a glamorous one. All-America selectors weigh team performances very heavily in their final judgments. After all, most of them have had very little contact with the players they select and, therefore, must rely greatly on reports, recommendations, records . . . and how well a man's team played, with the assumption following almost automatically that if a team played well someone on it must have been good enough to be an All-American. Because what, after all, is an All-American? In most cases, some player who played well on a good team. This is not to say that he was not deserving of the honor. But for every All-American from Notre Dame, Alabama, Southern California, Texas, Arkansas, Tennessee, Louisiana State, Penn State and all the rest of the schools who rank highly each fall, you can find men who are just as talented and just as worthy from the Oregon States, Californias, Iowa States, Indianas, Wake Forests and other schools with similar less-glamorous reputations who, nevertheless, play good, tough football. The Buffaloes made a major breakthrough into these ranks in 1971, climaxing a steady rise to prominence under Eddie Crowder which has produced four bowl teams (and a 3-1 record in post-season play) in the last five years. One of the major beneficiaries of this surge will be men like Bud Magrum. Bud is a tough, rough interior lineman who wages war in the trenches as well as anyone we've ever had. He isn't huge, 6-3 and 225 and he played at about 10 pounds below that weight as a sophomore, but he is exceptionally strong and very quick. Quickness is the quality which separates the men from the boys in the line. Everyone has brute strength or they wouldn't be starting in those positions. But the great linemen have the agility and quickness to embellish their strength and flee that hand-to-hand battle with another lineman and get to the ball. That, after all, is what they're there for. Magrum is perfectly machined for greatness. He has great strength for the action on the line of scrimmage, great quickness to get out of the trenches and get after the runner or passer and, just as importantly, the maturity to get it altogether early in his college career. The maturity, of course, comes from three years in the Marine Corps with a tour of duty in Viet Nam where he was a member of a bomb demolition crew. College football has got to be fairly tame for a man who wears the Purple Heart and several combat citations as does Bud Magrum. Bud stepped into a starting job immediately in 1971 and became the leader of the interior for the CU defense. That defense got away impressively as it overshadowed Louisiana State's renowned forces in tumultous Tiger Stadium. But that performance was considered an early season upset and, besides, LSU never is too impressive in their first game - hadn't they blown one to futile Texas A&M just 12 months earlier at Baton Rouge? Wait till this Colorado team plays at Ohio State and we'll see if they're for real, chorused the experts . . . and a lot of us ordinary Monday morning geniuses in Colorado. That confrontation came two weeks later and Magrum and his mates were even more impressive if that was possible.

    After the Buffaloes, with a good drive and a blistering punt return by Cliff Branch, had jumped into a 13-0 lead the Buckeyes fought back. But the CU defense stopped them on successive drives, at the end of the half and at the start of the second half, when Ohio State had reached first-and-goals inside the CU eight. Those defensive stands were just plain brawls. Nothing fancy. Woody Hayes doesn't believe in subtle football, especially down around the goal line. It was physical strength against physical strength on those stands and Colorado more than passed the test and Magrum was right in the middle of it all. Maybe his finest hour came at Iowa State two weeks later as the Buffaloes fought for their lives against an upset-minded Cyclone team which was much better than anyone, including a slightly flattened-out CU team, realized. This was an Iowa State team which was to become the first bowl entry in the school's history and which was to give Louisiana State a full afternoon before bowing to the more talented Tigers in the Sun Bowl. On this crisp afternoon in Ames, the Cyclones were primed for the ambush of the year. All the conditions were present and, as the season was to prove, it wouldn't have really been as big an upset as it would have seemed at the time because this was an excellent Iowa State team. The conditions were, in addition to a fine, well-prepared Iowa State team, a considerably battered CU team which had lost such line aces as Stu Aldrich, Rick Kay and, for the most part, Herb Orvis; a team which was ripe for a mental letdown following massive efforts against Ohio State and Kansas State on the two previous Saturdays; and a foaming-at-the-mouth crowd which was just beginning to really believe in the gridiron gospel being preached and displayed by that Rhett Butler-like rogue rebel, John Majors, a Tennessee thoroughbred right out of the breeding barns of one of the nation's best football families. There it was: Upset-ville, USA. Waiting in the bushes of Ames, Iowa, right there in the middle of all those cornfields of mid-America. Right there waiting for the unsuspecting Buffaloes. Right there at Ames where the Buffaloes had lost only one game in their last 10 visits. The Buffaloes almost played right into Iowa State's hands as Cullen Bryant gambled and got beat deep on a touchdown pass and John Stearns tried to run from deep punt formation on fourth-and-long inside his own 30 and just barely got back to the line of scrimmage. And a lot of bad things like these happened and suddenly it was 14-14 in the fourth quarter with Iowa State at third-and-two on the CU 36. At this point Magrum took charge: On the third down play he helped string out the Iowa State sweep which got knocked out of bounds for no gain. On fourth down, he clawed his way through to mangle the timing on a handoff, mauling the quarterback and forcing him to throw the ball wildly to his tailback who desperately tried to handle the high toss and promptly got assaulted by John Stavely and Brian Foster, who separated him from the ball and recovered it but didn't need to inasmuch as the Buffaloes had possession anyway on the failure to make the first down. This stand turned the tide and the Buffaloes quickly drove into field goal position then added a touchdown in the closing minute for a 24-14 escape which let them fly back to Boulder still unblemished and caused a lot of Iowa State fans to stagger home and wash off all that foam with the consolation beers of defeat instead of the wine of victory. Save that champagne for later, Johnny Reb, I'm sure you'll have lots of occasions to drink it in future seasons as you steadily change the Cyclone cardinal and gold to more impressive football colors, like orange and white.

These were just two impressive moments in Magrum's young college football life. But they were great ones and there'll be many more. Despite being several years older than his classmates, Bud still retains that boyish enthusiasm so necessary to a great performer. If he stays healthy he'll be an All-American. And CU will prosper from his presence.

Behind Magrum on my defensive team is a stocky, hawk-nosed

infighter who starred on the 1967 and 68 teams, 6-1, 223-pound Ron Scott, who had to work his way into a starting position from a long way back but who did a day-after-day, game-after-game great job when he got there. Scotty, whose chief early claim to fame was a beautiful wife, floundered around as a freshman then through a redshirt year, too small to be a tackle, too slow to be a linebacker. But he had that burning desire and the flame never wavered and if you keep hustling you just have to find somewhere to play. Because desire can overcome a lot of physical deficiencies. A coaching staff can eventually fit a man who desperately wants to play somewhere in the lineup where he can make the best contribution. That's a relatively easy part of coaching. The almost-impossible job is to light the fire in a young man who has everything but the will to work. You can't very often find the key to that problem and a lot of good coaches have climbed a lot of walls in frustration at watching a body-full of talent go to waste because the motor wasn't of the same quality as the body and wheels. A football player, or any athlete for that matter, is just like a car. No better than his, or its, motor. Stick a great motor in an average body and you'll have a darned good car which may break down once in a while but when the tires are up, it will go like crazy. Stick a weak motor in a great frame, though, and you've got a pile of nothing. A car which looks great in the show room, then in a lot of used car lots, but which doesn't do the job. Like a lot of great-looking football players who are magnificent men on Picture Day and tremendously impressive during the official weigh-in and set a lot of young maidens' hearts afire standing at attention while the band plays the alma mater but who are nothing at all after those annual and weekly rituals are finished.

Ronnie Scott had the motor and he functioned at full speed through his junior and senior seasons, ripping through roadblocks from his middle guard job and doing everything his coach, Rudy Feldman, asked of him. I guess the word to describe Ronnie as a football player is "fanatical." He literally was on fire every minute he was in the game, just burning and scratching and fuming to knock somebody down. So he knocked a lot of people down, many of them with the ball in their possession. That's what middle guards are for. And Ronnie was an outstanding one. Like so many good men, he didn't get a lot of acclaim outside of his own teammates and coaches. But he hung up his uniform with the most satisfying feeling of all, knowing he had done a good job and that the men who counted most, his teammates, knew it. And on top of everything, he had that good-looking wife as his ultimate reward. And you just can't beat good-looking, nice wives for ultimate rewards.

Pushing Scotty for the backup role on the team is Bill Collins, the quick, strong, intelligent, personable middle guard and tri-captain of the 1969 team. Bill was a man with great explosive quickness, somewhat on the order of Oklahoma's Granville Liggins, who was the quickest middle guard I ever saw. Collins (6-1, 220) was bigger than Liggins and, consequently, stronger at head-on assaults but not quite as adept at quick-stepping through the cracks in an enemy offensive wall. Bill had shoulder problems as a junior and, like Scott, he groped a bit before he and the coaches discovered that middle guard was where he belonged. Once he recovered from surgery and built the repaired shoulder back to full strength with a very conscientious weight and exercise program, he was ready for a fine senior season. Bill was secretary of defense for the Buffaloes and his work in the middle of the line was an important stabilizing factor for the Buffaloes in a fine 8-3 season.

The moment I'll always remember Bill for is the coin toss to start the 1969 Liberty Bowl game in Memphis against the legendary legions of one of the south's greatest plantation owners, Bear Bryant and his lean, mean (but not as lean and mean as in other seasons) ravagers of rebel country, Alabama. Bill was selected by his tri-captain mates, Bob Anderson and Mike Pruett, to call the coin toss. The Bear sent out all his seniors to serve as game captains so the Buffaloes were out-manpowered by a big margin there in the center of the field with 51,000 people waving their small American flags which are part of the tradition of that game and national television putting the ceremony into every living room in the country. It was an impressive sight. At least to us Colorado people. A lone black man flanked by two white teammates on one side of the coin toss. And on the other side, a group of good-looking, cleancut young men who might have formed a body guard for Jefferson Davis a century earlier. I think this moment portrayed one of the beautiful things about sport in this country. It transcends almost every prejudice and social barrier. Bill Collins might still have trouble buying a lunch in Birmingham. But he was accepted as a man, and a good one, by every one of those Alabama players. His color was Silver and Gold. Theirs was Crimson and White. There was no other color on that Liberty Bowl field. And that is as it should be and it is a shame that that is not how it is at every level of life. But it will be some day and when that day arrives, sports - and college football, in particular - will have played a tremendously important role in that progression to sanity and equality and love.

Incidentally, Bill won the toss and cost himself a chance to be on the field for the start of the game because CU received. But he had plenty of opportunities before the game was over and, as always, he was a perfectly-tuned instrument in the Colorado defensive orchestration which played its always important role in the victory. Bill Collins won't be remembered as the first black man ever to captain a Colorado football team. He'll be remembered as simply one of a long line of great young men who have begun their adult lives as college athletes and, in particular, at the University of Colorado and, with the highest honor, being selected as captain of his team. Bill Collins came a long way. From the time he hitchhiked to Boulder because of the telephoned promise that he could get an opportunity to come out for the squad and, if he was good enough, earn a scholarship after he had proven he was good enough. That's all Bill wanted. A chance to prove himself. Not four years on the athletic dole handed to him on a silver platter, as it is to a lot of young men. Just the chance to earn it. That's what I like about Bill Collins. He was a man for his time. And he'll be a man for his time throughout his life. That's the only way Bill Collins knows.

LINEBACKERS

My starting linebackers are a trio of get-with-it, rough and tumble tigers who let nothing stop them from getting to the ball. Rocky Martin (1966-7-8), Roy Shepherd (1950-1-2) and Steve Sidwell (1963-4-5) are my men and what a lot of havoc they'd have created had they ever been assembled on the same team.

Rocky was a fight-to-the-death battler from the normally gentle regions of Cherry Creek high school who jumped into a starting role as a junior and was always in the thick of the action thereafter. Rocky was perfectly named. Nobody, in fact, ever knew his real name which is Robert. But the name is Rocky and I doubt that he'll ever be called anything else until the day he dies. The proper first names of all guys named Rocky fade into obscurity quickly and you never know what they were unless the guy happens to be an Italian in which case you can be pretty safe in assuming that it's Rocco but you'd better not call him that or you might get punched because Italian Rockys are generally last-named Marciano and Graziano which is Italian for take-10-and-get-up-and-go-home-or-you-might-end-up-getting-
killed. Rocky Martin had a lot of great moments for CU as a regular in 1967 and 68 but the one I remember him for came during spring practice of his sophomore year. He and Bob Anderson were two of the most heralded young Buffaloes that April, both of them having earned their high school reputations in the general area of Folsom Stadium. Bob was a freshman and Rocky was coming off an obscure sophomore fall. I'll never forget their first meeting as varsity candidates. It was in a middle-of-the-week scrimmage early that spring. Bobby rolled out to this right and got around the end and roared up-

field, those powerful legs churning at full speed. Rocky was playing middle linebacker and he got in the pursuit and got in front of Bob. The collision was as hard a one as I've ever seen. It was like two automobiles head-onning. Both men went over on their backs, momentarily stunned by the impact. The coaches, who generally delight in foolish displays of courage and foolhardiness like this one, didn't know how to react for a moment either. There were two of their finest young prospects, prone on the ground. If there was one thing these men were, though, it was durable. The cobwebs cleared quickly. Rocky was ready for the next play and Bobby was back in one play later and the coaches went around the rest of the spring slapping each other on the back and relishing the memory of that collision which was probably about eight G's harder than any collision any of them had ever been involved in when they were playing. It may have been the hardest Anderson was ever hit. And Rocky certainly never ran into many other runners who hit as hard. Rocky is still decking halfbacks and quarterbacks and fullbacks but only on an annual basis as one of the regular returnees for the Alumni game. Andy, of course, limits his contact to the fall season upon the good advice of his agents and lawyers and pro coaches and girlfriends and all those people who cluster around a professional athlete today and build up his portfolios and Security and future and all those things but who maybe drain a little fun, and some 10 percents, out of their lives. But that meeting between Rocky and Andy, back in April of 1967, was something to remember.

Roy Shepherd may have been, pound for pound, the toughest linebacker we've ever had. And as tough a one as ever played in the Big Eight. He was a scrawny, mean competitor who'd tear your head off with a grin then pick you up and apologize in that soft drawl with which he spoke. Then tear your head off again on the next play. Shep listed his measurements as 6-0 and 185 but I'd guess that 185 was the most he ever weighed and, if the truth were known, he played most of his career at closer to 175. Shep was just closing out his career when I arrived at CU in1952. My first road game as sports publicity director was at Missouri. Don Faurot was one of the great old masters of the game at more things than just inventing the split-T offense. One of his coaching talents involved lopping about 20 pounds off his players for the program roster. Players, and in particular, smaller ones like Shep always check out the size of the man they'll be facing. The Missouri offensive lineman who would be coming out after Roy much of the time was listed at 180. A pretty close matchup with Shep and maybe old Shep was even a pound or two heavier. When they tangled for the first time that Saturday, however, Shep saw that his opponent was about 210. His arms were bigger around than my legs, Shep snorted after the game. But despite the weight differential, Roy gave as much as he received. He came from a long line of Shepherd brothers in Boulder and they were all tough battlers even though Roy was the only one to play college football. Roy had been a good fullback at Boulder High so he had the quickness and speed to be a good linebacker. His offensive position in college would have been center but he was used strictly on defense. Speed and quickness can generate a lot of momentum and momentum can overcome lack of weight at the moment of impact. That was the formula Roy used so successfully at CU. He later became an excellent high school coach, too, and helped develop such CU-stars-to-be as Dan Kelly, John Farler and Kerry Mottl at Aurora Central.

Steve Sidwell was the biggest of my three linebackers and looked bigger than the 6-0, 212 he played at as a senior. He might have been a shade slower than the others, too, but he made up for lack of great speed by being an extremely intelligent player. And you can save an important step by recognizing where you need to go immediately and having your legs almost perfectly synchronized with your eyes so that you are moving toward the ball almost before you see where the play is going. Sid had a lot of problems with a neck injury which involved a nerve which was always getting pinched and causing him a lot of pain and, in some instances, some temporary paralysis. He always wore that big collar and looked a little bit like Sir Walter Raleigh but he specialized in throwing his body in front of ballcarriers not his cape in front of lovely ladies. He must have done some impressive things with lovely young ladies, though, because he ended up marrying as pretty and nice a one as you'd ever find. It was poetic justice because the quarterbacks and halfbacks, not the linebackers, generally end up with the campus beauties. Sid had a lot on the ball, on or off the football field. He was a sharp business major who stayed on after graduation as a specialist in the department to work in fund-raising and did some coaching on the side. Sid quickly decided coaching was what he liked to do best and signed on as a full time member of the CU staff and a good one. One other thing about Sid. He was excellently bred for a role as a CU star. His father had been an outstanding basketball player for the Buffaloes, one of the deadliest set-shooting guards the school ever had. So Steve, and his bigger and younger but not as good a football playing brother, Dave, had a lot of silver and gold shoved up their arteries while they were growing up. Sid carried the family banner in football. Dave tried but had bad shoulders and knees and wore out a couple of sets of surgical instruments getting repaired and eventually gave it up to become a Golden Gloves heavyweight. And a pretty good one.

My backup linebackers are a pretty impressive crew, too. My first backup team includes John Stavely (1970-1-2), Rick Ogle (1968-9-70) and Don Greenwood (1951-2). Behind these men are Kerry Mottl (1965-6-7), Jim Dalthorp (1950-1-2) and Phil Irwin (1968-9-70).

Stavely is as fine a young man as I have watched come through the program. Most of his ability is on the inside although he has good speed and power. But he isn't a big man (6-0, 205) or a fleet pursuer. He was a good high school fullback at Fairview in Boulder and was one of the stalwarts of a team which went all the way to second place in the state playoffs in his junior year. John, the son of freshman coach Dan Stavely, was only a minimal college prospect but, just as in so many other cases, his abilities were those you can't measure with a set of scales, a tape measure and a stopwatch. Intelligence, initiative, energy and an all-overcoming desire are what make the John Stavelys of the world successful at anything they try, beginning with their work in the classroom, extending onto the athletic field and reaching into every endeavor they attempt throughout their lives. John was shoved into the breach quickly, taking over as a starter early in his rookie season. He ended up as one of the young veterans at the end of the year and ranked high in one very important category which reveals his ability to be in the right place on the field: he intercepted three passes as a sophomore, then three more as a junior. That's already more interceptions than a lot of linebacker squads get in a career. And John still has a year to go!

Rick Ogle was an outstanding high school athlete from the shadow of Montana State College in Bozeman who had a bright future in either football or baseball and chose to pursue it at CU. I can remember an instant in his young life when he might have come close to deciding against enrolling at CU. It was during his visitation to the campus in the spring of 1967. Dan Stavely, who was escorting him around the campus, had brought him by a spring practice mid-week scrimmage. Dan had to run into his office to make a phone call and asked me to visit with Rick while he was gone. Rick and I were small-talking along the sideline when the quarterback, a son of a former pro quarterback named Don Zimmerman who was a fairly fast good-throwing junior who really wasn't tough enough to operate at the physically-demanding quarterback position in Eddie Crowder's offense, rolled to our side of the field and couldn't find a receiver open so had to run. He was a rabbity runner and the sideline was a favorite bramble patch when he got in trouble and he was getting into trouble because Rocky Martin and Kerry Mottl both were closing in on him. Don didn't reach his sanctuary and Rocky got to him first and knocked him sprawling, and unconscious, at Rick's feet. Rick's eyes got as big as silver dollars and he gulped a couple of times and grinned, weakly, that people really like to hit in the Big Eight, don't they? The sight probably didn't bother Rick as much as it did me because he signed right up with CU and became an excellent linebacker who went on to make the St. Louis Cardinals after he graduated. Rick also was a pretty good pitcher for the Buffaloes although he never reached the stardom in that sport that he did in football and he signed a professional football contract before his senior spring and was ineligible for what would have been his last baseball season. Rick had a blazing fastball but he never really got it under control and the only thing he ever really burned real good was a big patch of grass in front of the CU dugout when he was working one summer as a groundskeeper and laid the fertilizer on a little too heavy in that area. We should have guessed that 6-3, 220-pound linebackers might doze a little on a balmy summer day, especially at the controls of a fertilizer. Rick never did doze much on the football field, though, and he had size and speed and power and, with just a teensy-weensy bit more fire, might have been one of our all-time greats instead of just a very good linebacker.

Don Greenwood was a swarthy, stubby (5-10, 190) who won a starting job as a freshman in 1951, the season that freshmen were eligible because of special Korean War rules. Don was strong for his size and quick and alert. He played very well and was destined for greatness but he had one basic flaw which did him in. He had an awful lot of trouble waking up in the mornings. And when he did wake up, most of the time he went right back to sleep. It was almost impossible to get him to a class before noon. And football players don't have too many classes after lunch because they have to save that time for practice. On those rare days when Don did get to class, he generally went right back to sleep about the time the roll got finished. So Don, a quick-thinking highly-motivated man on the football field, never got it going in the classroom and threw in the towel after his sophomore season. It's always sad to see someone with talent waste his educational opportunity. Don wasn't a dummy by any means and I'm sure he's doing something, besides sleeping, very well today. But sitting in classrooms just didn't appeal to him in those days. I'll bet he'd like to do it all over again but life isn't built that way and too many people discover that too late. And so Don Greenwood exited before his time. But he did a pretty good job of whacking enemy ballcarriers around in the two seasons he did play. And he also kept a lot of CU coaches busy trying to figure out ways to get him to be a better student.

Kerry Mottl (6-1, 216) learned his linebacking under a first-stringer on my team, Roy Shepherd, and he learned it well. I had a lot of fun with Kerry's publicity because he had taken tapdancing lessons as a youth and while he never did become too hot of a tapdancer, he could back up a line a hell of a lot better than Gene Kelly or Fred Astaire ever did. Kerry also looked a little bit like a young Marlon Brando who was at the height of his movie stardom back in those days. So we had all kinds of angles to write about but the best one was that he was a crisp-hitting, fine linebacker. Kerry got an additional coaching break when young Pat Culpepper, who had been an All-American linebacker at Texas, joined the CU staff in the spring when Kerry was a freshman and coached him then and during Kerry's sophomore season. Pat was a great influence on CU's young linebackers and no one benefitted from Pat's presence more than Kerry. When you've been trained by a pair of aces like Roy Shepherd and Pat Culpepper, you just can't help being a fine linebacker and Kerry was. His picture is on the wall in the Byron White room on the CU campus where undergraduate Buffaloes assemble to study and meditate and watch color television and read hometown newspapers and look at pictures on the wall. It is an action shot of Kerry striking down a runner during his sophomore season. It's a perfect illustration of a perfect tackle. Kerry has his helmet buried in the runner's chest and his arms firmly around the player's waist. The going-to-the-ground runner is bent over backwards, sharply, at the waist. Pat Culpepper thought it was the best picture of a tackle he'd ever seen and he was involved in a pretty good one himself during a goal line stand against Arkansas when Pat was playing for Texas. Old linebackers love the feel of contact like that and Kerry continues to get it every spring in the Alumni-Varsity game. It's his way of teaching current young Buffaloes what the game is all about. He does it well.

Phil Irwin was one of my favorite Buffaloes. Younger brothers of famous athletes are often doomed to obscurity and no younger brother ever had a bigger shadow to fight his way out of than Phil, who arrived at CU as a freshman just two years after older brother Hale had been an All-Big Eight safety for two years and won the NCAA golf championship in his senior year. Phil had been a smallish journeyman fullback and linebacker at Boulder High and got his scholarship mostly on his own merit but the fact that he had the same blood in him as Hale had to lift his stature a little in the eyes of the CU recruiters. Phil followed in Hale's footsteps but built his own career, one which paralleled his older brother's in football but didn't include the same golf ability. Like Hale, Phil was a gritty, tough, undersized battler, a skinny-ish 6-2, 200-pounder in a time when 200-pound linebackers were quickly getting to be an exception. Phil had a lot of smarts and always managed to be somewhere around the right place. He could level a devastating tackle, too. The Irwin brothers may have been on the small side but I've never seen anybody come flying in for a tackle any harder than they did. Phil made a pair of interceptions which did as much to propel CU into the Liberty Bowl against Alabama as any two single plays of that 1969 season when he was a junior. In a down-to-the-wire, 31-24 victory over powerful Missouri, he went high into the air to pick off a Tiger pass halfway between the thrower and the receiver to stop a last-ditch Missouri rally which had carried beyond midfield. It was a tremendous effort. Linebackers don't normally have great jumping ability. And nobody intercepts many passes where the ball is at its highest arc. But Phil did it this time and it saved the game. A few weeks later he made an even more dramatic interception, jumping in front of an Oklahoma State pass in the CU end zone with the Buffaloes leading 17-14 and about to be killed by a furious Cowboy rally which had sent them nearly 80 yards in less than a minute and a half.

Phil was a little linebacker who made a lot of big plays. He didn't make All-Big Eight and he wasn't a golf All-American like his older brother. But he matched Hale in an even more important honors department. He was selected by his teammates as co-captain, along with Don Popplewell, of the 1970 CU squad. Hale had been co-captain, with John Beard, of the 1965 team. There are all kinds of honors to be won in football. All-conference and All-American teams can include players who may have made the team for a number of reasons, not all of them entirely fair ones. But to be chosen captain of your team by your teammates is the highest honor which can come to a player. You can't fool those people. You've got to be a good player and a good man. Phil Irwin was. He made his own footprints.

Jim Dalthorp, like Roy Shepherd, was a senior on the 1952 team which was halfway through the season when I joined the CU staff. Jim was a fine linebacker, a steady, smart football player whose major characteristic was dependability. He was a member of that first wave of very good football players which Dal Ward brought into the program and who helped raise the quality of the program so dramatically. Dal Ward used to work the north central part of the country pretty hard for young talent during his early years at CU. It was a carryover from his Minnesota days when the Bernie Bierman staffs used to pluck a lot of outstanding young men from North and South Dakota and even as far west as Montana. None of those three states have ever had major football powers among their colleges so that the best of their athletes inevitably go outside the state to pursue their college and athletic careers. Jim Dalthorp was from Brookings, S.D., one of the first of several fine athletes to come to CU from that state. Carroll Hardy (Sturgis) and Bob Stransky (Yankton) followed Jim and there were several others who didn't reach the performance level of these three men but who nevertheless, were good, solid squadmembers. Jim Dalthorp went on to become an excellent high school coach at Arvada before joining the FBI where he now serves today. Like Shepherd, he wasn't a big man (6-0 and 185) but he was tightly-wound and size was no handicap. There's an old saw which says that it isn't the size of the dog in the fight that counts, it's the size of the fight in the dog. I don't want to infer that either man was a dog but that cliche gives you an idea of why Shepherd and Dalthorp are on my offensive squad even though they played in the days when they weren't building football players in the awesome dimensions they are today. There was a lot of fight in Dalthorp. And that's the quality that counts.

HALFBACKS

The two halfbacks on this defensive platoon were both great athletes who could have been just as good on offense and would have been great two-way players. Tom Brookshier (1951-2-3) and Charles Greer (1965-6-7) both had long professional careers, impressive testimony to their football ability. Tom was a senior on the 1952 team when I came back to CU and one of the things that I've regretted is that I didn't get the chance to observe this fellow's entire CU career. He was a great athlete but an even greater character. There was nothing that Tom Brookshier wouldn't try and he probably got into and out of more trouble than any other athlete in the history of the school. That covers a lot of ground but Tom Brookshier used to cover a lot of ground. Tom had a lot of fun, whatever he was doing. He was the personality boy to end all personality boys. He had the face of a movie star, the daring of a burglar and the mischievousness of an imp. And whether he was walking across a parking lot over and through the tops of convertibles or slyly starting a fight in the coffee shop, he did it with a flourish. Tom kept the Phi Gam house in an uproar most of the time and his brothers were either carrying him on their shoulders in celebration or trying to catch him so they could punish him. There was no in-between with Tom. In baseball he was a wild righthander who could throw a fastball right over the backstop, grin boyishly at the bench and fire the next one even higher. On the football field, though, he was a tightly-wound ball of fire who was as good a man at roaring up to the line of scrimmage to make the tackle on a running play as any halfback I've ever watched. He didn't get beat deep, either, even though his first choice on any play was to get up there and drill the ballcarrier. His teammates called him ''Kamikaze'' because he was always crashdiving into the side of a ballcarrier. I wasn't around Tom long enough to know many of his legendary accomplishments, most of them off the football field. I do know that Brookshier always took his choice of the nice things in life and one of the nicest things he ever took was his wife, Barbara, who was one of the Homecoming queens of 1952. No handsomer couple ever became man and wife, on any campus or in Hollywood. For all his wildness and for all his great ability to get into almost inescapable jams, Tom had a lot of class. Lovable class. Had he not had it there would have been very little chance he'd have escaped getting killed before he reached voting age by someone on whom he had perpetrated a practical joke. One of my favorite Tom Brookshier stories, and you've got to get with some of his old fraternity brothers if you want to hear the really good ones, took place when he was a star with the Philadelphia Eagles, the only pro team he ever played with and a team which he helped become NFL champions in 1960. Tom's pro career was ended by a badly broken leg in a game against the Chicago Bears not long after that championship but before he left the playing ranks he had left the same sort of a legend as he had established at the Phi Gam house. This story is a true one. You don't have to make up Tom Brookshier stories. The Eagles did their pre-season training at Hershey, Pa. and Hershey isn't a very big town which is why the Eagles probably trained there and about all they do in Hershey is sit around and make milk chocolate and eat hot fudge sundaes and stuff like that. They did have a couple of night spots downtown but these were off limits to the players. The reason, probably, they were off limits to the players was because that was where the coaches did their night-lifing and they didn't want any competition from the younger, handsomer men in camp. There were the usual devices rigged to beat bed check. It remained for Tom Brookshier to come up with the most elaborate fake body anyone has ever come up with. Most guys wad up a few blankets beneath the covers and jam a pillow over the top of the bed and go merrily on their way. Tom just had to improve on this ruse, however. So he went down to the city park and removed a statue from it- it was probably one which had been erected in honor of the guy who invented chocolate covered peanuts or something, maybe it was even General Hershey with his hand in a fishbowl - and tenderly laid it in his bed, covered it up, kissed it goodnight and sailed off into the night. The substitute body worked beautifully. Only one thing went wrong. Tom promptly jumped into his T-Bird and drove downtown and parked it right smack in front of the town's top bar and went in and was having some laughs and probably a beer or two. Everybody in Hershey knew Tom by this time and everybody knew what his car looked like, including the coaching staff which hustled right down to the spot as soon as bed check was over. So Tom got caught. I've never heard how the story ended. But I'm sure Brook gave out with that innocent-little-boy look and escaped punishment or fine. And I'm equally sure he got somebody else to put the statue back in the park. Every team needs a guy who can keep things loose and happy and alive. We have one of the all-time greats at this in Tom Brookshier. In case you think Tom was a complete screw-off, don't ever believe it. He had the brains to go along with his good looks and personality. He could have been an excellent coach. He did, in fact, help Ben Martin on the Air Force Academy staff while he was in the service. But he went a more stable route and has become one of the nation's top radio and television sports announcers and is one of the CBS stars in Philadelphia from where he does several national television shows, including NFL color. It's almost unfair for a guy to have everything like Tom has - looks, talent, flair for life, great family - but it couldn't have happened to a nicer guy.

Charles Greer came to CU from a tiny town on the outskirts of Atlanta, Ga., an outstanding athlete who needed to get out of the restrictive atmosphere of the south so that he could star at a major university. They called him "Sonny" at South Fulton High but he got rid of that nickname quickly when he got to Boulder. I guess it still wasn't too popular in 1965 in Boulder although I don't know why. We called him Charles the Swift and he was as agile an athlete as I've ever seen but he really wasn't all that swift on the straightaway. But he was exceptionally quick and had great reactions. He could jump around and stop and start and when he caught a punt or intercepted a pass he was really hard to corral. But, inevitably, he'd break into the open and get caught from behind. Charles was one of the top punt returners in the Big Eight for three straight years, finished second twice and sixth once, but only scored one touchdown in 66 punt returns even though he was on the verge of doing it at least a dozen other times. Charles was one of the most exciting runners I've ever seen, though, and he could have been a great running back or an outstanding wide receiver. He had the moves of a cat and great hands to go along with his moves. Charlie, in fact, was an excellent basketball player and a fine rebounder even though he was only 5-11 and he managed to squeeze in one year on the CU varsity in between football seasons. I think the thing I remember most about Charlie, aside from those spinetingling punt returns, was the way he took to men's fashions. Charlie was from a fairly modest background in Georgia and didn't own too many threads when he arrived in Boulder. But some of his older brothers took him over to the Regiment and introduced him to some of the finer garments of his time and Charlie quickly became a fashion plate. There was never a more impressive sight than Charlie strolling onto the scene as the Buffaloes left for a road game. Bowler, cane, vest, spats. Charlie had them all and wore them with authority. All he had to do was get out of the south where he could let himself go. A lot of pro scouts questioned his future in pro football because he didn't have great speed or height and all those physical attributes that pro scouts like to have you believe you have got to have or you ain't got a chance to be a success in that mysterious, superhuman world of pro football. But, like most of the old bird dogs who criss-cross the country looking at old movies and collecting spring and fall brochures and padding expense accounts and doing a lot of dozing in Holiday Inns, that's a bunch of hogwash. A good football player is a good football player. I'm sure I've said that somewhere before. But it's an undeniable fact. High school, college or pro. The guys who don't make it at the next level generally come up short in the head or heart. Charlie Greer had more than his share in these two vital areas. He wasn't too badly endowed physically, either, and promptly became a regular with the Denver Broncos as first a corner back then a safety. Of course that wasn't exactly like making a real pro football team but, nevertheless, it was a team of sorts and a lot of men didn't make it. Charlie will be carrying his share of the load for a long time. He always has.

Behind Brookshier and Greer, I choose Jim Cooch (1968-9-70) and Leon Mavity (1961-2-3). Cooch came to CU as a quarterback and could probably have become a pretty good one had he not been needed more badly somewhere else. Just exactly where that somewhere else was, the staff wasn't certain. But they knew he was too good an athlete to spend his life backing up Bobby Anderson. Jim had good hands, was a very smart player and had excellent speed and size and agility and was the starting tight end as a sophomore and caught 13 passes. The next spring he was moved to cornerback to fill a void there and he became a fine regular for the next two seasons. Jim was a lot like Charles Greer when he got the ball except that he was never a deep man in the punt receiving formation so that the only time he ever got the ball was on an interception. But he got eight of those in two seasons so he got more chances to run with the ball than a lot of cornerbacks. Maybe the biggest one he ever got didn't include a runback, though. That was a leaping, falling-to-the-ground interception he made at the CU 35 to preserve a come-from-behind 17-14 victory at Kansas and keep the Buffaloes on track to the 1969 Liberty Bowl date with Alabama. Jim was one of those quality young men who stand just a cut above the crowd of fine young men who pass through a program. He was the kind of man you like to have around. For his playing ability and for his personable presence off the field.

Leon Mavity was mentioned as one of the two-way halfbacks who was good enough to have been on my two-way team but who finished out of my top three. But Leon makes my defensive platoon with ease as he concentrated on defense in his senior year on the first team that Eddie Crowder coached. Leon was smart. He was tough. He had good football sense. And he was an excellent runner. He was one of the leaders of that 1963 team and while it didn't compile an impressive record because it had been a broken down team the year before and it was breaking in a new coaching staff this year, it was still a tough team which gave a good account of itself always and which took the first step on the road back for CU football. Leon had some fine offensive moments during his first two years for the Buffaloes and even played a little quarterback for a while in spring practice in 1963. But he closed his career as a sterling defensive back, one of CU's best. He was also one of CU's best in baseball, a smooth-stroking outfielder who could whiplash the ball out of the park impressively. A bad shoulder curtailed his baseball career and kept him from moving further up as a pro than he did. Leon was a good man. I'll take him in my secondary anytime.

My third pair of defensive backs is Brian Foster (1969-70-1) and Cullen Bryant (1970-1-2). Brian was a slender little scrapper out of Lexington, Ky. who was cut from the same cloth as the Tom Brookshiers and Eddie Doves and Leon Mavitys and all those guys who liked to come blasting up to the line of scrimmage and hit somebody. Brian was a good pass defender and a deadly tackler. He had a little bit of Homer Jenkins in him, though, and hit people harder than his body would take. He broke his arm making a tackle against Iowa State during his junior year and his absence was very costly as Cullen had to move into the starting lineup as a raw rookie and got beat deep a couple times before he settled down. Brian had some injury problems through the middle of his senior season, but he came back and finished well. I remember a typical suicide play by him at Nebraska in 1971 when he came diving into the knees of the Cornhuskers' hard-running Jeff Kinney and got knocked cold for his trouble. The contact came at about the CU two and Kinney just stepped over the body of Brian and lurched into the end zone, a la Steve Owens. But Brian was back a week later doing business at the same old stand and his unflinching qualities gained him the great respect of his teammates who voted him one of the tri-captains in 1971.

Cullen Bryant might just be the greatest athlete ever to play on the corner for CU. He's 6-2 and 215 and looks bigger. He can also run a :04.6 forty which ain't too bad. Cullen had to come in the hard way, starting his first game as a sophomore against Oklahoma and having to defend right away against a super sophomore runner and receiver like Joe Wylie who dealt Cullen and everyone else in the CU secondary a full afternoon of misery that 1970 afternoon in Boulder. But Cullen has come on strong ever since. He did a good job against Air Force's All-American Ernest Jennings in the final regular season game of his sophomore year and was a steady performer for the Buffaloes last fall and should have a super senior season. Cullen has it all. I probably ought to wrtie an ode about him. But what can you say, poetically, about a man named William Cullen Bryant?

There is one more corner back who I must mention because he was good enough to make this team but finished seventh on my list. Eric Harris, the younger brother of William, came to CU as a good quarterback prospect but had the misfortune to be in the same class as Bob Anderson and there wasn't much room for quarterbacks behind Bobby because he was very good and very durable. Eric was too good an athlete to waste as a seldom-used reserve quarterback so he was moved to defense which caused some unrest in the black circles of Boulder and Eric was used as one of the examples in a discrimination charge which was leveled against the CU staff in early 1968 but the matter was settled peaceably and Eric became a very good cornerback for the Buffaloes and was one of the solid starters on the fine 1969 team and was drafted fairly high by the St. Louis Cardinals but hurt his knee while playing in the Coaches' All-America game at Lubbock, Texas in the summer following his graduation and required surgery and never really got it going again.

SAFETY

This was the hardest single position on the defense for me to pick because I had four fine ones to choose from in Dick Anderson (1965-6-7), John Stearns (1970-1-2), Hale Irwin (1964-5-6) and Pat Murphy (1968-9-70). I rate them in that order and there isn't much difference between the first and fourth man.

Dick Anderson was a great competitor. He was just as great an athlete as his younger brother except that he didn't play as glamorous a position in college. But he did in high school and was a ripping, stomping fullback for Emerson Wilson at Boulder High and led his team to the state championship as a senior. Bobby was the sophomore quarterback on that 1963 Boulder team and it was the only time these two brothers were in the same backfield. I'd have loved to have seen them operating as a quarterback-fullback tandem at CU but Wilmer Cooks came in with the same class as Dick and they were both bluechippers so one of them had to change and Dick was the kind of man you could ask to move to defense and know he would do a great job even though it meant playing a less prominent position on the team. Dick's major characteristic was that he was a tremendous competitor. In the fury of the fray he was capable of stomping on his grandmother to get to where he was going. Sharing top place with competitiveness among his component parts was intelligence. He was a very smart player and having him in the secondary was just like having a coach on the field. Dick was an exceptionally good broken field runner who seemed to have eyes all over his head and, although he wasn't real big, he was still a pretty good man at 6-2 and 204 and had very strong legs so that he could tear himself out of a tackle. Dick was a good punt returner although that was never a primary assignment. He also was one of the longest punters since Boyd Dowler. But he kicked it so long, and often too low, that a good safetyman, like Eddie Hinton of Oklahoma, had too much time to set up a return. I can remember one time against Oklahoma in 1966 when Andy booted the ball about 70 yards and Hinton promptly returned it 93 yards. Andy worked more at kicking it shorter and higher after that but he still averaged 41 yards on 23 punts as a senior when he shared the kicking assignment with William Harris. One of my happiest moments as a publicity man came at the end of the 1967 season when Andy was named to the Associated Press All-American team, a tough thing for us to get done because he had not been mentioned at all in the pre-season discussions about potential All-Americans and it's pretty difficult to make an All-American team if you haven't had some sort of a pre-season buildup. He had been a regular for the preceding two years but he hadn't been that tremendous. Andy got off to a fantastic start and intercepted seven passes in the first five games. But then they stopped throwing into his territory and he didn't get another the rest of the fall. We couldn't get Andy on the Football Coaches' or the Football Writers' teams because they are picked early in the last month of the season. The A.P. team, however, is selected after the end of the regular season and the reason they do it then is so that they can put somebody on like Andy who has had a great season but who hadn't had any kind of a pre-season ranking. Jim Van Valkenburg was sports editor of the Kansas City office of the A.P. and he's a good old buddy who really went to bat for Andy as did another good friend, Mickey Holmes, publicity chief for the Big Eight conference. Andy made the team and I know there wasn't a more deserving man on that team. Later on, another old friend, Murray Olderman, came through with a spot for Andy on the N.E.A.All-American team. Dick made everybody look good when he became a standout in the Miami Dolphin secondary where he was picked as one of the top defensive rookie backs of the year. He continues to get better every year and I predict he'll be an all-pro safetyman before he finishes his playing career. It won't take many more plays like his interception and touchdown return against Baltimore in the 1971 playoffs to elevate him to a first team NFL berth. And he'll come up with many more. Of that you can be sure.

 John Stearns is cut from the same cloth as Andy. Break the Bad Dude down into his component parts and you can't really find the makings for an outstanding player. But, again, you can't measure head and heart and stomach and this is where the John Stearnses and the Dick Andersons are heavyweights. John picked up the name Bad Dude because he was a bad dude on the football field in high school and as a freshman. He liked to hit people. Went out of his way to do it. As a sophomore, in fact, he forgot about covering deep a couple times in his haste to get up to the line of scrimmage and clothesline somebody. John doesn't have the speed to be yo-yoing up and back, whacking people up close and covering the deep route in back. So he eased off in his eagerness to go get somebody as a junior. Don't get the impression that he stopped hitting people when the opportunity arose, though. He hammered Houston's All-American tight end, Riley Odoms, with brutal force three different times in that game. Once he jarred Odoms loose from the ball at the goal line to avert what looked like a cinch Cougar touchdown. Another time he knocked Riley flying out of bounds and clear beyond the Houston bench. John can gather up a lot of velocity in a short distance. A lot of it is mental. He loves contact. He can also come up with the big play. By almost willing it to happen. His almost back-to-back saves against Houston in the Astro-Bluebonnet Bowl game were classics, the first exemplifying total effort when he dove to deflect a touchdown pass which was only inches away from the receiver's hands, the second a tremendous impromptu play when he scooped up a bouncing snap from center on the short hop in the end zone on a fourth-and-nine from the CU 10 and raced 12 yards, stepping out of bounds at the 22, just three yards beyond the first down stick even though it was located on the other sideline. Talk about instinct! But the play that I remember John best for was a similar recovery after a bad snap on a fourth-down punt in the second quarter of the opening game in 1971 against LSU. It was fourth-and-long at the CU 33 and the snap went high over John's head and back to the end zone. John chased the ball and speared it on the bounce just as he crossed the end zone. He danced around a bit then stopped and punted it high and to the 48. There was no return on the punt. John's great reactions meant the difference between LSU getting the ball down close to our goal line instead of at midfield. The game was still up for grabs at this point and that play could have meant the game for the Buffaloes. That's the kind of competitor John Stearns is. He has that mystic ability to come up with the big play. Maybe he's a great athlete and we just don't have sense enough to realize it. We're always measuring people ourselves, just like those pro scouts. John's great ability carries over to baseball where he was the All-Big Eight catcher in 1972 after a sensational season in which he batted a stratospheric .491 to lead the league. Cancellation of the final series of the year because of rain kept him from setting a new record for basehits during the season . . . he was only two short of the record going into that three-game series which never came off. John is also one of the best baserunners in the Big Eight. And an outstanding receiver. Bad Dude is also a good dude in the class room. When you get right down to it, he's just a plain Good Dude.

Hale Irwin was a slenderish 6-0, 180-pounder who didn't seem to be that big until you saw him deck a runner. But size wasn't his big thing. He was an exceptionally smart safetyman who always seemed to be in the right place at the right time. He intercepted nine passes in two seasons as a defensive specialist after beginning his career as an offensive quarterback and safety when Eddie Crowder was still playing his best men both ways in 1964. Hale wasn't a bad quarterback although he was a much better defensive back because he wasn't a great passer or runner and really didn't have the offensive skills of the other two quarterbacks in his class, Bernie McCall and Dan Kelly. Hale got some ribs battered and a shoulder bruised by a late hit at Oklahoma State when he was a rookie and that pretty much ended his quarterback career. Then came the specialization at safety in a switch which paid big dividends to the Buffaloes. I can remember when Hale was graduating from Boulder High and was really torn between going to CU and playing football and golf or going to a southern school, like Houston, which really had a fine golf program. Our coaches really worked hard on Hale because they knew he'd be a winner. I'll say this about Hale. When he decided to enroll at CU, he gave football everything he had. There was no saving anything for the golf season. Even though he barely topped 170 as a sophomore, he wound up and flew at people and never avoided a collision. Once a competitor, always a competitor! The play I remember Hale best for was the final one of the first half at Oklahoma when he was a junior. The Buffaloes were ahead but Oklahoma was on the one-yard line with time for just one more play. The Sooners came out of the huddle and Hale alertly saw that the Buffaloes were short a lineman. Oklahoma saw it, too, and ran right at that empty spot. But Hale jumped into the gap just as the ball was snapped and made the tackle and the half ended with Oklahoma unable to get off another play. In the second half he came up with two clutch interceptions to help preserve a 13-0 victory. He was All-Big Eight and also on the conference All-Academic team for two years, as salty a player as there was in the league. Hale's golf career worked out okay, too. He won two Big Eight individual titles and was the national collegiate champion as a senior and was All-American twice in golf. Did he make the right decision when he elected to play football at CU? I have to think he did. Maybe he'd have been better off to have concentrated on golf but he made more than $94,000 in official earnings on the 1971 professional tour and it would have been difficult to improve on that performance. I really believe that the lessons he learned on the tough physical scenes which make up college football will pay dividends for him as he keeps going in golf. I don't have a lot of concern about what Hale does because I know he'll do it well. That's the way he's built and he is one of the best Buffaloes who ever knocked down a pass or cut down a tackler or drilled an iron shot dead to the pin. In short, he was, and is, a winner. And winning is the name of every game.

    Pat Murphy was a roundish butterball with a wit as sharp as his performances in the secondary. Dan Kelly was the original Irishman in my nickname book and Pat inherited that handle and was most worthy of it. Pat's strong point was intelligence and if I sound repetitive it's because you've got to have more than the average share of smarts to be a good deep defender. Mistakes cost touchdowns back there so it's no place for a slow thinker or a bad thinker. Pat had good quickness and speed, too, and he knew what to do with an interception or a punt, the only two ways he could get possession of the ball. I think the thing I remember most about Pat was his sly sense of humor and the ever-present grin that was always on his face and the twinkle that was always in his eyes. He enjoyed life and he made life enjoyable for the people around him. He and Jim Cooch were inseparables, two of a kind. They did a lot of patrolling together and did it well, most of it on the football field where they supplied leadership in the secondary in 1969 and 70. Before that Pat was a regular in 1968 as a rookie when Jim was playing offensive end. Pat was in a class with the three safeties I've placed ahead of him. And that's pretty

high class company. He belongs there.
THE DEFENSIVE THREE-DEEP
E — Herb Orvis, Mike Schnitker, Mike Veeder.
T — Bill Sabatino, Carl Taibi, Dave Capra.
G — Bud Magrum, Ron Scott, Bill Collins.
T — Bill Brundige, Frank Bosch, Jim Stander.
E — Bill Fairband, Don Branby, Ray LeMasters.
LB — Rocky Martin, John Stavely, Kerry Mottl.
LB — Roy Shepherd, Rick Ogle, Phil Irwin.
LB — Steve Sidwell, Don Greenwood, Jim Dalthorp.
HB — Tom Brookshier, Jim Cooch, Brian Foster.
HB — Charles Greer, Leon Mavity, Cullen Bryant.
S — Dick Anderson, John Stearns, Hale Irwin.

THE CAPTAINS

In looking back over 25 years and selecting my personal choices for the two-way and platoon squads during that period, I've mentioned more than 100 men. All of them were outstanding football players. Practically all were fine young men. But two men, Joe Romig and Bob Anderson, stand out vividly even among such a group as this. They are without peers. I challenge any university to come up with two men to match these two who I have selected as the captains of my squad: Romig for the line, Andy for the backfield; Romig for the two-way team, Andy for the platoon team. A lot of men in athletics can go through a career without knowing one man like them. I've been lucky enough to have worked with two. And, please remember, that Frank Bernardi and Eddie Dove, complete my top four and that they rank right up there with Romig and Anderson. These four are in a class by themselves.

Joe Romig was a fanatic. He didn't have enough physical talent to be as great as he was. Simply wasn't big enough or fast enough or tall enough or anything enough. Joe might have a tough time getting offered a scholarship in the 1970's. He'd almost certainly be considered a borderline case, not endowed enough physically but you might take a chance on him because he was a great competitor and you still have to weigh in that vital ingredient when you're evaluating a prospect.

Joe's success story was simply a case of mind over matter and that old formula still works as well today as it did in those old Horatio Alger books. Now I don't want to give the impression that Joe was a physical weakling without any ability at all because that was not true. He was quick. And he was tremendously strong in the upper body. But his was not a physique that would stand out in a crowd. Romig's greatness was in his mind. The mind is where toughness and intensity and determination and drive and fire and tenacity and all those things are developed which make an effective fanatic. And in the mind is where Joe Romig stood 6-8 and weighed 280 pounds in contrast to his actual physical measurements which were 5-10 and 199 and that 199 was what he weighed in at picture day not what he

played at most of the season. Which was more like 190. Joe had to get on his tiptoes to hit 5-10, too. Not-so-big guys like Joe and Eddie Dove and Homer Jenkins and Roy Shepherd never got on a pair of scales unless they absolutely had to because for some reason they were always embarassed about their size. Almost as though they figured they were intruders in a sport in which everyone is supposed to be big. Joe was one of the first men to get intelligently serious about a weight program. He studied different programs and determined the one which would help him most, then worked at it diligently. Joe was also fortunate to have played his high school football at Lakewood under Tom Hancock, who was in the process then of establishing himself as one of the top developers of a prep program in the state. Tom, a former CU center (1948-9-50) and a fine one, recognized the importance of a year-around conditioning program and put together an outstanding one which paid him annual dividends at Lakewood where his football teams were annually among the finest in the state. So Joe Romig had two important things going for him early: (1) his own great drive and (2) his exposure toan excellent high school program. Joe became a state champion wrestler and an all-state football player for the Tigers, playing fullback on offense and linebacker on defense. At CU he was quickly moved to guard as a freshman and just as quickly became a fine one. Joe wasn't an overpowering offensive lineman. He didn't have the size to be. But he was quick and smart and tough and could fire out straightaway or get into a blocking pattern quickly so that he was a completely effective guard. But it was as a linebacker that he was really impressive. Until Rich Glover came along at Nebraska in 1971-2, I had never seen another defensive man as good at moving laterally to the ballcarrier. Romig never took his eyes off the ball. His upper body was so strong that he could fight his way through blocks or through a maze of bodies by using his hands and shoulders almost by instinct, always keeping his eyes on the ball. This ability also requires great agility. Romig working his way toward the ball was like an artist at work. It was almost as though the ball was a magnet and Joe was a big chunk of steel. There was hardly any way you could escape him with a wide play. The best play against Romig was one in which a mis-direction step was taken to get him to begin moving in the wrong direction, then come back with a quick play right at him. Your ballcarrier might get past him before he had a chance to recover and your blocker wouldn't have to hold his block very long. But if you dawdled anywhere along the way, Joe would get you. And there was no way you could escape him if you went wide where he could claw his way toward you.
his way toward you.

Great as Joe's accomplishments on the football field were, his accomplishments off the field were even greater. He was an outstanding student, majored in physics, won a Rhodes Scholarship and studied for two years at Oxford, returned to CU to work on his doctorate and was completing that work and also working in this country's Outer Planet Exploration program when this was written. Joe wanted to be an astronaut when he was an undergraduate but his eyes weren't strong enough — he wore glasses off the field — and he could never have passed the physical. But don't bet that he won't log a lot of hours in outer space before he retires because eventually spaceships will be large passenger-carrying ones which will be able to take scientists and scholars of all sorts and not just pilot types. That will open the door for men like Joe Romig and, when it opens, he'll be one of the first to enter.

Joe was a young man of many contrasts when he was playing at CU. He was so intense about everything he did that you wondered how he could continue to keep it up through a lifetime. But as Joe matured, he leveled off and took on some of the steadying influences which come to most average men. Like a wife and family and a less fanatical attitude toward life in general. That leveling off helped Joe's personality tremendously, too. Super-intelligent people very often don't understand us average people and can have a difficult time communicating with them. It used to be a real problem to get Joe to take time off to be social or to talk to people about something besides the moon and stars or his religious feelings which were extremely strong before he went to Oxford. Not that Joe wasn't a friendly, gregarious type when he was in college. He was, when he wasn't thinking too hard about something else. But most of the time he was thinking hard about something else. I can remember an occasion midway through his senior season when the Buffaloes were undefeated and had just beaten Missouri to get the inside track on the Big Eight championship and Time magazine scheduled an in-depth feature on him and sent Barron Beshoar, Time-Life's Denver bureau chief, to Boulder to interview him. Despite realizing that Time was a prestigious national news magazine and that the exposure would enhance his reputation, Joe resented the intrusion on his time and was almost hostile toward me for playing a role in arranging the interview. He sincerely did not want to do it because he felt there were more important things to do. Like study. Barron Beshoar is a very nice man, a native Coloradoan and an excellent reporter who knew how to lead his subject through an interview. Barron's poise and patience settled Joe down quickly and the interview went well although Joe was never one to go into too much detail during an answer to a question. Barron got his story and it was a good one. Unfortunately, CU got upset by Utah that Saturday for its only regular-season loss in 1961 and the Time sports editor killed the Romig story and replaced it with a standby one on an Ohio State fullback who probably would have had a hard time figuring how to get Joe's slide rule out of its case, let alone read it.

That single-mindedness was a great aid to Joe in critical times, though. He could almost will things to happen. I remember the start of his senior fall when he suffered a severe knee injury in a Friday afternoon workout just one week before the first game of the season. The Buffaloes were working on blocking extra point kicks late that afternoon near the finish of a light workout before the final intra-squad scrimmage the following afternoon. Joe came charging in from his position and a CU back who was blocking for the kicker stepped back, accidentally, into Joe's path. The collision produced a freakish situation in which Joe came down wrong on his knee and strained the ligaments in it. Normally, a man would have missed at least a month. But Joe Romig wasn't a normal man. He was lifting weight with it before the middle of the next week and I'll never forget the sight of him sitting on a table in the training room raising his leg with the iron boot on it, his eyes closed, teeth gritted and big beads of sweat popping out of his forehead from the pain. The sight of CU's All-American captain fighting back despite the mental and physical miseries he was going through was enough to bring tears to a lot of eyes. It even impressed such hardened young cynics as Claude Crabb and Mike Wolfe, a couple members of that squad who required a lot of impressing before they were impressed. But Joe never wavered in his determination to be ready a lot sooner than everybody said. And, sure enough, he played against Oklahoma State on the second Saturday after the injury. He was still limping a little but he played and he never missed a turn the rest of the season as he repeated as a consensus All-American and led his team to the conference championship and into the Orange Bowl.

Joe Romig is a unique human being, one who achieved greatness early in his lifetime. In athletics despite not being greatly endowed physically. As scholar, he was greatly endowed intellectually. But most of all as a great human being and, here again, he achieved this greatness despite coming out of a background which could have turned his energies and talents into the wrong direction. Joe's parents were divorced before he was a year old. He was raised by his mother who was a nurse in Boulder for the first 12 years of his life then moved to Lakewood and died when he was a junior in high school. At that point, Joe was taken in by the father of one of his closest friends in Lakewood, the Rev. William Spence, a Presbyterian

BOB ANDERSON

I especially like this picture because it shows Bob blocking for Jimmy Bratten during Bob's senior year after he had been switched to halfback. Bob Anderson did whatever needed to be done for the team.

minister. Joe's father is a prominent physician in Anchorage, Alaska and Joe has had the capacity to love him and his children as much as though they had all been raised together.

Joe Romig, then, was a player to end all players, a captain to end all captains, a man to end all men. As I've said, you are lucky to run across one person of his quality in a lifetime. But you keep hoping there'll be another. And there was.

The second one to come across my path was Bob Anderson, who was Joe Romig 10 years later except that he was more of a social lion and less of a classroom cougar than Joe.

I don't mean to infer that Bob wasn't a good student because he was just as good as he wanted to be and most of the time he wanted to be just as good as he needed to be-a solid, average student but not the brilliant scholar Joe was. But a good one, nevertheless. Bob had been a high school superstar at Boulder under Emerson Wilson where he quarterbacked a state championship team as a sophomore and in the championship game took over the offensive load after his brother Dick, the star senior fullback on the team, was injured early in the game. As a senior Bob led the Panthers to an undefeated season and number one ranking in the state but his team was upset in the semifinals by a Ft. Collins Poudre team quarterbacked by Monte Huber. Ironically, the two young men were to wind up as teammates at CU where they combined to form one of the finest passing combinations in the history of the school.

There was great recruiting pressure on Bob after he had finished his prep career as schools from every section of the country tried to attract him to their campus. Bob actually signed a Southeastern conference letter-of-intent with Florida and appeared to be headed to that faraway school. But late in the summer, Florida withdrew its scholarship offer to Bob with the explanation that they had over-committed their scholarship budget and had to reduce the number they had offered. Whatever their reason, Bob decided to stay at home, a decision which he never regretted and one which enabled CU to land a young man who was to be one of the school's all-time athletic greats. In addition to being a football star at CU, Bob was the starting catcher for the baseball team as a sophomore but gave up that sport after one season to concentrate on improving his football ability.

Bob didn't waste any time proving to a lot of people who didn't think he was fast enough or a good enough passer to be a good college quarterback that they were wrong. Bob had developed very quickly as a youngster and was tremendously strong so that he had been able to run over a lot of high school tacklers. He wouldn't be able to do that in college, a lot of cynics said. Others said he wasn't tall enough and couldn't throw deep well enough to be a good enough passer to reach stardom in college. But Bob had a most impressive freshman season as he gained 760 yards in four games, 462 of them on the ground, where he didn't have any more trouble running over college freshmen than he did high school players, and 298 in the air. He gave an indication of what was to come as he scored five touchdowns and passed for two more. His next test came the following spring when he faced a strong alumni team which included two of my all-stars, his brother Dick and Eddie Dove, in the deep secondary and another, Ralph Heck, at linebacker. Bob riddled that defense, passing for 181 yards and running for 51 more. It appeared as though he was more than ready for his varsity debut coming up in four months. But before that, he found time to make All-American as the number one catcher on the Boulder Collegians baseball team which won the national semipro championship at Wichita in August.

Bob came out firing at full blast in his first varsity game, silencing all his critics forever as he scored three touchdowns and won Big Eight "back-of-the-week" laurels while leading the Buffaloes to a 27-7 victory over Baylor in Boulder, totalling 212 yards, 83 rushing and 120 (11 of 21) passing. Getting into the end zone was to be an Anderson trademark and playing sensationally in opening games was another. In the 1968 opener against Oregon, Bob scored three more touchdowns and was again named Big Eight back of the week. Then, as a senior, he scored four TD's in the opener against Tulsa for a total of 10 touchdowns in the three opening games of his varsity career. Overall, in those three seasons, Bob scored 40 touchdowns, the most ever by a CU player.

Bob wasn't too bad at winding up seasons, either, winning "the outstanding back" award in both bowl games he played in and setting a school passing record of 234 yards in the final game of his junior season. Bob came on dramatically near the end of the first half of the Bluebonnet Bowl game against Miami in his sophomore December to rally the Buffaloes from behind and propel them to a 31-21 triumph, scoring two touchdowns, the second on a rampaging 38-yard run down the left sideline to move the Buffaloes in front in the fourth quarter, 24-21. As a senior, he was even more sensational against Alabama in the Liberty Bowl, running over and around and through the Crimson Tide defenders for 254 yards in 35 carries to wipe out the old CU school record of 238 yards by Carroll Hardy in 1954. Bob scored three touchdowns against Alabama in the most sensational performance by any back in any bowl game that season.

When Bob graduated, his name was in the CU record book in 18 different categories, the greatest one-man assault on the school records in the history of the school.

But statistics are a rather cold way to tell about a man and the story of Bob Anderson must include the warmth of his personality, his infectious enthusiasm, the driving determination which made him such a great athlete and, more importantly, such a great person. Dedication was something Bob Anderson learned early. You don't have to go back any further than his parents, Herman and Marietta, to see where his character comes from. They are warm human beings but both are tremendously, and effectively, competitive. The genes do get passed down. Their sons, Dick and Bob, are two of a kind, totally determined and totally competitive. And totally successful.

Bob was a great physical conditioner, with that rare ability to drive himself to greater condition without the aid of a coach watching over him. Dan Stavely loves to tell his freshmen the story about the time he was driving to work at six o'clock one summer morning and saw a sweat-suited person with a towel wrapped around his head running up a hill in Boulder's university hill area. As he got closer he saw that it was Bob Anderson, still in high school at the time, running with heavy lead weights attacked to his ankles. Bob did it every morning and those unattended workouts helped develop the strongest pair of legs I've ever seen and knees which were never damaged in eight seasons of high school and college football and through his first two seasons as a professional which is where his career stood as this was written. I can remember discovering Bob was back from the national semipro baseball tournament in Wichita in the summer before his sophomore season at CU by seeing him running — running not jogging — around the intramural field which adjoins Folsom Stadium. And in the winter of 1970 I took up jogging and by that June could do a mile in somewhere around nine minutes without collapsing and was somewhat proud of myself for reaching that level of performance (a level, incidentally, which I dropped from in practically no time and have never regained.) One afternoon I was wheezing around the fieldhouse track on about my second lap of an 8-lap mile when a big and somewhat familiar figure shot past me. It was right behind me in about two more laps and I looked over my shoulder to see who it was. It was Bob Anderson and he was in his third mile. Getting ready for the fall, he grinned as he slowed down momentarily to exchange greetings.

Bob Anderson is also an inspirational worker in the Fellowship of Christian Athletes and he and Dan Stavely have teamed up for a half-dozen years now to work very conscientiously in that great organization dedicated to increasing the influence of religion in young men's lives. Bob Anderson is a Christian man, one who is proud to give his testimony before groups of young people and his leadership in this most important of all walks of life eclipses all the other achievements he has attained in his relatively short career.

Another Bob Anderson quality that impresses me tremendously is his loyalty. Despite the many demands upon his time which have come with his great popularity and, I might add, also because of his great ability and charm as a speaker, he has always been extremely co-operative and available to help CU in any way he's asked. That includes fund-raising, recruiting, meetings...any type of activity. Bob Anderson always has time to help his alma mater. Not every star of his magnitude has that attitude. But, then, not many men have his character.

Bob Anderson left a lot of great scenes stamped into my memory. I can remember during that baseball trip to Hawaii in 1968 when we had been asked by Dan Stavely to look up a young man in Honolulu who was a fine college prospect he was trying to recruit by mail. Bob and I drove across Honolulu early on a Sunday morning to see the boy and his parents and what a tremendous impression Bob made on those people. And on me, too, because it was one of the first times I'd ever seen him in action without an athletic uniform on and I was amazed at the poise of this college sophomore as he visited with a group of people he had never seen before. We didn't get the young man at CU as he went to UCLA — it's tough to get Hawaiians past the west coast although we've done as well at it as any school. I can also remember vividly, Bob's response at Memphis a couple of months earlier when he had been named the outstanding player in the Bluebonnet Bowl. Bob was almost as articulate as an Adlai Stevenson in modestly giving credit to his teammates for his performance then proudly giving thanks to his parents for having given him the kind of character and upbringing which had enabled him to take advantage of his opportunities. He was tremendously sincere and tremendously impressive and no one who attended that post-game awards banquet will ever forget it, I'm sure.

On the field, many memories burst to the front of my mind when I think of Bob Anderson in action as a Buffalo. That opening game against Baylor, both his bowl games, his great efforts in two losing causes as a junior when he total offensed for 343 yards at Oklahoma State and 286 more against Air Force. But two individual plays and one game stand out in my memory.

The first play was against Oklahoma in Boulder during his junior season. CU was reeling in the face of a furious Sooner comeback which had reduced a late third quarter CU lead of 34-6 to only 34-27 with five minutes left to play. The way Oklahoma was scoring, you just knew they'd win 35-34 if they ever got the ball again. But they didn't. At least until CU had scored a clinching TD. The play I'll never forget was a fourth-and-four at the Oklahoma 16. Anderson went back to pass but couldn't find anyone open. Oklahoma's interior linemen were watching for Bobby to run because they knew he'd go for the first down if he saw the slightest opening. There was no opening but Andy went for it anyway and in one of the greatest individual efforts I've ever seen, literally ripped through a half-dozen tacklers. When they finally got him down, he was at the 10 and CU had a first down and, two plays later, the touchdown which ended Oklahoma's hopes.

The next play was also against Oklahoma, a year later in a losing effort at Norman. This time it was the Sooners who got far ahead early and the Buffaloes who almost came back to win. The Buffaloes were behind 35-23 in the fourth quarter and had the ball on a first down at the Oklahoma 17. Andy got the ball on a pitchout from Jimmy Bratten and bolted around his right end. Two Oklahoma tacklers converged on him at the three yard line but he dove for the flag and crashed into the end zone, literally flying over the top of the two defenders. It was a superhuman effort even though the Buffaloes were almost hopelessly behind with time running out. But Andy has never given up for one second in his life and he went for that end zone just as though the score was tied.

The game I remember him for was against Indiana on the first Saturday in October of his senior year. The Buffaloes had just been mauled badly at Penn State and the CU offense was almost at a standstill with only Andy an effective runner in the backfield with tailback Steve Engel injured. Penn State had concentrated on stopping Andy and did. Something needed to be done about the offense and Eddie Crowder decided to move Bobby to tailback and bring in Paul Arendt or Jimmy Bratten at quarterback to add a new dimension to the CU attack. Not many men with two years of brilliant quarterbacking behind them could have accepted the switch to a less prominent total offense spot. Bobby had 5000 yards of total offense within his reach. But moving to quarterback meant not being the primary passer any more and probably losing his shot at 5000 yards. No other back in Big Eight history had reached that plateau and a lot of magnificent men have passed through the portals of the national's finest conference. Bob's reaction to the switch was completely typical and totally predictable. I'll move to tackle if it will help the team, he replied. And meant it. Andy's performance that Saturday was typical, too.

Despite a field which had been reduced to a giant mudbath by a freak early fall snowstorm, Bob rushed for 161 yards and scored three touchdowns to lead a 30-7 victory over the first Big Ten team ever to play in Colorado. The new dimension did all right, too, as rookie Arendt made a smashing debut at quarterback, running for 72 yards, completing eight of 15 passes for 103 more yards and directing the CU attack almost flawlessly despite the miserable conditions.

And justice was served in the end, because Bob's sterling play at halfback helped the Buffaloes to a 7-3 record and the Liberty Bowl invitation. In that game, Bob's 295 yards pushed his career total to 5017 yards so he did become the first man in the history of the Big Eight to reach 5000 yards.

This, then, was Bob Anderson. A handsome, dedicated, driving, intelligent young man. Joe Romig ten years later. It's probably foolish to expect still another. But somewhere in the future there'll be a Joe Romig-Bob Anderson strapping on a pair of CU shoulder pads. I just hope I'm still around when he arrives. When he does, I'll have tri-captains for my all-time CU teams.

SOME OF THE OTHERS

When you run down a list of men which covers 25 years, you pass over a lot of good ones and tough ones and wild ones and unsung ones even though you pick three 33-man squads. Here are some who I remember but who there wasn't room for on my all-star teams. But even though they don't show up on those teams, they still show up in a special place in my memory. One reserved for all old Buffaloes and, in particular, for old Buffaloes who were something special. Here are some little men who were something special:

Woody Shelton (1950-1-2), as great an escape artist who ever zig-zagged through an open field.

Gary Nady (1955-5-6), a scrawny, slowish end who was better then he had a right to be because he was so brash and cocky that he just forced himself to be good.

Ellwin Indorf (1956-7-8), a 170-pound reserve who overcame an epileptic condition to become a fine placekicker and whose two pressure extra points against Missouri in 1956 helped the Buffaloes to a 14-14 tie which clinched an Orange Bowl berth.

Bill Elkins (1958-9-60), a 6-2, 170-pound string bean end who was as tough as any Buffalo who ever played despite being built like a refugee from a concentration camp.

Ken Vardell (1959-60-1), another under-sized Texan who came on to play well for the Buffaloes at guard despite weighing only 180.

Jim Raisis (1960-1), a furious little 173-pound fullback who was tough as they come and who came from a tough section of Pittsburgh to play well for the Buffaloes and eventually graduate from medical school.

Ed Coleman (1960-1), still another tough little halfback at 176 cut from the same cloth as a pair of men who came along after him, William Harris and Brian Foster.

Dan Patterson (1967-8-9), a 179-pound safety who never played much but who always gave it all he had, in practice or in a game, and who played well when he did get in.

Mike Bynum (1966-7-8), a 185-pound fireplug who delivered some of the hardest hits from his safety position that I've ever seen and who almost killed himself at Kansas as a senior when he smashed into Bobby Douglass.

Mel Warner (1955-6-7), a 175-pound wingback then fullback who became a fine starting center in 1957 and whose most traumatic moment came in a hilarious post-game celebration which developed into a free-for-all with some service personnel following the final game of 1956 when he took out his dental plate to keep from getting it broken and it fell off the table and somebody stepped on it and broke it and Mel was so upset that he quit fighting and sat down and cried.

Bob Boyer (1955-56), a 155-pound tailback who didn't know he was too small to be a tailback but who was a pretty good one and who later graduated from medical school.

Malcolm Miller (1947-8-9), a 166-pound halfback who was one of the first fine running backs to play for Dal Ward.

Don Evans (1944-6-7-8), a good 170-pound tailback who ranks among the finest punters we've had.

Bill Simons (1947-8-9), a 185-pounder who was one of the steadiest centers CU has ever had.

Stan Hendrickson (1941-2-7), a slashing 6-2, 172-pound end who had the sharpest elbows I've ever seen and who knocked people around like he weighed 200.

Continuing on with some of the better unsung men who have performed for CU during my time:

Jack Swigert (1950-1-2), a ski-footed 185-pound offensive guard for Dal Ward who used superior intelligence and aggressiveness to become an excellent lineman. Those same qualities also got him to the moon and back as an astronaut in 1970.

Dave Jones (1954-5-6), a squatty 5-9, 210-pound guard who was one of the veterans on the 1956 Orange Bowl champions and whose life came to a tragically early end in an auto accident just when he was building an excellent highway construction business.

Jim Howell (1957-8-9), a sleepy-eyed tackle from Montrose who came to CU with a minimum of high school fanfare and played at CU with a minimum of fanfare but who became a very solid tackle.

Frank Montera (1959-60-1), whose only flaw was bad timing because he arrived at CU at the same time as Gale Weidner and played in Gale's shadow most of the time but who played well every chance he got and who led the Buffaloes to a 21-6 win over a tough Iowa State team in 1960 when Weidner was shelved by a hip pointer.

Jerry Steffen (1958-9-60), a hard-working halfback who worked his way steadily to the top and who became a solid starter as a senior, beating out Ted Woods for the number one spot.

Frank Rogers (1963-4-5), who came to CU from Del Norte as a

quarterback but wound up as a fine wide receiver and placekicker, catching 13 passes as a senior and leading the Buffaloes in scoring with 61 points, including 13 of 17 field goals and 16 of 18 extra point kicks plus one touchdown.

Bart Bortles (1965-6-7), who was a 170-pound halfback at little Fruita High but grew up to 200 and into a tough guard for the Buffaloes.

Steve Dal Porto (1968-9-70), son of a former CU star who came as a running back but developed into a fine runner and receiver at slotback.

Bill Kralicek (1969-70-1), another solid citizen from a small Colorado town, Olathe, who put on nearly 40 pounds (to 243) while at CU and who developed into an outstanding offensive guard who was a tri-captain in 1971 and who was also a fine heavyweight wrestler for the Buffaloes.

Willie Nichols (1969-70-1), a talented young man from Pueblo who became an outstanding wide receiver for the Buffaloes and an equally-proficient infielder-outfielder for Irv Brown.

Ed Pudlik (1947-8-9), whose older brother John preceded him as a fine CU end and who was a solid all-around end himself and captained the Buffaloes as a senior.

And there were some wild men who played for the Buffaloes, good men but somewhat unpredictable:

Leroy Clark (1956-7-8), nicknamed "Crazy Horse" because he was always talking about the famous old Indian chief of that name but who was a very good fullback with the speed of a halfback and the temperament of a lefthanded pitcher. Leroy was the kind of guy who could run a punt back 70 yards, which he once did, or fumble a screen pass and have it get intercepted and run back for a touchdown, which he also did and it happened to be the touchdown that beat CU in the last game Dal Ward ever coached.

Bill Eurich (1958-9-60), a burly 220-pound tackle from Pueblo who nearly killed a little Iowa State wingback named Mickey Fitzgerald in 1960 on a kickoff return when he stuck out his arm and caught Fitzgerald just under the chin as he was about to escape on a good move. Fitzgerald skinned the cat with his neck around Eurich's brawny arm and collapsed at Bill's feet.

Gary Henson (1959-60), a devil-may-care end with great speed and hands who was a fine deep threat but whose finest moment may have come one spring vacation when he escorted three girl friends to Las Vegas and kept them all happy during their stay.

Dan Grimm (1960-1-2), a hulking 230-pound guard and tackle and linebacker who was always angry about something and who always felt like he was getting short-changed by somebody but who was a pretty good ballplayer who made it in the pros.

Tom Kresnak (1962-3-4), a good but somewhat reckless guard who captained the 1964 Buffaloes and who once was caught fishing in the artificial pond that used to be part of the May-D&F complex in downtown Denver. Tom was a great fisher and hunter and figured if there were fish in that pond, which there were, he should be able to catch one. Which he did.

Rich Varriano (1968-9-70), a swarthy, 5-8, 225-pound blockbuster who was nicknamed the "Italian Stallion" a full year ahead of Alabama's Johnny Musso and who was a very tough, aggressive defensive tackle for the Buffaloes who once lost his 1969 Liberty Bowl watch because he left it in the glove compartment of his car which somehow got driven to the bottom of one of the lakes surrounding Boulder by someone.

Roland Gregory (1946-7-8-9), an ex-paratrooper who was a rampaging fullback for the Buffaloes when a bad knee was functioning.

And closing up this list with a trio of men who ranked among the toughest of the Buffaloes I have seen:

Mel Semenko (1958-9-60), who transferred to CU from Wyoming after breaking an usher's jaw at a basketball game and who settled down to become a fine end and who graduated to return to his native Pennsylvania as a teacher. Mel dealt out a lot of punishment once he learned to hit football players not ushers.

Chuck McBride (1959-60-1), who once played a series with a broken neck and who recovered to become an outstanding offensive end on the 1961 Big Eight champions. He also was the team barber and used to give Jack Rockwell and me free haircuts in the training room. I remember that he was the only barber I've ever known who trimmed your neck with a safety razor. Rockwell wouldn't let him bring his straight-edge into the training room.

John Farler (1965-6-7), was a very good slotback and a very good placekicker who was always at his best in the clutch. John was tough and mean and never backed away from anyone and inspired his teammates with his toughness. He drilled a clutch 34-yard field goal with five minutes left to play to give CU a 10-9 win over Air Force as a junior and the next year booted three of four, including a key 3-pointer against Miami in the Bluebonnet Bowl. John had good quickness for a big (6-0, 208) slotback and he was very effective on the inside reverse. He'd have made it in the pros if his legs had held up. But they didn't.

These, then, are some of the Buffaloes who come to mind as I look back over the years. The list would be longer, I'm certain, if I went over the rosters more laboriously. But this recollection of players has been primarily one of men who come readily to mind for one reason or other. So I'll stand on it and apologize to those Buffaloes who should have been included but who weren't.

THE 25 SWEETEST SATURDAYS

There are no highs like there are in sports. Nor no lows quite like the lows. Life in an athletic department isn't exactly feast or famine because even when you're wallowing around in a drought you're still a long way from famine because you're still working in athletics and no matter how tough things get it's still a great life. And at the other extreme, the feasts can be fantastic when things are going well. There is no greater exhilaration than being part of a team which is playing well and winning. There is no greater frustration than being part of a team which is playing well but not winning as much as it should be. There is no greater disappointment than being part of a team which is not playing as well as it could. But there is no greater satisfaction then being part of a program in which every man is doing his damnedest to make it a fine one. That is, basically, the kind of a program which I have been associated with at Colorado for the past 20 years as a member of the athletic department and for five years before that as a student and-or observer. Every human being has his particular weaknesses. I certainly haven't noticed any perfect people during my time at CU although I've seen several great persons, many more than most people have been privileged to work closely with. But 95 percent of the men I've been associated with at CU have had one important quality: they have had almost endless mental and physical energy and have not hesitated to dedicate themselves totally to their job. Part of that, I realize, is because working in athletics, with and for young people, is a rewarding and satisfying effort. It's not like an 8-to-5 job overloaded with monotonous routine. And it's only natural that when a person has an enjoyable and interesting job, he spends more time on it. There is always excitement and anticipation in the atmosphere...at least there has been in the air I've been breathing for the last 20 years. There's always a new kickoff or a tipoff or a first pitch or an opening event right around the corner. Maybe all the finishes aren't all that exciting. But the start of every game or event or season is and that constant anticipation is what keeps the excitement churning.

It's a great life and it is never greater than on a Saturday afternoon in the fall. All Saturday afternoons in the fall are exciting. So are most of the evenings. In looking back over the last 25 years of CU football that I've seen, I'd like to share with you some of the sweetest Saturdays I've ever spent. I'm sure many of you have relished them as much as I have. To those of you who haven't, it has been your loss. And all I can say is that there'll be many more sweet Saturdays which you can savor if you care to join the team. I have selected the 25 games during the past 25 years which, to me, have been particularly significant. Some of the reasons are strictly personal but most of these CU victories have had great impact on the school's athletic history. It's somewhat foolish to rank them in order of their importance but I am a somewhat foolish person so I have rated the games and I'll work from the bottom to the top. This isn't meant to be a suspenseful book so if you can't stand the strain flip on ahead to the end of this section and work your way down from the top. And please note that all of these 25 games are CU victories. There isn't any way a defeat or a tie can make this list and I realize that there have been some semi-glorious ties during these 25 years. Like the 21-21 deadlock with Oklahoma in 1952 when the Buffaloes should have won but didn't as they didn't so many times during the Wilkinsonian Dynasty at Norman. And the 16-16 tie with Nebraska later that fall when Carroll Hardy ran a Cornhusker kickoff back 84 yards to the Nebraska nine to set up a tying touchdown which came with 1:33 left and every Nebraska fan and player screamed that Preacher had run behind the Husker bench on his flight down the sideline but he was going so fast that nobody really could tell. And the 19-19 draw at Missouri in 1954 when Frank Bernardi got his face bashed in blocking what would have been the winning extra point. And the 14-14 tie at Missouri in 1956 when Boyd Dowler and Frank Clarke and Ellwin Indorf teamed up to pull the Buffaloes out of a 0-14 hole to take a big step toward the Orange Bowl. But the only total satisfaction comes from winning and my sweetest Saturdays were all winning ones. After we played Washington to a 6-6 tie in Seattle to open the 1957 season, Huskie coach Jim Owens commented afterwards that playing a tie is like kissing your sister. That's an old saying but it was the first time I'd heard it and I've always thought it was a pretty good description of a tie. But enough of these preliminaries. It's time to start doubling back up and down those switchbacks which crowd the road to senility. This ride is all downhill, readers, so fasten your seatbelts and tighten your trusses!

A VERY SPECIAL PIECE OF PERSIMMON

Once upon a time, the Big Eight Skywriters, aware of my plight as a golfer, presented me with an 8 Wood, a Big 8 Wood, at the Kansas game in 1966. It is a very formidable club. Built for very unformidable golfers. I received it for being a very good guy and a very bad golfer. Laughing his head off while I unwrap it is Pete Hansson, a very good guy and a very good golfer. Out of sight behind the partition is Bob Hurt, who was then sports editor of the *Topeka Capital*, who made the presentation.

I NEVER DID MEASURE UP TOO WELL

After the 1962 Orange Bowl game, the nice people down there held a fishing derby and players and people from both CU and LSU went deep-sea fishing and, afterwards, Joe Romig and I compared our catches.

No. 25: CU 19, NEBRASKA 6 (BOULDER, OCT. 9, 1948)

There is never any time quite like the first time. No matter what you are doing. CU's first victory in the Big Eight Conference was one of the big highlights of my past quarter-century and, although I was involved only as a screaming senior in the stands, it still earns a spot on my list even though I was not part of the inside operation as I have been in every other of these 25 games.

The circumstances going into the game were not tremendously sensational. Nebraska hadn't had a winning season since its Rose Bowl year of 1940 and had just gotten clobbered by Minnesota a week earlier, 39-13. But the Cornhuskers were still living on high hopes based mostly on the heights they had attained during the 1930's when they had been one of the top football teams in the nation under D.X. Bible and Biff Jones. The 1948 team was to spiral downward to a 2-8 record but this was early in the season when even bad teams have high hopes. And besides the Cornhuskers had an All-American center named Trainwreck Tom Novak and a 240-pound tackle named Charlie Toogood who was to go on to a long and notable professional career. These two spearheaded a big Nebraska line which would supposedly be too much for a smallish CU team to handle. And if Nebraska wasn't coming off an impressive performance, neither were the Buffaloes. Rookie head coach Dal Ward's forces had just received their Big Eight indoctrination a week earlier at Kansas, getting wiped out by the Jayhawkers, 40-7, after leading 7-0 with just seven minutes left to play in the first half. And two weeks earlier at Boulder, the Buffaloes had suffered through the humiliation of a 9-6 upset to New Mexico in Ward's coaching debut. So Nebraska was an understandable two-touchdown favorite going into the game and the Cornhuskers acted the part as they casually strolled down the road from their dressing room in the men's gym to the north end zone. Led by Novak, a 204-pound stallion out of the stockyard section of south Omaha who looked even bigger and meaner in the Huskers' all-white uniforms, the Nebraskans nonchalantly rolled their headgears onto the field and got ready to administer the second Big Eight lesson to the Buffaloes.

The Buffaloes were a somewhat shabby collection of runts and war veterans and rookies and they cavorted unimpressively in pregame preparations, clad in those old gold uniforms which had all the sparkle and sheen of a thousand stacks of chips left by a departed herd of real buffaloes. But, like coach Dan Stavely always says, the only thing you can judge by how it looks is a statue . . . it's what's inside a man that counts. Colorado certainly wasn't the better physical team this day but they were in better shape mentally - Nebraska had to be looking ahead to its meeting with Notre Dame the following Saturday - and the Buffaloes got a lot of help from the Cornhuskers who were to lose three of five fumbles before their long afternoon was over. This was a confrontation between the solid, unspectacular, but very effective, single wing power attack of Ward and a gimmick-laden Husker offense prepared by Potsy Clark which featured the spread formation which Clark labeled the North Platte Spread and the South Platte Spread. The Platte river is an old, meandering stream which crawls through Nebraska and that's just about the way the Cornhuskers played that day.

The Buffaloes had only two starting linemen over 200, end John Zisch at 209 and guard Dick Stevens, 204. The rest of the CU line included Capt. Bob Spicer, 182, at the other guard; Ed Pudlik, 194, at the other end; tackles Frank Krone, 191, and Pete Thompson, 199; and center Bill Simons, 190. The starting backfield included such behemoths as quarterback John Strobel, 182; tailback Harry Narcisian, 173; wingback Malcolm Miller, 167; and fullback Don Hagin, 172. This team wouldn't have been too tough in a tug of war but they were ready to play football on this day.

A record crowd of 26,500 was in Folsom Stadium as Nebraska won the toss and chose to kick off and was promptly rocked back on its heels by a savage CU march which carried to a first and goal at the Nebraska 10 after an opening Narcisian aerial barrage which saw the stocky speedster, who was nicknamed "Roaring Twenty" because of the way he played and his uniform number, hit Zisch for a 20-yard gain to midfield then Strobel for 31 more to the 10. But the big Cornhusker line braced and stopped Narcisian on the Buffs' favorite off tackle play on fourth down from the two and took over on downs at the one.

As the first period ended, tackle Doug Nelson recovered a Nebraska fumble at the Cornhusker 40 and the Buffaloes promptly drove deep again with Miller twisting 15 yards on a reverse for a first down at the two. Three plays later it was fourth down at the two and Novak intercepted Narcisian's pass in the end zone to halt that threat. But on Nebraska's first play following the interception, halfback Cletus Fischer fumbled and Stevens recovered at the 18 and Narcisian promptly bolted 13 yards around end to the five and Hagin plunged over from the three two plays later and for the second straight week the Buffaloes were in front of a Big Eight opponent in the second quarter. That big Nebraska line then set up a 6-6 tie with 1:40 left in the half as Toogood blocked Don Evans' punt and the Huskers recovered at the CU one-foot line and scored. But CU still had its biggest explosion of the game to detonate before the end of the half. After quarterback John Ferrier passed to Pete Cook for eight yards and Hagin burst through for 14, Narcisian dropped back and hit Pudlik with a perfect pass at the five and Ed went on in to put the Buffaloes ahead at the half, 13-6.

That quick retaliation pumped new life into the Buffaloes and drained a lot out of the Cornhuskers and Nebraska never crossed midfield until late in the game after the Buffaloes had made it 19-6 early in the fourth quarter, driving 33 yards after guard Chuck Breinig's fumble recovery and scoring on a 21-yard pass play from Narcisian to Miller.

Statistical heroes for the Buffaloes were Narcisian, who had a 195-yard day on 19 rushes for 78 yards and five of eight passes for 117 yards, and Hagin who hustled for 116 yards in 25 carries and Miller who ran for 42 in 15 carries and caught a 21-yard touchdown pass.

CU was to win only two more games that fall, Narcisian turning in tremendous performances to lead the Buffaloes over Kansas State 51-7 at Homecoming and 28-14 over Utah State. But Ward's first season was made a success by that convincing 19-6 upset of the Cornhuskers. And, even more importantly, Colorado fans had been convinced quickly that CU could win in the Big Eight, a fact which Ward and his teams were to establish soundly during the next decade.

No. 24: CU 28, AIR FORCE 23 (BOULDER, NOV. 21, 1964)

This victory was significant because it marked the turning point in Eddie Crowder's young head coaching career, ending a season of frustration on a winning note and launching a period of success which saw Crowder's teams, beginning that day and over the following three seasons, win 23 games while losing but seven and tying two.

The 28-23 win over a typically sharp and aggressive Air Force team, primed for battle with the Buffaloes by the always-resourceful Ben Martin, was particularly satisfying because the Buffaloes won it despite being heavily outgained (Air Force had a 22-8 first down and a 412-170 lead in total offense.) The outcome was a reversal of most of the previous games that fall (CU was 1-8 going into this one) in which the Buffaloes had been a tough-luck team, losing five of eight games by a margin of one touchdown or less and earning the unsatisfying designation as the best 2-8 team in the country that fall. Only Southern California and Nebraska had scored as many as 21 points on the CU defense going into this game and the Buffaloes had lost such tough decisions as 14-7 to Oregon State, 16-14 to Kansas State, 14-10 to Oklahoma State, 14-11 to Oklahoma, 16-7 to Missouri and 10-7 to Kansas. In seven of the preceding nine games, CU had out-firsted downed its opponent and five times had outgained it. But the record was still 1-8 and Air Force, with a somewhat disappointing 4-4-1 record of its own after a 7-3 mark the season before, was a slight favorite at the kickoff.

Crowder's CU record in one game less than two seasons was an unimposing 3-16 and at the joint luncheon held by the two schools' boosters in Denver on Monday, a not-so-waggish Falcon wag in the audience asked Crowder if he planned on being back at CU in 1965. It was a foolish question, foolishly intended to be humorous, and superfluous because Crowder was only halfway through a 4-year contract but more than halfway through the massive CU rebuilding program. He was, in fact, through with the rebuilding. The Buffaloes were back in business and Ben Martin must have shuddered when he heard the question.

Only 26,500 fans were in the stands on a sunny but chilly 42-degree day and the game started on a sour note for the Buffaloes as Air Force drove impressively 68 yards with the opening kickoff to take a 7-0 lead, using up nearly eight minutes during the march. But the Buffaloes came right back with a march for the same distance following the next kickoff with the biggest gainer a 17-yard run off tackle to the Falcon nine by halfback Robert Lee. Fullback Ben Howe pushed over from a yard out and with less than two minutes remaining in the first quarter it was 7-7 and the battle was joined. Two possessions. Two long touchdown drives. An impressive offensive beginning. But the fireworks, mostly in the form of long CU kick returns, were still to come.

Air Force kept going and drove to the CU six from where they kicked a field goal to take a 10-7 lead with 1:18 gone in the second period. Two series later, however, CU broke Ted Somerville for a 54-yard punt return to the Falcon 21 and the Buffaloes scored in four plays from there, Lee getting the TD from the three and Frank Rogers' placement making it 14-10, the halftime score.

After Rogers hit the goal post from 44 yards out on the Buffs' first possession of the second half, George Lewark peeled off a beautiful, twisting 50-yard punt return to the Air Force 17 and on the first play Howe broke around a perfect block by Bill Symons to go all the way to make it 21-10. But Air Force struck back with a 74-yard drive, interrupted by a brawl during which CU captain Tom Kresnak and his Air Force opponent were tossed out of the game, to make it 21-16 and bring the cadet cheering corps to its feet, a position they are in most of the time anyway.

At this point, Symons, who was closing out a frustrating CU career, switched sides of the field with his fellow deep back Lee because he wanted to handle one more kickoff and he had noticed that Air

Force was kicking to the east half of the field. Symons got the kickoff at the nine and took off. Bill Fairband gave him a beautiful block at about the 20 and that was all Symons needed as it got him to the east sideline into the open and he outran the pursuit to the end zone to give the Buffaloes what appeared to be a commanding 28-16 lead with 14:45 left to play.

Air Force-CU games don't die that easily, though, and the Falcons sailed right back with a 67-yard touchdown drive to tighten the collars of CU fans. Air Force quarterback Tim Murphy was in a pure pass offense now and completed five straight in the Falcons' next possession. But the last one was a short one over the line of scrimmage and Lewark jolted the ball loose with a vicious tackle and Dave Peercy covered it at the CU 32 and the Buffaloes hung on to win, 28-23.

It was a great finish for Symons, who was awarded the game ball by his teammates. And to make it a big day for the western slope men on the team, Peercy's fumble recovery put the final clincher on the victory. Symons was from tiny Nucla, Peercy from Rifle and their play was significant in that it signaled a return to key roles in Colorado victories by young men from the state. Colorado men have always been important to CU athletic teams and it was only fitting that the men who engineered this victory were Coloradoans. Like, in addition to Symons and Peercy, Somerville (Greeley), Lewark (Lakewood), quarterback Bernie McCall (Yuma), center Steve Sidwell (Denver), tackles Stan Irvine (Denver) and Jerry McClurg (Grand Junction), ends Ray LeMasters and Dick Taylor (Pueblo) and Rogers (Del Norte.)

Yes, the Buffaloes were back! And back, healthily, with a fine sophomore cast ready to move ahead in 1965. And the voice from the crowd was noticably silent the following Monday as Crowder accepted the CU-AFA trophy at the Monday luncheon.

No. 23: CU 7, OKLAHOMA 0 (BOULDER, OCT. 29, 1960)

This was the victory that CU fans had been awaiting since the Buffaloes entered the Big Eight and began meeting Oklahoma annually in 1950. It had been a frustrating series with only the 21-21 tie in 1952 to show for Colorado's efforts. Ten straight times the Buffaloes had gone down to defeat and, in the majority of these games, the defeats were bitterly disappointing ones which more often than not sent the Buffs plummeting into a season-ending tailspin. Those nosedives ultimately did Dal Ward in and so it was with extreme irony that he was not on the sideline as head coach when the victory finally came. But the last freshman team which he and his staff had recruited for CU was on the scene, as the seniors who led the victory, a 7-0 mild upset - the Sooners were only a half-point favorite at the kickoff.

The 1960 Oklahoma team was far from the powerhouses that Wilkinson had put together during the previous decade when he had dominated college football. It was only 2-2-1 going into this sixth game of the season. But it had served notice on the Big Eight that it would not yield its championship lightly, hammering Kansas State into 49-7 submission the previous Saturday. Colorado, meanwhile, had ticked off four straight impressive victories after an opening loss to Baylor and only the magic of Wilkinson's name kept the Buffaloes from going into the game as the favorites.

It was, however, a typically alert, opportunistic and aggressive Wilkinson team and the CU victory did not come easily even though the Sooners were to skid to a 3-6-1 record that season. The Buffaloes built a solid statistical edge: 17-7 in first downs, with 16 of CU's coming on the ground, as Gale Weidner passed only five times, and 267-193 in total offense. The CU hero was fullback Chuck Weiss, who led all runners with 75 yards in 22 carries and scored the game's only touchdown and, just as importantly, made the game's biggest single defensive play.

That play came late in the third period on this dark, gloomy afternoon when Oklahoma's reserve quarterback, Bennett Watts, broke open down the east sideline on a keeper play from the Sooner 14. Weiss, showing almost unbelievable speed and a perfect pursuit angle, burst through two Oklahoma blockers and knocked Watts out of bounds at the CU 17 after a 69-yard gallop. The Sooners promptly moved to a first down at the five but linebacker Joe Romig led a fierce goal line stand, making two key tackles with captain Bill Elkins getting the third and Jerry Steffen jarring the ball loose from the receiver on a fourth-down pass. That broke the back of the Oklahoma effort and the Sooners never threatened again as Steffen and Ed Coleman led a punishing CU ball control attack which moved from the four to the Sooner 39 in 13 time-consuming plays before Chuck McBride punted dead on the Sooner eight with only seven minutes left to play.

The Buffaloes had started the game as though they were going to have a big offensive day, driving from the CU 27 to the Sooner nine with a Bill Eurich recovery of a fumbled punt keeping the drive alive. But they stalled and Jerry Hillebrand missed a 30-yard field goal attempt. The Buffaloes then got the lone TD of the game with a 61-yard drive in 15 plays to score with 5:33 left in the first half. Weiss, behind the fine blocking of Tom Wilscam and Chuck Pearson, was the workhorse in the march, carrying the ball seven times and going over from the one for the score after the Sooners had stopped he and Weidner on successive tries from that point. The getaway gainer which launched the drive was a 12-yard burst by Ted Woods and two spectacular catches by Hillebrand kept it alive. The first was a catlike grab of a deflection for a seven-yard gain to the Oklahoma 19 on a fourth-and-four play and the second was a leaping spear of a high throw from Weidner with Jerry getting possession just before his momentum carried him out of bounds at the one. It was a 13-yard play.

And so an amazing Sooner Big Eight string came to an end. It was the first time a Wilkinson-coached Oklahoma team had ever been shut out in conference play and only the Sooners' second Big Eight loss in 14 seasons under Bud's direction.

CU heroes? They were all over the field. There was Weiss and Steffen and Woods and Coleman and Dave Rife and Eurich and Pearson and Wilscam and Hillebrand and McBride. But the man around whom the Buffalo defense revolved was iron man Romig, who played the entire 60 minutes with his usual ferocity and was the first man to hit the ballcarrier 10 times and got assists on six other tackles.

The jubilation over the victory was dampened somewhat at the Monday meeting of the Denver Buff Club when Sonny Grandelius snapped at Rocky Mountain News columnist Leonard Cahn publicly for hinting in his Monday morning column that Dal Ward deserved some of the credit for the victory for recruiting the seniors on the team. After his brief verbal attack, Sonny stalked out of the room, turning over the mopup duties to Buck Nystrom. The column by Leonard, one of the best football writers I've ever read and a man who always gets his facts straight, was properly sentimental and properly accurate. Sonny's outburst was simply a sign of the times. A good man had been fired two years earlier because he couldn't beat Oklahoma although he almost always came close. And when the long-awaited victory finally came, that man was instructing volley ball classes and teaching golf in the physical education school instead of standing on the sideline. A lot of us felt sad because Dal was not the first man to lead a CU team to victory over Oklahoma. But that feeling didn't detract from the flush of the victory. It was a truly Sweet Saturday. But it would undoubtedly have been much sweeter had it come a few years earlier against one of those Sooner powerhouses.

And mentioning Leonard Cahn brings up some of the other sportswriters who have covered the Buffaloes during my time. There have, literally, been more Denver Post sports editors than I can remember but Harry Farrar, who served a double hitch on that treadmill to oblivion, was the finest master of the written word I've ever known around these parts (he ought to assemble a collection of his best columns as a book) and George Franco was as good a friend and as effective a running mate as I've ever had and Chuck Garrity was as sound a newspaper man as I've ever been around. And Frank Haraway who has done most of the CU game stories since 1956 is the nicest, most enthusiastic, good writer I've ever seen, always bubbling over with energy and pleasantness, like anyone lucky enough to be covering sports ought to be. And Chester Nelson, one of the real old pros in the country, has been a sports editor as long as anybody alive, I guess, and a good one who I was privileged to observe in action at close quarters, not only as a before-and-after-dark ally on many road trips when he was covering the Buffaloes but as an employee during the summers of 1955-6-7 when I moonlighted as a fill-in night worker at the Rocky Mountain News. And his longtime assistant who has recently succeeded him, Bob Collins, is truly one of the finest and nicest and gentlest persons I've ever known and maybe the best newspaper man. Bob used to catch us for one trip every year, either to Iowa State or Nebraska, and having him with us was a real delight.

The reason the News let him out of the slot, where he is a genuine master at ripping apart pages and putting them back together and making every edition with a new sports section, was to let him get back home. Bob is a native Iowan who married a girl from Omaha so the Iowa State and Nebraska trips were naturals for him. But one year he went to Iowa with the Air Force and the Falcons tied one of Forest Evashevski's greatest teams in a huge upset and Bob wrote an award-winning story about the game and, after that, just had to become the Air Force football regular so we haven't seen him in our press box as much as we would have liked. Two other men who have not covered CU football but who I respect greatly as football writers are Dick Connors of the Post, who I first knew when he was a fellow sports publicist at Regis College, and Dave Nelson, one of my former student assistants at CU who escaped from my influence to become a solid regular at the News. At the Boulder Camera, Don Ceiber and Lu Monroe were doing CU football when I arrived and both were dedicated CU loyalists. Don was one of Frank Potts' former quartermilers and a good one and a fine newspaper man who did a lot of things besides being sports editor of the Camera and who soon moved up and out and is now one of the top men in the business department of the Denver Post. Monroe has long been a great friend and he has helped me as much as any person in Boulder and he is probably the number one CU football fan of all time and I was sorry to see him retire from the newspaper scene in 1970 but he had certainly earned the right to take it easy although you always hate to see a good horse put himself to pasture no matter how hard or how long or how well he has worked. And Lu was a very good horse. Howard Baxter has been sports editor of the Camera since 1954 and he is a great friend and one of the nicest guys I've ever met and a very sound editor and an exceptionally dedicated and thorough and good track and field writer but a very ordinary horseshoe pitcher who I have conquered more often than not despite the fact that he once won a lower classification championship in a city tournament. The best young sportswriter in the country today, and I'll match him against anyone young or old, is Dan Creedon, the Buddha-like fountain of information and ability who now covers the Buffaloes for the Camera. I first knew Dan back in 1958 when he succeeded Dave Nelson as my student assistant. Dan was as bright and able a student helper as I've ever had and his star has risen steadily as a sportswriter, first with the Grand Junction Sentinel and, since 1962, as Howard Baxter's strong right arm at the Camera. Big Dan can do it all. He has a deep knowledge of every sport and almost limitless energy. And tremendous perception. He would be great anywhere but I hope he elects to confine his career to Boulder and that he always covers the Buffaloes. There have been lots of others who have been good friends and allies but these are the ones who have been especially significant along the trail of the last 25 years and the men who I wanted to publicly acknowledge in this stroll through the high spots of this past quarter-century.

No. 22: CU 53, AIR FORCE 17 (BOULDER, NOV. 20, 1971)

I liked this game very much because it was a fitting finish to a great season and one in which the most exciting and explosive team in CU history put on a tremendously exciting and explosive exhibition to whip an outmanned Air Force team which made a game battle of it for nearly two quarters but finally wore down. Going in, the Buffaloes were 8-2 and coming back after a mid-season sag in which some injuries to key linemen contributed to losses to Oklahoma and Nebraska and the Falcons had a good looking record although five of those victories were against such 1971 gridiron have-nots as Wyoming, SMU, Colorado State, Army and Tulsa. But Ben Martin teams can always crank up for a big game and the Falcons, earlier in the year, had come within seconds of upsetting a Penn State team which was to trounce Texas in the Cotton Bowl on New Year's Day. So it figured to be an interesting game and one the Buffaloes could win. But only if they played somewhere near to their potential. You don't take naps and beat the Air Force.

The Buffs got a quick 7-0 lead when John Tarver covered 28 yards in two carries after Herb Orvis had caused a Falcon fumble which Chris Havens recovered at the AFA 32. Ken Johnson gave the cadets a scoring opportunity by losing a fumble on the Air Force 45 and the Falcons got a field goal out of it and it was only 7-3 at the quarter with neither team showing any great ability to sustain a drive.

Johnson then hit his slotback, Larry Brunson, on a crossing pattern and Brunson laid a couple of great moves on two Falcon deep men and it was good for a 55-yard touchdown and it looked like the Buffaloes might be on their way. But, hold up! Air Force stunned CU with a 50-yard bomb from quarterback Rich Haynie to flanker Frank Murphy and it was 13-10 almost before the CU fans had had time to screw the caps back down on their coolers. The Buffs gave their followers lots more opportunities to hoist their canteen cups before the end of the half, though, as Charlie Davis dashed 17 yards in two plays for a third touchdown and Cliff Branch fled down the east sidelines for 34 yards on his pet reverse to make it 27-10 at the half.

Air Force drove 50 yards to draw first blood in the second half but that was all they could produce in the face of a CU barrage which included touchdowns by tight end J. V. Cain on an 11-yard pass play from Johnson, a 30-yard sortie by Davis, a terrific twisting 65-yard punt return by Branch in a perfectly breathtaking final display of his open field running ability and sensational speed, and a closing one-yard smash by sophomore fullback Bo Matthews.

The win gained the Buffaloes an invitation to the Astro-Bluebonnet Bowl and the 46,362 fans who almost filled Folsom Stadium raised CU's home attendance total to a record 220,782. It was indeed a sweet Saturday to end a sweet season. The Buffalo offense had ripped out 556 yards, 352 on the ground and 204 by air, and a 26-15 first down advantage with the incomparable Davis following up his 341-yard effort against Oklahoma State a week earlier with 196 yards against the Falcons and Tarver closing out his regular season career with his biggest afternoon, 139 yards and Johnson passing for 130 and Branch running back five punts and one kickoff for a total of 168 yards in addition to his lone scrimmage carry of 34 yards.

No. 21: CU 45, KANSAS STATE 32 (BOULDER, NOV. 22, 1969)

This was Bobby Anderson's final home game and was against the surprise team of the Big Eight that year, Kansas State which had used the deadly right arm of Lynn Dickey and the jackrabbit running and receiving of little Mac Herron to jolt Oklahoma 59-21 and take the conference co-champions right down to the wire before losing (to Missouri 41-38 and to Nebraska 10-7). It figured to be a wild battle and it turned out to be one of the wildest ever played in Folsom Stadium. To add to the tension, the winner would receive the Liberty Bowl bid to play Alabama.

It was one of the longest games ever played and was finished in near-darkness as the Wildcats passed an amazing 63 times with Dickey throwing the ball 61 times and completing 28 for an eyepopping

439 yards. Buffalo quarterback Jimmy Bratten didn't have too bad a day himself, completing 11 of 21 for 251 yards. Both quarterbacks threw two touchdown passes including one each in the opening 28 seconds of play in the most electrifying exchange of touchdowns I've ever seen to begin a game. And when the smoke had cleared from a pair of offensive explosions which totalled 903 yards (459 by K-State and 444 by CU) it required a roughing the kicker penalty on an over-committed Kansas State lineman (and perhaps a skillful bit of acting by CU punting specialist Dick Robert who had one of his finest days as a kicker with a 42-yard average) late in the game to keep a CU drive to a clinching touchdown alive and also keep red-hot Kansas State from gaining possession with plenty of time remaining and behind by only six points.

The game began with an unusual pair of CU bombs. The first one thrown from halfback by Anderson in his first pass since he was moved to halfback in the third game of the season. Andy barely missed Marv Whitaker for what would have been a touchdown, then, on the next play, broke wide open down the middle to take a perfect toss from Bratten for a 44-yard touchdown. Dave Haney's extra point made it 7-0 with just 14 seconds played. K-State only needed one play, a 70-yard bomb from Dickey to his flanker Chuck Collins, to make it 7-7. Time elapsed in the game: 28 seconds!

After that spectacular opening, there was no further scoring in the period but the two teams got hot again in the next one as Bratten hit slotback Steve Dal Porto for a 30-yard TD with Dal Porto taking the ball on the dead run as he crossed the goal line. K-State seemed to react violently to CU touchdowns. This time they broke Henry Hawthorne for 60 yards on the following kickoff then went the remaining 25 yards in six plays to tie it again.

Bratten, more than holding his own against Dickey in these first 30 minutes, promptly hit Whitaker for a 31-yard play after Steve Engel had returned the kickoff 47 yards to midfield and the Buffaloes were quickly at the K-State 20 and Anderson got his second touchdown from four yards out five plays later to give the Buffaloes a nervous 21-14 lead which they stretched to 28-14 by halftime on a 7-play, 83-yard drive started by Bratten's deep completion to Monte Huber for 62 yards all the way to the Wildcat 21. Huber got the TD from the three on a deep reverse, going into the end zone at the southeast flag with just 41 seconds left in the half.

Running was almost non-existent in that first half as K-State passed for 242 yards and CU for 201. On the ground they had 35 and 63 yards, respectively. The third quarter was relatively calm with the Cats getting a field goal near the end of it then making it 28-24 on a

15-yard Dickey touchdown pass. The Buffaloes rammed right back with an 80-yard march with Anderson getting his third TD from the one early in the fourth quarter after the drive had gotten rolling with a 26-yard Bratten-Huber completion, a 20-yard sprint by Engel and a series of short, jolting thrusts by both Anderson and fullback Ward Walsh. When Jim Cooch intercepted a Dickey pass and returned it 18 yards to the Wildcat 15 from where Haney kicked a field goal to make it 38-24 with 9:44 left, it looked as though the Buffaloes might have that Liberty Bowl berth sacked up.

But Dickey was just getting warmed up. He completed five straight passes for 76 yards and a touchdown then hit a 2-point conversion and it was 38-32 with 7:50 left. The Wildcat ace was red hot and everyone of the 37,400 fans present just knew that he'd get the Cats into the end zone again for a 39-38 lead if they could only get the ball back. And just when it appeared as though they had, with the Buffaloes punting on fourth and one from their own 28, an overanxious Wildcat deflected Robert as he was getting a 50-yard punt away. Robert did a cartwheel, the referee flipped his flag and the Buffaloes were still in business with a first down at the 43. CU didn't score but they chopped valuable time off the clock with Walsh ripping out good gains to move to a third and four at the 16. But Bratten misfired on a pitchout to Engel and K-State recovered the loose ball at the 28 and Dickey was still alive. But the Buffaloes, knowing he had to pass on every down, put on a wild rush led by Orvis and Bill Brundige and Dickey completed only one of seven and was wiped out once by Orvis for an 11-yard loss and the Buffaloes took over on downs at the Wildcat 32 and scored in four plays, three of them keepers by Bratten, the score coming on a 20-yard whirl through the secondary by the scrappy CU quarterback.

It was all over. CU was in the Liberty Bowl. Dickey and Bratten had limp right arms. The Folsom Stadium scoreboard was about to blow a fuse. And there was a lot of worn down sod in both end zones. And Saturday night was as sweet as any Saturday night ever was.

No. 20: CU 41 IOWA STATE 34 (BOULDER, OCT. 31, 1953)
This was another game with a wild start except that it was the Cyclones of Abe Stuber and, in particular, a little 147-pound scooter named Gary Lutz, who provided most of the opening fireworks. Lutz literally tortured the Buffaloes with 131 rushing yards and a 37-yard pass reception. It took great afternoons by CU's touchdown twins, Carroll Hardy and Frank Bernardi, to finally overcome an Iowa State start which, if you can believe it, saw the Cyclones jump in front 21-7 in less than 10 minutes with CU putting the ball in play from

scrimmage only twice during that period of time.

The barrage went like this. Iowa State received the kickoff and drove 79 yards with Lutz scoring from the four. CU's Ronnie Johnson took the kickoff and raced 97 yards to tie the score. Iowa State scored in three plays following the CU kickoff with Lutz racing 22 yards to midfield and quarterback Bill Plantan passing to end Kim Tidd for a 50-yard TD. Bernardi lost a yard on the Buffaloes' first scrimmage play and lost the ball on the second. Iowa State recovered his fumble at the CU 41 and scored in two plays, the second a 37-yard pass from Plantan to Lutz. And so it was 21-7 with only 9:34 played.

But CU maintained its poise and, with Hardy going right and Bernardi reversing back to the left and fullback Don Shelley ripping up the middle, drove 80 yards to make it 21-13. CU came right back with a 64-yard drive capped by Bernardi's pass off the wingback reverse to Gary Knafelc for a 31-yard touchdown and it was 28-20 at the half. There had been 10 possessions in the first 30 minutes. Seven resulted in touchdowns and CU was on the Cyclone 30 with a second down when the half ended.

The Buffaloes did the exploding to start the second half. On the first play, Bernardi broke open on the reverse and fled 46 yards and Hardy's conversion drew the Buffs to within one point, 28-27. Bernardi promptly intercepted a Plantan pass and returned it 18 yards to the Cyclone 30. One the first play, Ronnie Johnson threw off the double reverse and hit wide open Knafelc for a 30-yard TD and Roger Hunt booted the extra point. CU led, 34-28, with only 3:29 gone in the third quarter. Iowa State tied it early in the fourth quarter as Lutz sparked an 89-yard drive with runs of 12 and 28 yards to get the Cyclones out of the hole. Plantan's kick missed, though, and it was 34-34 with 14:17 left in the game and both defenses slightly punchy by this time.

At this point, though, the defenses tightened up. Or maybe the two offenses were leg-weary. Whatever, there was no further scoring going into the final three minutes and it looked like it might wind up in a tie. But the touchdown twins had one more salvo left. Bernardi returned a punt five yards to the Iowa State 46 as the clock ticked into the final 2:30. Then Hardy broke open on a double reverse and looked like he might go all the way. But he cut to the inside and was chopped down from the side after a 19-yard gain. Bernardi then swung around on the wingback reverse and looped a perfect pass to Knafelc, good for 10 yards to the 17. Now Hardy took the snap from center Dave Hill, stepped back and faked a pass, then headed off tackle. He shot through an opening and broke to the west sideline and literally disappeared down the sideline with his tremendously explosive speed. There was 1:22 left to play and that score finally decided the game.

It was a typical performance in the lives of CU's touchdown twins who were to become the All-Big Eight halfbacks a year later. Bernardi finished the game with 104 yards in 12 carries, hit three of four passes for 45 more and caught one for 17 yards. Hardy had 103 yards in 17 carries, completed one of five passes for 25 yards and punted once for 39 yards. Iowa State netted 448 yards of total offense; CU got 395. And, for CU fans, it was a sour beginning but a sweet finish. And sweet finishes are very important parts of Sweet Saturdays.

No. 19: CU 24, OKLAHOMA STATE 0 (BOULDER, SEPT. 30, 1961)

After two straight near misses into a bowl in Sonny Grandelius' first two seasons at CU, 1961 was a fall filled with promise. The Buffaloes had dropped a frostbitten 14-12 game in icy Lincoln in 1959 and missed an Orange Bowl bid which would have accompanied a victory. A year later they were 6-1 when injuries or illness wiped out both starting guards, Joe Romig (broken hand) and Tom Wilscam (hepatitis) and both starting halfbacks, Dave Rife and Jerry Steffen (leg injuries). Badly crippled by these losses, the Buffs lost three of their last four games to finish 6-4, although a later decision changed the record to 7-3 when Kansas had to forfeit its game because of the use of an ineligible player. Now 1961 was here and the Buffaloes had a veteran team with a record of success and CU entered the Big Eight season as one of the favorites, along with a strong Kansas squad and a suddenly-potent Missouri under Dan Devine.

The Buffaloes had to come out at full speed because they opened the season with two tough conference games. The opener was against Oklahoma State followed by the big early season matchup with Kansas. Both games were scheduled for Folsom Stadium and CU fans licked their lips in anticipation. And no team ever came out with all guns blazing any better than the Buffaloes did against the Cowboys who were in their second season under Cliff Speegle.

Oklahoma State won the toss and that was the last thing they won on this sparkling 57-degree September afternoon. After three plays, the Cowboys punted to CU and the Buffaloes started from their own 34 after Eddie Coleman's 11-yard return. On CU's fifth play of the game, Gale Weidner pinpointed Jerry Hillebrand with a perfect strike. The play covered 40 yards and Hillebrand scored untouched. Time elapsed was 3:27.

After three plays gained only nine yards, the Cowboys kicked again. This time Ted Woods took it at the 20, stepped back to the 18, found his lane and blasted 82 yards up the east sideline, literally running away from the pursuit. Hillebrand's second conversion made it 14-0 and only 5:47 had been played.

Oklahoma State ran three more plays and punted, this time to a sophomore CU back, Leon Mavity, who was handling the ball for the first time as a collegian. Mavity caught it at the 40 and zig-zagged 60 yards in a beautiful broken field run in which he left five tacklers groping in his wake. Now it was 21-0 and only 8:10 had spun off the scoreboard clock. The Buffaloes had detonated three long scoring plays in their last three plays and had netted 182 yards in a period of less than five minutes. It was a blitzkreig worthy of Hitler's legions and served notice on the Big Eight that the CU threat was for real.

The Buffaloes didn't score any more touchdowns on this afternoon. But big Hillebrand put a fitting finish on the impressive opening day performance by drilling a 54-yard field goal midway through the second quarter. It was the longest 3-pointer in the nation that fall. The CU defense effectively choked off every OSU scoring attempt, intercepting four passes among other things with two of the beefy CU linemen, tackle John Denvir and guard Ralph Heck each getting one and backs Loren Schweninger and Coleman also coming up with one each. It was a proper beginning to a championship. The Buffaloes never got off that explosively again although they finished almost as impressively a week later. But that's the story of another Sweet Saturday.

No. 18: CU 21, NEBRASKA 16 (LINCOLN, OCT. 21, 1967)

Most of the games on this list so far have been wild offensive exchanges. This one was for the defense and the CU defense is what won this game, the Buffaloes' fifth straight triumph of 1967 and one which lifted them into third place in both national polls. The CU defense certainly didn't rest much on this afternoon. Among other things, the Buffaloes intercepted four passes and recovered four fumbles to save a day in which the CU offense, minus several starters, could gain only 182 yards as compared to Nebraska's 402. But such unlikely heroes as Jeff Raymond and Mike Veeder came up with long TD runs following interceptions and the Buffaloes escaped with a tense victory.

Nebraska opened the scoring midway through the first quarter, recovering a Bob Anderson fumble and going 42 yards to take a 7-0 lead. The Buffaloes got a big break when Nebraska gambled on fourth and one at its own 29 and the middle of the CU line with Ron Scott leading the charge stopped quarterback Frank Patrick cold and linebacker Kerry Mottl drove the ball out of his hands and sophomore linebacker Steve Blair recovered it. Anderson promptly rolled out for 10 yards and, on the fifth play, halfback Larry Plantz sprinted around left end for six yards and the tying touchdown. CU took a 14-7 halftime lead as Dick Anderson intercepted a Patrick pass on his own 30, threaded his way up the east sideline to the 50, flipped the ball to Veeder as he was being tackled and the big defensive end then rambled the remaining 50 yards with the help of a great block by Mottl. Pass interference by Ike Howard gave the Cornhuskers a first and goal at the CU four with time for just one play left in the half. But big Frank Bosch jarred the ball loose and fell on the ball at the goal line as the half ended with CU nursing its slender lead.

Nebraska drove 80 yards following the third quarter kickoff and sent Joe Orduna flying into the end zone from 27 yards out but Dick Anderson broke through to block the extra point kick and CU still led, 14-13. Nebraska came ripping right back on its next possession, moving from its own 19 to the CU 33, mostly on a 34-yard pass play with the 6-7 Patrick hitting halfback Ben Gregory. On second-and-eight at the 33, however, Patrick flipped a short pass into his right flat. Raymond, who was playing defensive left halfback in place of Charles Greer, who had suffered a slight concussion late in the first half and who did not play in the second half, timed his move perfectly and intercepted in front of the intended receiver and sped 76 yards to make the score 21-13 and give the Buffaloes a bit of breathing room. Nebraska countered with a fourth period field goal and threatened again on its next possession but Orduna fumbled on a first down play at the CU 14 and Mottl pounced on the ball. The Huskers got to the CU 36 following William Harris' punt but Raymond came up with his second interception. And on the Cornhuskers' final possession of the game, at their own 49, Tom Kmetovic intercepted a desperation Patrick pass and ran it back 28 yards as the game ended.

It was a valiant effort by the defense and Mottl and Anderson were the ringleaders. Kerry got five unassisted tackles and was in on three assists in addition to his big fumble recovery and key block for Veeder. Anderson made five unassisted tackles, got eight assists, blocked the extra point kick, intercepted the pass to launch CU's second TD and batted down another pass. It was a Sweet Saturday, the only one the Buffaloes enjoyed against a Bob Devaney Nebraska team in his first 10 years at the Cornhusker controls. But it proved to be a costly triumph for CU as several regulars were injured and their absence sent the Buffaloes into a 2-game tailspin which knocked them out of the national rankings. Nobody was anticipating the following Saturday's Homecoming upset at the hands of lowly Oklahoma State, though, and it was a sweet plane ride back to Denver and a Sweet Saturday night.

No. 17: CU 13, BAYLOR 7 (WACO, SEPT. 24, 1966)

This one was another victory for the defense. More importantly, this game marked the biggest victory to date for an Eddie Crowder-coached CU team, coming over a fine Baylor squad which was ranked tenth nationally going into the game. And, just as critically, the victory turned CU's fortunes around after a bad start and started the Buffaloes to a fine 7-3 record. Baylor, behind the four touchdown passes of quarterback Terry Southall, had humbled mighty Syracuse on national TV two weeks earlier, 35-12, completely dominating a team which had been ranked nationally in pre-season polls. Southall's pinpoint passing had humiliated Syracuse and its great All-American halfback Floyd Little. But it was Southall who was the toast of the national TV audience after the game. CU, meanwhile, had faltered badly in its opening assignment against Miami in Boulder a week later, crumbling 24-3 after taking a 3-0 lead into the second quarter. It was an error-filled performance by an experienced Buffalo squad which had entered the 1966 opener with high hopes after building a 6-2-2 record the preceding fall. Going into the night game at Waco, then, Baylor was riding high and the Buffaloes were faced with the problem of bouncing back. Baylor fans, enveloped in the longest championship drought in the history of the Southwest Conference, were understandably, if somewhat prematurely, enthusiastic about their team. Despite the fact that the season was only one-game old, a giant banner which announced, "On to the Cotton Bowl!" spanned Waco's main street to greet the Buffaloes when they arrived. The Bears had momentum. But the Buffs had some adrenalin flowing for them, too, most of it the quietly desperate determination of good men with their backs against the wall. So the battle lines were formed. Baylor's wide open aerial attack matched against a hard-hitting Colorado defense built by two masters of defense, Crowder and his chief assistant Rudy Feldman. The Buffaloes were not an explosive offensive team. Rather they were a powerful, crunching team which moved grindingly behind a fine junior-dominated line. The principal backs were Bernie McCall, William Harris, John Farler and Wilmer Cooks - all power runners rather than will-o-the-wisp types.

The game began quietly in the gloom of the Southwest's biggest burial ground for football coaches. The Buffaloes got into trouble early as they got no further out than the 12 with the opening kickoff then gave the ball to the Bears at the CU 47 on a short punt by Dan Kelly. But a third down play from the 41 indicated the kind of night it was going to be for Southall. Ronnie Scott came charging through the pocket and dumped the stocky Baylor passer for a 9-yard loss. Before the night was over, he would turn the ball over five times, once by fumble and four times on interceptions. After another short Kelly punt, Baylor started from the CU 35. But on the first play, the Bears fumbled and big Sam Harris, who along with his running mate at defensive end Bill Fairband played an outstanding game, picked the ball out of the air to get the Buffaloes out of their early jam. A series later, Harris leaped high at the line of scrimmage to deflect a Southall pass attempt then caught the ball before it hit the ground to set up a CU threat at the Bear 32. An interception stopped the Buffaloes but Fairband promptly nailed Southall for a 10-yard loss back to the 11 and CU took advantage of its field position following the punt to drive 47 yards in six plays with Farler quick-stepping 23 yards on an inside reverse to score and Dave Bartelt adding the extra point. But Southall found the range following the kickoff and hit four straight passes to lead a 72-yard drive which tied the score on his perfectly floated lob pass into the far corner of the end zone for a 10-yard TD.

There was no score in the third period although Baylor had to stop Cooks on fourth-and-two at the five after Frank Bosch had recovered a Southall fumble at the Bear 46 to set up that deep penetration. Bosch got the Buffaloes headed goalward again early in the fourth as he made a diving stab of a Southall pass which had been batted down just off his hands by the flailing Fairband. Bosco got it at the Bear 27 and McCall quickly hit fleet little Larry Plantz for a 24-yard completion to the one from where Cooks mashed into the end zone. But Bartelt's extra point kick wafted weakly into the air and fell futilely short of the goal posts. There was still 12:08 left and the Buffaloes, with that precarious 6-point lead, faced the full fury of a Baylor counterattack.

It came quickly as Southall passed and ran to take the Bears to a first down at the CU 17. But Hale Irwin, Dennis Drummond and Ike Howard came up with good defensive plays in the secondary and the Buffaloes survived that threat. When Irwin intercepted and returned 48 yards to the Baylor 30 a few minutes later, the Buffaloes appeared to be out of trouble. But Bartelt missed a 34-yard field goal try and Southall had one last chance, starting from the 20. Three completions and an interference call on Steve Graves moved the Bears to the CU 31 with 1:08 remaining. At that point, Baylor came up with a wild trick play which involved a double reverse followed by a lateral to Southall who threw into the end zone. Baylor's fleet flanker, Paul

Beckton, appeared to have caught the ball for a touchdown and one quick-triggered official did, in fact, signal a touchdown. But Beckton couldn't control the ball and it bounced into the air where it was pawed frantically by both Irwin and Graves with the latter making a shoestring interception to preserve the CU victory.

It was the most magnificent moment in the football career of Graves, an obscure battler from Estes Park who was one of the scores of good athletes who work their way through their athletic careers without great fanfare but always do their job and, accordingly, fill a vital role for their team. It was a magnificent evening for the Buffaloes, too, as they redeemed themselves after the preceding Saturday's great disappointment against Miami. This 1966 crew almost became Crowder's first bowl team but just missed out in the shuffling which goes on each December as the bowl pairings are made. And it was a Sweet Saturday for all of us in Waco. It was a somewhat memorable evening for me, too, because it marked my debut as a color announcer for my great friend John Henry who was doing the play-by-play for KOA then. John pressed me into service as an extra pair of eyes, weak as they were, to help him in the shadows of Baylor stadium. I worked with John for four seasons, including 1969 when we became the Lame Duck Network as John and KOA parted company. My broadcast career came to a halt less then two seasons later when an oversupply of enthusiasm and an undersupply of talent combined to do me in and bring about my demise as color man for another great buddy, Jim Kithcart the voice of the Colorado Network, with whom I'd first worked with in 1965. I've worked with many other fine broadcasters in off-the-air capacities, including Starr Yelland, the dean of CU play-by-play men and a great friend and ally in and out of the press box and at home or on the road; Pete Hansson, who came to KBOL about the same time I went to work for CU and who has remained one of my dearest friends despite moving out of the broadcast business several years ago; Pete Smythe, another great friend and one of the most loyal of the CU loyalists who did some color work for John Henry in addition to his daily work for the Buffaloes and his Tincup Titans on his KOA early morning General Store show; Don Roper, another good play-by-play alumnus of KBOL; and a current crew of very able KOA sportscasters which includes the impeccable Bob Martin, the suave Bob Rubin and the lively Larry Zimmer. Not to mention such old off-the-air radio friends as Bill Day, Bob Seymour, Ned High, Don Lee, Roger Cracraft and a lot of other good men who have done a lot of the important behind-the-scenes work in CU football broadcasts.

No. 16: CU 38, KANSAS STATE 14 (BOULDER, NOV. 20, 1954)

This victory is memorable because it marked the farewell performance of Frank Bernardi and Carroll Hardy and what an unforgettable farewell it was as the greatest halfback combination in CU history led an offensive onslaught which completely buried a fine Kansas State team which would have earned an Orange Bowl bid with a victory. It had been another close-but-no-cigar season for the Buffaloes who had reeled off five straight lopsided triumphs before sagging in mid-season when a serious back condition sidelined Dal Ward for nearly a month, reducing his coaching contribution tremendously. And inasmuch as Ward ran practically a one-man coaching show, his absence hurt the Buffalo preparations badly despite the valiant efforts of his assistants, Ray Jenkins, Marsh Wells, Frank Prentup and Hugh Davidson. The Buffaloes were upset by Nebraska 20-6 then dropped a typically tough decision to Oklahoma a week later, 13-6, after leading 6-0 going into the fourth quarter. Those two conference losses knocked them out of the Orange Bowl berth which would go to the Big Eight runnerup that year. Nebraska would go unless Kansas State whipped the Buffaloes in the season finale in Boulder. Wildcat fans streamed into Boulder to boost the bid of Bill Meek's men and the K-State band even had gone so far as to put a specially-written Orange Bowl march into their halftime routine.

But most of the marching on this beautiful 59-degree late-fall afternoon was done by the Buffaloes. Aside from the sad march back to Manhattan for the wilted Wildcats and their fans who could now look forward to an unobstructed Christmas holiday. The two teams sparred cautiously in a scoreless first quarter, and a lot of sparring went on that day as a total of 18 penalties for 155 yards were whistled by a quartet of officials which included such illustrious flagwavers as John Waldorf and John Lloyd, before the exploding began early in the second period. Hardy began it with a 46-yard liftoff through right tackle and a helplessly outraced secondary on the third play of the quarter. On CU's next scrimmage play, Bernardi bounced 50 yards on the single wing reverse back to the weak side. And on the second play in its next possession, CU sent Emerson Wilson straight up the middle for 95 yards. On that dash, Emerson outraced K-State's halfback and track star, Corky Taylor who had been selected already as a member of the West squad for the post-season Shrine game in San Francisco. Hardy and Bernardi were to make the squad the following week, primarily on the strength of their great performances in this contest. This 3-touchdown explosion which produced 191 scrimmage yards within a 4-play span was the greatest CU offensive eruption to that point and ranks right alongside the opening outburst against Oklahoma State in 1961 as the most scintillating sequence in the history of the Buffaloes.

It was 19-0 at the half and the K-State brass section wasn't getting much lung into their horns and a New Orleans funeral march might have been more appropriate than their Orange Bowl melody. But the Wildcats got the lone touchdown of the third quarter and were still alive until Hardy took a lateral from Wilson and streaked 75 more yards up the east sideline. And when K-State came right back with another touchdown, Bernardi got back into the act, zig-zagging 30 yards to the 20 to set up a John Bayuk scoring blast in which Big John just burrowed beneath the two lines and carried practically everybody into the end zone. And to lay another layer of icing on the cake, Hardy finished the day by reversing his field twice on a fake pass then racing 46 yards to the 13 where he got roughed and K-State got penalized to the one, from where Carroll plowed over on the next play which came with only 31 seconds left.

It was a beautifully savage exhibition of single wing execution at its best. The Buffaloes got 493 yards on the ground in only 36 rushes, an average of nearly 14 yards per try. Hardy had 238 in 10, Wilson 124 in 7, Bernardi 113 in 9. Homer Jenkins completed the only pass the Buffaloes connected on in five tries, a 5-yarder to quarterback Bill Lamont, who was Sam Maphis' backup man. It was a fantastic farewell for CU's touchdown twins and a fitting finale to the careers of two great Buffaloes. And a sweeter-than-usual Saturday night for a young CU publicist who had seen two of his favorite people performing at their finest for one of his favorite coaches.

No. 15: CU 15, AIR FORCE 7 (BOULDER, NOV. 28, 1959)

Mark down another victory for the defense in this 15-7 triumph over Air Force in 1959. This one was led by all-time great Joe Romig and his great supporting cast of fellow sophomores who were to grow into Big Eight champions two years later. The victory also helped to ease the pain of the preceding season's loss to the Falcons in the first full-fledged varsity football game between the two schools. Air Force was coming off a cinderella season in which they were undefeated, winning nine games and tying mighty Iowa before tying Texas Christian in the Cotton Bowl. The Buffaloes were coming off a coaching change, with Sonny Grandelius replacing Dal Ward who had been axed following the 1958 campaign. And one of the big reasons for the decision to lower the guillotine on Ward's CU coaching career was the Falcon's 20-14 upset to close the '58 season. The Falcons, new royalty in college football, soared into the 1959 campaign with high hopes. CU entered it uncertainly, under the youthful direction of Grandelius after 11 years of single-winging it with Dal. Neither team fared particularly well in 1959. CU was 4-5 but on the upswing going into this finale. Air Force had suffered through some flameouts en route to its 5-3-1 mark. But as Ben Martin so fluently proclaimed on the eve of the battle, "The prefabricated tradition of the Colorado-Air Force rivalry has become a reality." The two teams were ready for their intra-state battle. Especially Air Force, which was the home team even though the game was played in Folsom Stadium because the Falcons did not yet have theirs completed. Quarterback Rich Mayo exploded a 44-yard bomb to halfback Don Baucom on the Falcons' first play of the game, the play going out of bounds at the CU five. From there Air Force scored in two plays to take a 7-0 lead with just 2:18 played. And that's the way it stayed throughout the first half as the game settled down into a gruelling defensive dual with neither Mayo nor CU aerial star Gale Weidner able to do any great damage aside from Mayo's opening thrust. Mayo completed only three more in 10 attempts for a paltry 17 yards after that first one. Weidner was only five for 18 and 26 yards. Air Force never got beyond the CU 47 the rest of the half. CU made one serious penetration set up by a punt exchange initiated by Chuck McBride's great 40-yarder which hit the sideline stripe at the Falcon three. CU got the ball back at the AFA 43 and drove to a fourth down at the eight. But from there, Weidner threw to end Mel Semenko, who didn't turn around in time to see the ball which flew past him and into the arms of Mayo.

    The Buffaloes wasted another scoring opportunity at the start of the third quarter when Weidner misfired on a fourth down pass from the Falcon 15 after guard Ken Vardell had recovered Mayo's fumble at the AFA 34. But Jerry Steffen returned the following punt 13 yards to the Falcon 39 and the Buffaloes, with Steffen, halfback Dave Rife and fullback Chuck Weiss doing the damage, moved it to the 12 from where Weidner, from tailback in the spread formation, danced around for several seconds before spotting Weiss alone over the middle and drilled the ball into his ribs for a touchdown. The Buffaloes gambled for two and this time Rife made the clutch catch, again right over the middle. Leading 8-7, the Buffaloes scored again early in the fourth period in a 16-play, 59-yard drive which began with Steffen's 7-yard punt return and ended with his full speed catch in the corner of the end zone of a 9-yard Weidner toss. The tough CU defense and the 45-yard punting of McBride kept the Falcons from any serious penetrations going into the final five minutes. But Mayo suddenly got hot and hit four straight passes for 47 yards to move the Falcons quickly to a first down at the CU nine. Fullback Ron Stoner hit over right tackle. Bill Elkins, Bob McCullough and Vardell smashed him down after a yard gain. The CU line was impressively dominant at this point so Mayo went to the air. His second down pass was batted down by Weidner. On third down, center Walt Klinker made a leaping save. On fourth down, the Falcons reached deep into Ben Martin's salty bag of tricks and came up with a halfback pass which fooled 10 CU defenders. Mayo pitched out quickly to left half George Pupich who looked to have some running room on a right sweep. But he pulled up suddenly and threw to his crossing left end, 6-3 Sam Hardage. Just as Hardage was reaching for the ball, Romig came roaring up from out of nowhere to smash the ball down. And that was the game. A well-earned triumph for Romig and his defensive mates. And a fitting 2-touchdown effort by Weidner, whose bullet passing from the spread had constituted much of CU's offense as the Buffaloes finished well with five wins in their last seven games. The Grandelius regime was firmly launched and the closing victory over Air Force in 1959 did as much to establish Sonny as a solid young coach as any. Because, to win, his durable defense had to overcome the attack of Martin, who had established himself quickly in his career as one of the nation's finest young offensive tutors.

No. 14: CU 31, MISSOURI 24 (BOULDER, OCT. 25, 1969)

This big CU victory was another reminder of the dangers of a Folsom Stadium visit by a nationally ranked team. Missouri was rolling along undefeated and ranked fifth in the nation when the Tigers arrived to serve as the villains in CU's Homecoming festivities. This was the last serious obstacle between the Tigers and the first undefeated season for Dan Devine, who had done such a tremendous job of overhauling Mizzou's football fortunes since taking over in 1958. The site of the confrontation resembled a North African battleground in World War II as several loads of sand had been wheeled into the soft spots of Folsom Field which was still mushy from a heavy wet snowfall of three weeks earlier. Irregular patches of sand, grass and dirt blotched the landscape as the two teams opened fire.

CU drew first blood on an 80-yard drive which got started when Bob Anderson bolted 30 yards down the west sideline after breaking a tackle just beyond the line of scrimmage. Quarterback Jimmy Bratten quickly followed up with a 35-yard completion to slotback Marv Whitaker, who made a sensational catch, ripping the ball away from a Tiger defender and tumbling to the ground with the ball. Anderson bulled over from the one on fourth down. After two exchanges, linebacker Rick Ogle recovered a fumble at the Missouri 21 to set up a 30-yard Dave Haney field goal. A strong factor in the early going for the Buffaloes was the tremendous punting of Dick Robert, whose first four punts in the game went for 62, 46, 49 and 40 yards, the latter one out of bounds at the Missouri four. Near the end of the half Bratten was kayoed by a hard Missouri rush and replaced by sophomore Paul Arendt, who had lost the starting job he had debuted in so sensationally against Indiana three weeks earlier. Arendt promptly hit Monte Huber, who had gotten all alone deep when two Missouri backs got mixed up in their defensive assignments, for a 79-yard touchdown play to make it 17-7 with 5:18 left in the half. Missouri had scored in the second quarter on a 75-yard bomb from Terry McMillan to Mel Gray. After a Missouri field goal made it 17-10, Arendt fired another bomb, this one to Whitaker for a 58-yard gain to the Tiger five from where Paul showed fine power in driving his way into the end zone on the next play. CU led 24-10 at the half, mainly on the strength of those long bombs to Whitaker and Huber.

Missouri showed why it was ranked No. 5 after the half, though, coming out with a fierce trapping game which repeatedly sent big Joe Moore barreling down the middle for big gains. Moore got 46 yards in five carries during an 8-play, 51-yard drive which made the score 24-17 at the end of the third quarter. CU pulled away again as Bratten's keepers sparked a 54-yard scoring drive with the biggest play a 9-yard dart inside his left tackle to the 15 by Bratten with a piling penalty moving the ball on down to the seven from where the Buffaloes required six plays to score against the powerful Tiger defensive line. But Anderson finally cracked through from three yards out and the Buffaloes again had some breathing room. But not for long. Fullback Ward Walsh fumbled away the ball at the CU 29 and the Tigers made it 31-24 in five plays, the touchdown coming on a 10-yard strike from McMillan to end Chuck Henley with 5:02 left to play. There was no scoring in those five minutes but there were some tense moments for CU fans as the Tigers moved to their own 43 in one last-ditch effort. But linebacker Phil Irwin made a leaping interception of a bullet pass over the line of scrimmage to kill Tiger hopes. Irwin had never made a bigger play than that one although he was to top even that with an end zone interception against Oklahoma State a month later. Phil's interception put the final touches on a very Sweet Saturday, one which wiped out much of the memory of the preceding bitter Saturday when the Buffaloes had been whipped 42-30 at Oklahoma. It also launched the Buffaloes into a closing surge which led to the Liberty Bowl date with, and conquest of, Alabama.

No. 13: CU 31, MIAMI 21 (HOUSTON, DEC. 23, 1967)
I particularly relish the memory of this game because it marked a sensational return to action by Bobby Anderson after the only injury of his college career, because it extracted a full measure of revenge for Miami's humiliating 24-3 victory over the Buffaloes in the season opener at Boulder a year earlier, because it came in the Bluebonnet Bowl before a national television audience and, finally, because it came practically on Christmas Eve and I can't think of a nicer Christmas present than a CU bowl victory.

Miami, led by its All-American defensive end Ted (The Mad Stork) Hendricks, was a solid touchdown favorite going into the game. Both teams were 7-3 and had finished the season impressively, Miami coming within inches of upsetting might Notre Dame before bowing 24-22 then toppling a strong Florida team 20-13. CU had punished Kansas State 40-6 and Air Force 33-0 in its last two starts. But Anderson had sprained an ankle badly in the closing seconds of the first half of that finale against Air Force and was not at top speed during the Buffaloes' preparations in Houston. Dan Kelly started at quarterback for the Buffs who took an early 7-0 lead when Larry Plantz sped seven yards with a pitchout to score after Mike Veeder had recovered a Hurricane fumble at the Miami eight. Miami came right back with a 55-yard kickoff return then covered the remaining 35 yards in 11 plays to tie the score. The Hurricanes went in front 14-7 with 10 minutes gone in the second quarter when defensive back Jimmy Dye intercepted a Kelly pass and brought it back all the way, 77 yards. When the Buffaloes couldn't move the ball on their next possession, Anderson took over the quarterback role and on his first play ran 15 yards on a keeper around right end to the Hurricane 30. On the next he ran for five more. Then he hit Monte Huber for an 11-yard gain in a race against the clock which ended with John Farler kicking a 31-yard field goal with 12 seconds left to make the halftime score 14-10. To start the third quarter, Bobby ran for 28 yards in five carries and hit tight end Mike Pruett for 11 more to lead the Buffaloes on an 80-yard drive for the go-ahead touchdown which he scored from the three. Miami countered with an 85-yard drive which started near the end of the third period and ended with quarterback Bill Miller's 9-yard touchdown pass to end Jerry Daanen with five seconds gone in the final quarter. A few minutes later, however, Andy got the Buffaloes rolling again, running for nine then six and throwing to Huber for eight in between some crunching power shots by big Wilmer Cooks. All this brought the Buffaloes to a first down at the Miami 38. From there Andy wheeled to his left toward the short side of the field, broke into the open and pranced down the sideline to score, getting a great block near the goal line from his slot end, Tom Corson, who cleared out the last two defenders at the 10 yard line with a domino block, knocking one man into the other and flooring them both. When Miami tried desperately to come back, cornerback Ike Howard intercepted and the Buffaloes quickly drove 34 yards to clinch it with Andy hitting Pruett for 15 and Cooks crashing over from the two. It was now 31-21 with only a minute remaining and Charlie Greer intercepted a Miller pass to wrap things up.

It was a very Sweet Saturday night in Houston as the Buffaloes celebrated their victory, Bobby Anderson was named the game's outstanding player, Rudy Feldman was named head coach at New Mexico and I took a hot bath, drank a cup of Ovaltine, ate a vanilla wafer and went to bed. Penniless but happy. That's how I always end up on Sweet Saturdays. When you've won that afternoon, material things really don't matter. It's that exhilaration which counts.

No. 12: CU 7, MISSOURI 6 (BOULDER, NOV. 4, 1961)

This game was the biggest of the 1961 Big Eight conference season as it matched unbeaten and 8th-ranked CU against unbeaten but once-tied and 10th-ranked Missouri in the game which would decide the conference championship and its accompanying Orange Bowl bid. 43,000 fans huddled in Folsom Stadium on a dreary, cold afternoon and millions of others in a large regional television audience watched from the comfort of their easy chairs as the league's two titans squared off for what promised to be, and was, a bruising, physical low-scoring duel. Missouri had yielded only 27 points in six games, the Buffaloes 40 in five. CU's board of strategy felt, though, that its defense could shut out the Tigers who were an extremely conservative, and consequently predictable, offensive team. The Buffalo brain trust therefore reasoned, and almost fatally, that if CU could score one touchdown it would win the game. That's the way it turned out, too, although the Tigers were a lot more dangerous offensively than the Buffaloes had estimated. Both teams made serious probes in the first quarter. Missouri's failed at the CU 17 when Claude Crabb intercepted a third-down Jim Johnson pass in the end zone for a touchback. Colorado's went awry when Jerry Hillebrand missed a 27-yard field goal after Gale Weidner's passes, Hillebrand's catches and some excellent power running by Ted Woods had moved the Buffs to a first and goal at the nine. A 25-yard punt return by Leon Mavity gave the Buffaloes another opportunity, starting from the Missouri 47, going into the final two minutes of the half. This time the Buffaloes didn't waste it. With Missouri looking for a pass, Weidner gave the ball to Woods on a counter play, an excellent call which picked up 12 yards. Now Weidner nailed big Hillebrand with a perfect pitch at the sideline and Jerry wheeled out of bounds at the 21. After an incomplete try toward Woods, Weidner rolled right, stopped and threw back across the field to his halfback Bill Harris, who had slipped out into the left flat. Harris caught the ball at the 10 and went into the end zone untouched. Hillebrand's conversion made it 7-0 with just 35 seconds left in the half.

The Buffalo defense kept Missouri bottled up, just as the pregame thinking had anticipated, throughout the third period. Deepest the Tigers got was to their own 49 and little Reed Johnson promptly swiped a pass to end that move. But Missouri, with round Ron Taylor directing the offense exceptionally well, began moving from its own 37 on its first possession of the fourth quarter and drove relentlessly to a touchdown in 14 plays, scoring on a smart call by Taylor, a halfback pass from Mike Hunter to end Don Wainwright on a third-and-ten play from the 10. There was 6:14 left and the Tigers gambled for two. And almost made it on the same play. But this time Hunter's pass was barely deflected by the desperate lunge of Johnson and went flying over the intended receiver's head. Colorado, in a full offensive shell which had failed to produce a first down to this point in the second half, tried to regain the momentum which had produced 12 first downs and 173 total yards in the first half but couldn't. They did manage a first down on their next possession. But it came on an interference call. So Chuck McBride had to punt and he got off a beauty, a high, spiraling 50-yarder which Missouri had to fair catch at its 25. Now Taylor began to puncture the CU secondary with short pegs to receivers cutting in front of the deep-conscious Buffalo defenders. He threw for nine, then 10, then 21, all to big 6-3, 206-pound Conrad Hitchler who went down with the last catch at the CU 29. After two incompletions and a 2-yard draw play, Missouri kicking specialist Bill Tobin placed his tee on the CU 34 for a 44-yard field goal attempt with just 32 seconds left. Tobin could kick it accurately that far and you could hear a heart beat as he awaited the snap. The kick was plenty long enough. But it sliced wide to the right at goal line and missed the right goalpost by several feet, although it looked awful close from where I was shaking in the press box.

So this became the Sweetest Saturday of all to us because it practically assured the Buffaloes of an undefeated conference championship. And to make it even sweeter, Capt. Joe Romig came to the press box after he'd dressed, made a typically short and blurting speech and handed me the game ball in honor of my 38th birthday which had been the day before. It wasn't a Sweet Saturday. It was a Great Saturday. One of the greatest of all time.

No. 11: CU 30, INDIANA 7 (BOULDER, OCT. 4, 1969)
   This was a multiply-memorable afternoon because it (1) produced the first CU victory ever over a Big Ten opponent, (2) marked the first appearance of a Big Ten team in the Rocky Mountain West, (3) featured two fantastic performances by Bobby Anderson, who had switched to halfback in mid-week, and sophomore Paul Arendt, who had never played a down in college but who started at quarterback in a big gamble, and (4) started a chain of events which eventually brought about the installation of Astro-Turf two seasons later.
   This was a solid Indiana team which as sophomores, had won the Big Ten in a cinderella season, played dramatically well against Southern California before bowing in the Rose Bowl, had then had disappointing junior seasons, but was ready to return to the heights as seniors. They didn't make it, though, and the snow-soaked drubbing they took in Boulder undoubtedly took a lot out of the Hoosiers. It probably took out what an opening loss to California in Bloomington a week earlier hadn't.
   But CU's fans weren't exactly doing handstands going into the game, either. The Buffaloes had been severely thrashed by powerful Penn State a week earlier, 27-3. Tailback Steve Engel was injured. His backup man, Ron Reiger, had hobbled out of that game early with a painful foot bruise. Slender Marv Whitaker had wound up as CU's only tailback and Penn State quickly concentrated its defense on stopping Anderson's quarterback keepers. It did that most effectively, hounding Bobby so thoroughly that he netted only four yards in 17 rushes and completed only eight of 26 passes for 81 yards with four intercepted. It was apparent that, without a strong running threat at tailback, the Buffalo offense was in real trouble. The CU staff deliberated late Sunday and Monday nights about what to do. Crowder had decided to move Andy to tailback and install either junior Jim Bratten or sophomore Arendt, whoever looked the best in practice that week, at quarterback. Most of Crowder's assistants were extremely nervous about such a radical change after the start of a season. But any good head coach always has the votes to win any election involving he and his staff and Crowder was no exception. The move was made. Anderson was called in and told about it. His reaction? "I'll play tackle if it will help the team," replied Anderson. His response was totally predictable. He is that kind of a young man. Very probably, the only four people who felt good about the change were Crowder, Anderson and the two young quarterbacks, Bratten and Arendt, who had just been given a new lease on their lives as CU quarterbacks. The security blackout was imposed on CU's workouts. Arendt had impressive practices Tuesday and Wednesday and won

the starting job. The secret was remarkably well kept. And unsuspecting Indiana came into Boulder along with a heavy snowstorm on Friday.

The extremely wet snow, more than 10 inches of it, dumped onto the stadium beginning in mid-afternoon Friday. CU officials, fearful that they couldn't get the field cover off with all that snow on it, ordered it removed at midnight. The snow continued to fall heavily into early Sunday morning. Pre-game sales had totaled nearly 32,000 with at least 10,000 more due to attend on Saturday. But less than 20,000 were on hand and all those got soaked by the large, wet flakes which made watching almost impossible, too. The field was a pigsty in a storm. Indiana's fleet runners, Harry Gonso and Jack Isenbarger, never could get going. But it was a great day for stronglegged men, longer in power than in speed. Like Anderson. And Arendt. And CU's fleet of Italian Stallions — Rich Variano, Dave Capra, Dave Perini and Carl Taibi —all of whom could run just as fast through a swamp as over pavement. Observers didn't have to wait long to see whether or not the Anderson experiment would work.

Colorado won the toss and received and Andy ran the kickoff back 20 yards to the 27. On first down he rammed off left tackle for nine. On second down he circled right end for nine more. Next time, Arendt faked the pitch to him and kept for five. The Hoosiers ganged up on Andy to stop him with just a yard on his third carry but on the next play he took Arendt's pitchout, cut inside his right end, got to the outside and slithered through the muck for 20 yards. The Buffaloes had to settle for a Dave Haney field goal and fell quickly behind 7-3 when Gonso took the Hoosiers on an explosive drive, hitting his split end Dave Stolberg for 47 yards then flanker Jade Butcher for 17 and a touchdown. Unperturbed, Arendt calmly directed an 80-yard drive, running once for 16 and another time for 25 and hitting Monte Huber for a 14-yard completion and finally sending Anderson into the end zone from the one with two minutes left in the quarter. CU was ahead to stay.

But Indiana took one more good shot before they laid down their guns. Trailing 10-7 early in the second period, they drove to a first down at the CU 15. But a diving interception by Irish Pat Murphy snuffed out that flame and the Buffaloes and, in particular, Anderson took over with authority. Starting just eight yards from their end zone, the Buffaloes drove the 92 yards in just 11 plays. Anderson, running like he was on a cinder track, carried seven times, netting 61 yards, including a 33-yard gallop to the Hoosier 18 and the touchdown from the one. Arendt chipped in with a 17-yard completion to Huber which moved the ball to the one. There was no scoring in the second half until Anderson tallied from the five after big Bill Brundige had forced and recovered a Hoosier fumble at that point. The final score came late on a short Arendt sneak.

Anderson liked the new position and the unfamiliar footing to the tune of 161 yards, nearly three times the Indiana team total of 56. And his three touchdowns also tripled Indiana's total. Arendt was the second best runner on the field with 72 yards. And the CU rookie hit eight of 15 passes for 103 more and handled the slippery ball almost flawlessly. The Buffaloes had made a 180-degree turn from the preceding Saturday at Penn State. The CU ship was again on an even keel, one which was to wind up in the Liberty Bowl where Anderson could show a national television audience what he could do on a dry surface. This was the soggiest Saturday I've ever seen at CU. And the field never recovered and was covered with AstroTurf 18 months later. But those scoreboard lights which twinkled out that 30-7 final score also made it one of the sweetest Saturdays.

No. 10: CU 49, AIR FORCE 19 (AIR FORCE, NOV. 21, 1970)

This turned out to be an extremely Sweet Saturday because the Buffaloes were trying to salvage something out of the 1970 season after they had lost three mid-season Big Eight games to Oklahoma, Missouri and Nebraska to fall out of conference and, apparently, bowl contention. Air Force, meanwhile, had collected another bottleful of lightning, bringing a 9-1 record which was good enough to earn a Sugar Bowl spot into this regular season finale and fresh from a 31-14 clubbing of Stanford's Rose Bowl entry on the previous Saturday. CU had recovered from its mid-season sag to roll up big scores against Kansas (45-29) and Oklahoma State (30-6) but neither of those teams were doing well at this point in the season so the Buffaloes entered the Air Force game as slight underdogs. That prefabricated instant tradition which had developed in the CU-AFA series was more than a decade old now and starting to take on the vines of genuine tradition and the Air Force cadets, who were to prove more resourceful than their football team on this occasion, slipped into Boulder late one mid-week night, backed a trailer up to the fence at the Hidden Valley Ranch and calmly kidnapped Ralphie, CU's 800-pound buffalo mascot. So there was proper atmosphere going into the game which was played in nearly perfect 65-degree temperature in beautiful Falcon Stadium located in the pine-dotted hills which lie below the marble and concrete and glass and spires which make up the impressive Academy complex.

Ben Martin's always finely honed Falcons are more often than not out-muscled. But they are always opportunistic and ready to pounce on any break the opposition might give them. Coaches like to talk about their rubber-band defense (it stretches but never breaks) in situations where they have to concede a stronger opponent its ball control tactics, hoping to come up with the big defensive play somewhere during a drive which will halt the march. Martin's teams do this as well as any in the country. But don't get the impression that the Falcons are a bunch of 175-pound weaklings who get by on raw courage and gallant effort alone. They aren't. But neither are they monsters and the Buffaloes of Eddie Crowder normally have a physical edge, especially in the line where it counts.

The matchup, then, was between a savage CU running attack and a well-conceived Air Force aerial attack. CU featured the adept option play of quarterback Jimmy Bratten and the crunching charges of big backs Jon Keyworth, John Tarver and Ward Walsh. With excellent deep threats in Cliff Branch, Larry Brunson, Willie Nichols and Steve Dal Porto. Bratten was a fine long thrower. Air Force could counter with All-American flanker Ernie Jennings, possibly the best receiver in the country, and 6-5 tight end Paul Bassa, also a fine receiver, catching the accurate tosses of Bob Parker, who had had a spectacular senior season after two years as a fairly obscure reserve. And the Falcons had a solid running threat on draw plays in tailback Brian Bream.

The component parts for a great battle were present and the game started on an impressive note for both teams. CU took the opening kickoff and promptly and authoritatively drove from its 17 to the Falcon 18, springing fullback Ward Walsh for 40 yards along the way. But on a second down play, Tarver lost the ball. It flew right into the arms of Falcon safety Scott Hamm, who blinked his eyes a couple of times at his good fortune then raced 80 yards into the far end zone. Just like any good alert Falcon would do. Just like that, CU had 73 yards of total offense and Air Force had seven points. Shades of 1958! And when Nichols fumbled a deliberately short Air Force kickoff and Branch finally picked it up and ran it out to the 25, it looked as though the Buffaloes might be involved in one of those days.

But Bratten warmed up to his job and pretty soon he hit Dal Porto for a 13-yard gain and squirted around end for eight yards on a keeper to move the Buffaloes to the AFA 42. Then he dropped backed and zeroed in on the flying Nichols who caught the ball on the dead run at the Falcon 15 and scored with no one around him. So the opening disaster was neutralized. The second quarter was just heavenly for the Buffaloes. They controlled the air. And the ground. And everything else. Even Ralphie, who had been turned back over to CU by the cadets before the game. Undamaged. (It's pretty tough to damage a buffalo unless you use an elephant gun and Air Force cadets are just mischievous not murderous.)

The Buffaloes scored four times in the second quarter. Falcon fans must have felt that halftime would never arrive. CU's celebrating legions were hoping it wouldn't. First Bratten bounced into the end zone from seven yards out to complete an all-on-the-ground 69-yard drive. Then Keyworth stampeded through the secondary for a 30-yard TD. On the next drive, Bratten injured a knee but Paul Arendt was waiting in the wings, anxious to get in on the kill. He did, quickly, lunging around left end for a 15-yard touchdown. As the half drew to a merciful end, Tarver ripped into the end zone from the five and, with Dave Haney chopping out extra points like they were coming out of the barrel of a mortar, the Buffaloes went into the rest period ahead by an amazing 35-7 score. Sugar Bowl officials, on hand to see their team perform, looked like they'd walked in on a convention of saccharine manufacturers. Their bowl was getting flushed. And Sugar Bowls aren't designed to be flushed. Especially by 5-4 teams. The CU secondary, and in particular Jim Cooch, Cullen Bryant and Pat Murphy, was giving Jennings a pretty good blanketing. Bream couldn't find much running room at the line of scrimmage either.

When the Buffaloes made it 41-7 on their first possession of the second half on a 64-yard Arendt to Brunson pass, those Sugar Bowl scouts headed back for the airport and New Orleans to prepare their defense to explain why they had picked a team which was going to carry this kind of a shellacking into the New Year's Day classic. At this point, CU relaxed and the game turned sloppy and nothing much else happened except that Jennings caught three passes to swell his game total to five and the Falcons scored a couple of touchdowns in the fourth period and CU got another and all the Air Force brass headed for the friendly booths of the officers club and the happy CU fans lurched northward while the unhappy AFA boosters lurched in any direction where they might find comfort and both teams just wanted to get the game over with so they could get on to the more important affairs of celebrating the end of the regular season.

But the CU statisticians had a great day as the Buffaloes rolled up 33 first downs, 482 rushing yards and 193 more passing for an awesome 675 yards of total offense, most in the nation for a single game in 1970. The impressive victory got CU a repeat bid to the Liberty Bowl. Unfortunately. They'd have been better off to end the season with this game because Bratten's knee never healed and Arendt couldn't move the Buffaloes and Tulane administered CU a sound

17-3 whipping at Memphis. The impressive loss didn't disqualify the Falcons from the Sugar Bowl, either, and they'd have been better off to have forgotten about the whole thing because they got another flogging there from Tennessee. But all this was in the future and on this Sweet Saturday life was never sweeter as we savored the victory en route home then stopped for a delightful dinner in the charming chambers of that Gracious Greek, Jimmy Fillas, the dapper former proprietor of the antique and atmospheric Denver Press Club who had moved onward and upward into his own joint after ministering to the physical and spiritual needs of the Denver press corps, and a more than occasional visiting fireman, for many years. Sweet Saturdays are good victories, good food, good drinks and good friends. This was an exceptionally sweet one.

No. 9: CU 23, MISSOURI 9 (BOULDER, OCT. 14, 1967)

This was a savagely-fought battle between a pair of powerful, unbeaten and nationally-ranked teams who disdained fancy-dan football and preferred to slug it out with each other on the ground. The result was a classic contest and Colorado was a classic winner, completely and somewhat surprisingly overpowering the tough and durable Tigers. Missouri teams in those days were head coached by Dan Devine whose defensive coach, Al Onofrio, was a master at setting up roadblocks for enemy offenses. There would be no trick plays on this overcast 50-degree day. Just a lot of halfbacks and fullbacks hitting up the middle and, for variety, just as many options to the outside. And not too many passes (CU was to throw 10 times, Missouri 16, nine of these in the fourth period when the Tigers were trying desperately to catch up.)

A near-capacity crowd of 44,517 massed in Folsom Stadium to watch this titanic between the undefeated co-leaders of the Big Eight. CU had conquered Baylor, Oregon and Iowa State; Missouri had whipped SMU, Northwestern and Arizona. The Buffaloes took it to the Tigers right from the start, carving out yards relentlessly through a good Missouri line and driving 61 yards in 16 plays, the longest a 14-yard Bob Anderson to Monte Huber pass, to take a 6-0 lead. Missouri shocked the Buffs with a countering touchdown in just three plays as quarterback Gary Kombrink cut inside his right end and caught the CU secondary moving in the wrong direction to go 75 yards and put Missouri in the lead, 7-6. CU's offensive unit got right back in business, however, and with Anderson zeroing in on Mike Pruett for 13 yards then bursting 17 off tackle himself, moved into position for a Dave Bartelt field goal to go back in front. CU's defense, with linebackers Kerry Mottl and Bartelt and middle guard

Rocky Martin playing extremely well and the entire line of Mike Schnitker and Mike Veeder and Frank Bosch and Ronnie Scott clogging up the line of scrimmage, pretty well muffled all the Tiger guns and they could get only two first downs during the remainder of the first half after Kombrink's shockingly easy scamper. The defense kept improving CU's field position and after William Harris had kicked dead on the Tiger seven, the Buffaloes began on their own 37 and, once again, chopped out a string of short gains to score in 14 plays with Anderson and Harris collaborating on a perfect pitchout to catapult Harris into the end zone from seven yards out. Reserve slotback Gary Kuxhaus, starting in place of the injured John Farler, chopped down gigantic Russell Washington with a perfect block around the knees to open up the outside for Harris. The halftime score was 17-7 and CU was completely dominating this power struggle to the great delight of its fans.

The second half was more of the first half with the Buffaloes getting a pair of Bartelt field goals early in the third period and Missouri getting a safety late in the game when the Tigers caught Dan Kelly trying to pass out of his end zone. CU's defense was even more restricting in the second half if that were possible, limiting the Tigers to just two first downs. In all, Colorado finished with a 20-5 lead in first downs and 309-149 in total offense. This stirring victory lifted the Buffaloes to a fourth-place ranking in the national polls which followed. But, more importantly, it proved that CU had the muscle to out-muscle one of the finest muscle teams in the country. Nobody shoved Missouri teams around like the Buffaloes did on this dark, dreary day. It was a loud and clear warning to the nation that Eddie Crowder's Buffaloes had arrived and that notice made this Saturday one of the sweetest.

No. 8: CU 29, HOUSTON 17 (HOUSTON, DEC. 31, 1971)

"Don't Play Houston in the Astrodome" is a pretty sound piece of advice for football teams. In particular, don't play them in the Astro-Bluebonnet Bowl game, a good 1969 Auburn team might have warned after it got crunched 36-7 by the Cougars. But CU chose to ignore the storm warnings and passed up a highly-possible Gator Bowl date with Georgia to take its best shot at the home town school in what over-enthusiastic Houstonites refer to as the "Eighth Wonder of the World." Houston was a lot closer to Colorado than Jacksonville for the fans to travel, CU officials considered. And, besides, the Buffaloes had several stars from the Houston area and was interested in showing some more potential ones down there what kind of football Colorado played. So the match was made and it figured to be a great dual between a pair of Texas tornadoes, Houston's piston-legged Robert Newhouse and CU's dancing dervish, Charlie Davis. And each team had an All-American end: Houston a tight end named Riley Odoms and CU its meanest man, Herb Orvis. Both teams had a lot more top individuals going for them but these were the four who got most of the pre-game headlines. And a lot of the post-game ones as Davis barely edged Newhouse for most valuable back.

The Astrodome was full of football fans, many of them peaking for the evening but a lot more just using the football game as a warm-up for the New Year's Eve partying to follow and the game started off a lot wilder than most of the parties which were going to follow. Davis quickly showed the home state people why he was considered the best sophomore running back in the nation as he chop-stepped for 49 yards in four carries, the last one a 27-yard touchdown spring to the flag, as CU marched 70 yards after receiving the opening kickoff. Newhouse matched him with 38 yards in eight carries as the Cougars came right back to cover 79 yards and tie the score. An interception halted CU on its next possession and Houston promptly slammed 34 yards in seven plays with Newhouse getting 25 of them in five rushes. He scored both Cougar TDs on short blasts as the CU defense had some early problems adjusting to a Cougar attack which was concentrating on the outside instead of the inside where they normally directed their early attention.

CU got back into the swing of things with the next kickoff, covering 61 yards and again Davis was the workhorse on the ground although quarterback Ken Johnson loosened up the Cougar defense with a 23-yard strike to Willie Nichols to get the drive underway and hit Bob Masten for 14 more critical yards early in the series. Davis carried five times for 32 yards before Johnson hit Larry Brunson on a quick out pattern for a 5-yard touchdown pass. But J. B. Dean's placement was wide and CU still trailed, 14-13. Dean made up for that kicking lapse with a 32-yard field goal to send the Buffs in front, 16-14, on the next possession as a 38-yard breakaway on a keeper by Johnson got the Buffaloes out of deep trouble. The Buffs had gotten possession at their own seven on a Houston punt which rolled dead there. Dave Orvis, not as ill-tempered as his older brother but just as aggressive, recovered a Houston fumble on the next kickoff after Dean's 3-pointer and the Buffaloes and Davis were off to the races again. Starting on the Cougar 33, Johnson hit Nichols for a quick 5-yard gain then gave the ball to Davis seven straight times. On the seventh Charlie went diving into the end zone and the Buffaloes had a 23-14 halftime lead.

CU's defense took over in the second half after a shaky start in which the Cougars moved to a first down at the 11 on their first possession. Quarterback Gary Mullins hit Odoms with a pass right over the middle and the big tight end whirled to the three. But John Stearns and Lorne Richardson waylaid him there and he coughed up the ball and Richardson plucked it out of the air. End of threat. A Davis fumble stopped a deep CU penetration at the Cougar 25 and Houston came back to kick a field goal and draw to 23-17 as the third quarter ended.

Back came the Cougars at the start of the fourth, all the way from their 35 to a first down at the 13. Two running plays netted only four yards as Herb Orvis and Bud Magrum made the big stops. Mullins went to the air on third down but Cullen Bryant knocked the ball down. On fourth down, Mullins, under great pressure from Orvis, threw hurriedly to Newhouse who appeared to be breaking open on a delay route into the flat. But Stearns came racing out of nowhere to bat the ball down. End of that threat but CU was still in deep trouble and looked to be in very tough shape as Stearns stepped back into his end zone to punt on fourth down. And in even deeper trouble as the snap from center came bouncing back. However, the incomparable-in-the-clutch Stearns scooped up the ball on the short hop like the All-Big Eight baseballer he is and, seeing Houston peeling back to set up a punt return, took off around right end. The first down marker was on the 19. Stearns skipped out of bounds at the 22. The effect on the CU team was tremendous. Pinned back against the ropes through all of the fourth quarter to that point, they began moving and, before they were finished, had gone all the way for a 91-yard touchdown drive to put the game out of reach. Clifford Branch, along with center Bill McDonald and tight end J. V. Cain a native Houstonite, was the man who kept this drive alive, speeding 13 yards on an end around then breaking open on a fly pattern and forcing Houston to interfere with him to prevent him from going all the way. It was a 32-yard penalty and took the Buffaloes to the 27 from where Davis blasted out 14 yards to set up a one-yard Johnson TD.

This was a beautiful victory, achieved in one of the most difficult settings a bowl team can find itself in - playing Houston in the Dome. In winning, the Buffaloes of 1971 became the first team in Colorado history to win 10 games. Their record was 10-2 and the final win was impressive enough to lift the Buffs into third place in the final national rankings for the year. Behind Nebraska and Oklahoma for an unprecedented sweep of the top three places by a single conference. This wasn't a Sweet Saturday. Because the game was played on Friday. But it was a Fantastic Friday. Just as sweet as any Saturday ever was!

No. 7: CU 31, LSU 21 (BATON ROUGE, SEPT. 11, 1971)

When the NCAA members voted to permit an 11th game for college football teams, the reason was to produce one more pay day to help offset the constantly-increasing expense of the sport. Accordingly, CU sought the game which would bring with it the biggest check. That meant playing a national powerhouse on its own field. CU assistant coaches shuddered when the message went out to Arkansas, Notre Dame, Tennessee, Texas and Louisiana State that the Buffaloes were anxious to play them. In their own stadium. Louisiana State made the date and the Tigers were possibly the toughest of all those foes to play in their own lair. LSU, playing six or seven home games annually, had lost only eight times in Tiger Stadium in the past 12 years. The Bayou Bengals played their home games at night because of the steamy temperatures of Baton Rouge. CU was used to neither condition, playing all of its games in daytime and most of them in the crisp, dry climate of more-than-mile-high Boulder. And this was a very youthful CU team, maybe a year away from its peak. And this was a veteran LSU outfit, right at the top of its game. The Tigers were, understandably, a two-touchdown favorite going into the game. Nearly 68,000 fans were on hand, licking their lips at the thought of their Tigers devouring these brash young upstarts from the mountains.

The game started as though all the pre-game predictions were true. LSU gained 10 yards on the first play of the game and 13 on the next. Right up the gut. They were at midfield almost before the nervous Buffaloes realized the game was underway. But CU braced and held only to have All-American tackle Ron Estay punt the ball dead on the three. So the Buffalo offense took the field for the first time in 1971 and huddled behind their own goal line and lined up with a sophomore center (Bill McDonald) handing the ball to a sophomore quarterback (Ken Johnson) who was backed up by a sophomore tailback (Charlie Davis.) Try that on for terror, sports fans! So what happened? Johnson and Davis, moving with the coolness and precision of veterans, carried the ball on five of the first six plays and moved the ball all the way out of danger, to the CU 33. That impressive beginning gave the Buffaloes early momentum and on their next possession they went all the way with Johnson's scrambling cross country pass to Willie Nichols covering the final seven yards of an 83-yard march against one of the finest defenses in the nation. LSU banged right back to tie the score in the opening minutes of the second quarter but another sophomore, J. B. Dean, kicked a 35-yard field goal and the Buffaloes were rattling at the touchdown door again as the half ended with CU ahead, 10-7. The Buffs' ace tailback, Jon Keyworth, had gone out for the season with a broken leg received early in the first quarter but the Buffaloes were taking the fight to their favored foes.

Early in the third period, Cliff Branch showed the Louisianans how to fly as he collected an Estay punt at the 25 and shot 75 yards down the right sideline. It was now 17-7 and CU threatened to make it a rout as end John Stavely dropped off the scrimmage line to intercept a pass in the flat at the LSU 29 and move to the 25. CU scored in four plays: Tarver for eight then two and Davis for 12 then three. Nothing to it, sports fans. Pack up your terror in your old kit bag and smile, smile, smile. If you got room, stick that tiger in that old kit bag, too. He has just been tamed. But not completely. LSU drove 71 yards, with reserve quarterback Paul Lyons providing the spark, to close to 24-14 at the end of the third quarter. But the Buffaloes drew away again on a perfectly executed Johnson-Davis maneuver which saw Kenny sliding inside tackle from the LSU 47 to draw in the secondary then pitch out to the trailing Davis who peeled back from the sideline to go all the way into the end zone at the far corner in a picture-book play. That finished off the Tigers although they never quit trying and scored a final touchdown with 3:02 left.

It was a most impressive beginning for the young Buffaloes who rolled up 375 yards of total offense against the Tigers. Davis got 174 yards rushing despite not getting the ball in the final 11:22 of the game. Johnson ran for 18 and passed for 82. It was truly a Sweet Saturday night. And so was the check. CU's share of the gate receipts was nearly $130,000. That would have been pretty good balm for a defeat. But with the victory and the accolades which followed - Crowder was coach of the week and Davis back of the week, nationally - it was almost too much to believe. I guess you'd have to say it was a good piece of scheduling. Good, hell! It was perfect.

No. 6: CU 20, KANSAS 19 (BOULDER, OCT 7, 1961)

This was the most dramatic comeback in CU history, one I still find hard to believe a decade later. Hard to believe because it wasn't just a case of a team coming off the deck with a desperate rally. It was a case of a team staggering off the deck after being almost brutally outclassed and beaten physically and just plain humiliated. These were two physical teams which had been picked as leading contenders for the Big Eight title. Both Jack Mitchell and Sonny Grandelius were devotees of power football. No basketball on grass for these guys. Unless you were far behind in the fourth quarter, maybe. The Buffaloes only got four first downs in the first half. Kansas got a big break to set up its first score as Chuck McBride sliced a punt out of his end zone which netted only six yards and gave the Jayhawkers the ball at the 13. John Hadl and Curtis McClinton got it to the one from where quarterback Rodger McFarland slipped over on a sneak. Later in the second quarter, KU punched 52 yards with Hadl throwing to McClinton for 11 yards and a 13-0 halftime lead.

Gale Weidner got his Buffalo offense untracked to start the third quarter, hitting four passes to take the Buffs to a fourth and five at the Kansas 11. But his pass intended for Hillebrand was no good and the Buffaloes had no other chances in the period as Kansas took over the initiative again and was driving at the quarter's end. When McClinton broke 19 yards around end for a touchdown to make it 19-0 with 13:18 left in the game, it looked like the end of the line for the Buffaloes. But Weidner and his receivers were just beginning to fight. On the first play after the kickoff he whipped a long pass to the speeding Ken Blair who took it on the dead run at the Kansas 20 and went all the way for a 58-yard touchdown. Hillebrand's conversion kept the CU fans from leaving although it was still a long hill to climb trailing 19-7 with 13:04 remaining and Kansas, which had chopped out 16 first downs to this point, due to get possession on the kickoff. But the adrenalin was flowing now for the Buffaloes and Kansas could gain only three yards in three plays and Hadl had to punt to Claude Crabb who advanced the ball only two yards to the CU 37. Four plays later from the Kansas 48, Weidner looked for Blair on the same pattern as had scored the TD. But McFarland who had seriously considered enrolling at CU before deciding on Kansas, was ready for the play and moved in for what looked like an easy interception. But, miraculously for the Buffaloes, the ball skipped off his fingers and straight to Blair who had put on the brakes to try to get back and make the tackle. Blair caught it, whirled around and went all the way again. Now it was 19-14 and there was plenty of time left, 10:02, and the Buffaloes and the 42,700 fans were on fire. Kansas made one first down but the Buffalo defense stiffened. McClinton made three yards on first down to the 40. On second down, Frank Montera, Ralph Heck and Blair stacked up Hadl but only after a 5-yard gain. Third and two. It was Hadl again. But center Walt Klinker met him head-on at the line of scrimmage and knocked him back for no gain. It was punting time and Hadl booted it to Ted Woods who was buried at the CU 21. Buried overzealously and Kansas got a 15-yard penalty for unnecessary roughness. CU was confident now. And cool. And in control. The game had turned completely around and Kansas which had dominated everything for three quarters was now enveloped in panic.

CU's winning march was a masterpiece. Weidner hit Crabb in the flat for three yards, then sent fullback Loren Schweninger up the middle on a draw for 12. Now it was Woods around end for four. And Schweninger on another draw, this time for 13 as Weidner calmly took advantage of a Kansas defense which was suddenly deep-pass conscious after the two bombs to Blair. At this point Kansas tightened up its defense and stopped wingback Ed Coleman for two then Schweninger for only two more. Third and six at the 17. Now Weidner threw. To his big end Hillebrand who slanted across the middle and took the ball in stride at the five and simply cruised into the end zone. Nobody was near him. Jerry added his third straight conversion but a CU holding penalty moved the ball back 15 yards and a Weidner pass then fell incomplete. But nobody cared by now. It was 20-19 and only 2:56 remained and the Buffaloes weren't going to blow this one. Hadl completed one pass for 18 yards to midfield but on a fourth down play he turned receiver and caught what was almost a lateral from Lee Flachsbarth. But guard Ralph Heck arrived at almost the same time as the ball and flattened Hadl for a 6-yard loss and it was all over.

The Buffaloes were on their way to the Big Eight championship. What a Sweet, Sweet Saturday! It was Easter in Boulder. Only this time it was the Buffaloes who came back from the grave. You had to see it to believe it!

No. 5: CU 47, ALABAMA 33 (MEMPHIS, DEC. 13, 1969)

A Liberty Bowl date with illustrious Alabama, a team which had more reputation than ability in this particular season, concluded the 1969 season and the game was significant because the Buffaloes had fought back to finish with three straight victories and climb back into the bowl picture and also wipe out the stigma of the 1968 ending when they had sagged to four straight losses to wind up 4-6, the only sub-.500 for Eddie Crowder between 1965 and 1971. It was also a memorable occasion because it marked the last appearance for Bob Anderson in a CU uniform. And like a pair of earlier CU halfback greats, Carroll Hardy and Frank Bernardi 15 years earlier, he put on a closing show to end all closing shows.

Alabama had only a 6-4 record going into this game. They had been clobbered 49-26 by Auburn in their final regular season game. Earlier in the fall they had been abused by Tennessee, 41-14. And Vanderbilt, which had dropped out of football's upper echelons after Red Sanders left more than 20 years earlier, had ambushed the Crimson Tide in October, 14-10. Alabama's six victories included such prestigious victims as Virginia Tech (Excuse me, Jerry Claiborne) and Southern Mississippi. But you must understand bowl economics, class. Most of them are played in the south. And it's almost imperative that there be at least one southern team in the game to make sure that its mass of cornpone chawing, magnolia bouquet-ed, confederate flag waving legions flock to that old ticket office. In recent years the major bowls like the Oranges and the Sugars and the Cottons have built up their followings so that they are practically assured of a sellout no matter who plays the game. But you still see a lot of Mississippis and Georgias and Auburns and Tennessees and Alabamas and Arkansases and people like that in them. At least one. But in the Libertys and the Gators and the Suns and the Peaches and the Bluebonnets and all those pre-New Year's Day classics you always have one of these southern regulars and lots of the time, two. So be it. (By the way, they also happen to be pretty good football teams most of the time: you have almost got to wind up with a pretty fair record if you can slip enough Virginia Techs and Southern Mississippis and, most of the time, Vanderbilts, on your schedule.)

Anyway, Alabama is a magic name and it was never more glamorous than in 1969 despite that 6-4 record and despite having gotten racked up real good by Missouri in the Gator Bowl 12 months earlier. So the stands were full of all those magnolias and confederate flags and crimson banners and southern accents and reeling rebels which make football in the south such a great and colorful tradition. And making it all perfect were those lean, mean, grim, good old Crimson Tiders down there on the field ready to give their lives if necessary for the honor of the old south and, in particular, the Southeast Conference which annually sends five or six teams into the bowls. And making it all even more perfect, if that were possible, was that almightiest of Alabamans, that living legend in his Rex Harrison hat and hounds tooth coat, with his personal honor guard clustered around him in the form of a partial platoon of Alabama state troopers, with the lines of 187 victories and 187 victory celebrations etched into his handsome face and perhaps some of the confetti from the preceding night's pre-game festivities at the Sheraton Peabody still clinging to his locks: the Bear himself. Right there in person on the sidelines. Radiating that mystique which turns Alabama players from mere men into maniacal monsters and, if necessary, invoking a miracle if normal super-human effort is not enough to carry the day. Add those 50,000 miniature American flags which are part of the Liberty Bowl's somewhat transient tradition and you can understand the impressive setting this game was played in and why it occupies such a scintillating spot in my personal memory bank.

Yea; verily, verily, it was so. All eyes were on the Bear. Hardly a soul paid any attention, though, to those 65 grizzlies from the Rockies who were bigger and stronger and better and much more unknown than these leathery Alabamans who were playing in their school's 11th straight bowl game. On with action, gang. Let's see what magical movements ole Bear and his boys are gonna come up with this afternoon. Alabama had its great Italian Stallion, Johnny Musso. Colorado had five times that many: Varriano, Perini, Taibi, Capra, Dal Porto. But CU's one man to match its mountains was Anderson and he wasted no time in letting everyone know who was the top man in the Liberty Bowl that day.

The Buffaloes won the toss and Jimmy Bratten teased the Tide on the opening play, faking the pitchout to Andy and keeping it and ducking inside for six yards. Now the fooling around was over. Time to get down to basics. And basics, for Colorado in 1969, meant pitching the ball to Anderson and getting out of the way. And so the assault began. Andy for four. Then 15. Then 10. And, just like that, Alabama is backed up to its 35. In four plays. Now they were Anderson-conscious - quickly they had become believers - so Bratten sent fullback Ward Walsh over left guard and he breezed 13 yards into the end zone. Untouched. 7-0 and just 3:24 gone. Awful early, 'Bama guys, but it's already sucking-up-guts-and-get-tough time. Take the blanket off that wild Italian Stallion and let's strike back! And when Musso ripped 20 yards on Alabama's first offensive play, it looked like another version of the roller derby was coming up. But suddenly Stallion Road got barricaded. Musso got three, then lost one, then got a tough two. Back to the drawing boards, Tide. Looks like we're out-stallioned. We'll punt and re-group and limber up ole Scott Hunter's arm. We'll just keep probing those people. Something will open up. Next possession, Hunter loosened up his arm. And Bill Brundige and Carl Taibi and Herb Orvis loosened up everything else on him, burying him for first seven then nine yard losses sandwiched around a harried incompletion.

Anderson then ran through a big hole and right over the top of a defensive halfback for 49 yards before he got blindsided on a cutback and dragged down at the 11. CU had to settle for a field goal but two possessions later the Buffaloes, with Bratten hitting Steve Dal Porto twice for 29 yards and Bob Masten once for 23 then bolting 29 himself, drove 80 yards in seven plays to send Anderson across from the four and make it 17-0. Now it was take-a-nap time for the Buffaloes and you should never take a nap against the Bear's teams. But this was a first meeting and the Buffaloes didn't realize this. It was also time to get this thing back into being a contest or else the TV audience might drift out into the backyard and play with their frisbies or girl friends or something. And horrors, not to watch all those Right Guard commercials. Which might upset ABC-TV and they might not be back next December! So, suddenly, All-Big Eight defensive halfback Eric Harris got called for interference twice and a total of 36 yards in penalties and before the Buffaloes could awaken, Hunter had ducked through a yawning gap - or was it a gaping yawn? - and quarterback-sneaked 31 yards for a TD. 31 yards on a quarterback sneak? Leave it to the Bear to come up with something exotic. A few minutes later the Tide drove again, with Hunter throwing very well now, and made it 17-13. Tighten up your trusses, men, this thing is getting out of control. But Bratten and Anderson continued to drive Alabama crazy with their option play and Jimmy went 21 in three carries and Andy ramrodded for 25 in two and the Buffaloes were quickly at the 15 and again Bratten gave the ball to Walsh on the first option and Ward waltzed into the end zone and it was 24-13 and Alabama came right back and went 62 yards in five plays (plus a roughing penalty and one more interference call, on Jim Cooch) and made it 24-19 and the touchdowns were coming faster than the Right Guard commercials now and everybody was happy except the two defensive staffs and all those frisbies and girl friends who were stacked in all those TV room corners, unnoticed. And just when everybody was leaning back limp in their seats with just 1:01 left in the half, the Buffaloes sprang the biggest shocker of all on those coming-back Crimson Tiders. A 91-yard kickoff return on one of the hoariest plays in football, a handoff. And it wasn't even a good handoff. Alabama didn't kick the ball far enough for the scheduled exchange. So Masten had to scoop it up and run back to where Steve Engel was coming across. Shades of the Statue of Liberty! Take that, Bear and your quarterback sneak. We got exotic stuff, too. So Engel sped up the sidelines with sore-shouldered Monte Huber getting him a block at the beginning and one at the end and it was 31-19 at the half and even Roone Arledge, not to mention Bill Dudley, was happy. Everything was going great and if it kept up even old Chris and Bud in that old broadcast booth were going to get excited and raise their voices. Anderson had 126 yards in 12 carries and one touchdown. Musso had 97 in 16 and a matching TD. But Hunter had gotten wiped out on the last play of the half and was not to return and Alabama would have to depend upon its backup quarterback, Neb Hayden, an unlettered junior, in the second half.

So Hayden promptly hit a 55-yard bomb on the fifth play after the third quarter kickoff and it was 31-26. Are those beads of sweat rolling off your humps, Buffaloes? Maybe the Bear does have more in his bag than Italian Stallions and quarterback sneaks! And you aint't seen nothing yet. Now comes an interception followed by an 87-yard drive. And no roughing penalties. Or interference calls. Just 14 good plays, seven of them runs for not less than two nor more than 11, three incomplete passes and four completions including a 10-yarder to Musso for the touchdown which moved the Tide in front 33-31 and yes, Virginia, those are beads of sweat - great big balls of sweat, in fact - rolling down those Buffalo humps. And when the Buffaloes drove all the way to a third-and-one at the Bama 11 only to fumble it away on a bad exchange between Bratten and Engel and the third quarter ended 33-31, it looked indeed as though the south might be rising again.

But the Buffaloes were aroused again and Anderson began butchering Alabama: for 52 yards in eight carries during a 12-play, 63-yard scoring drive in which his two-yard thrust sent CU ahead for keeps at 38-33 with 10:57 left. Near the end Orvis and Brundige obliterated Hayden in the end zone for a safety after Bratten's fumble had ended another CU penetration at the 17 and Anderson rampaged for 11 yards in three carries just before the end after Bill Collins, Brundige and Taibi had thrown the desperately-trying-to-pass-or-at-least-escape-with-his-life Hayden three straight times for a total of 25 yards and set up that final score.

It was just one of the sweetest of the Sweet Saturdays I've ever had and if I have seemed effusive about it it is because it was that kind of a day. Anderson wound up with 254 yards and three touchdowns in 19 carries. Musso, as gallant as they come, wore down in the second half and netted only 10 more but still finished with 107 and two touchdowns. He caught three passes for 22 yards. Andy lost his only reception, a 31-yarder, on a motion penalty but hit three of four passes for 41 yards. It was a game to remember. And I, obviously, have.

No. 4: CU 27, CLEMSON 21 (MIAMI, JAN. 1, 1957)

This was a momentous occasion because it was CU's first visit to a bowl since the days of Whizzer White when that All-American Rhodes Scholar led the Buffaloes to a perfect 8-0 record in 1937 and into the Cotton Bowl where he scored two touchdowns in a 28-14 loss to Rice. It is also memorable because the Buffaloes won and, like Will Walls said when we were on our way to Miami that December, bowl games ain't of much benefit unless you win. It was also the first appearance for the Buffaloes on national television and CU needed an impressive showing to make its mark on the national football map. It was also my first visit to a gala vacation spot. Unless you count Seattle in 1953. And that ain't exactly my idea of fun city although you can stir up just about anything you want there if you work hard enough at it. And, even though the Big Eight is an exciting land of such wonderful way stations as Columbia, Mo., Ames, Ia., Manhattan and Lawrence, Kans., and Stillwater and Norman, Okla. and Lincoln, Neb., it still doesn't compare with that magnificent tribute to concrete and neon and sand that is Miami Beach in the wintertime. All hail you, magnanimous men of the Orange Bowl Committee. May your blessings continue to multiply and may the bluebirds of happiness continue to sail over your causeways and may the sanctions of Allah continue to waft down on all those wonderfully kind and gentle little people who sift down from Manhattan Island from December through March to make your fiscal joys complete. And may you occasionally invite us Buffaloes to your New Year's Day fun and games, dear and gracious sirs.

This was a memorable event and to an impudent little Italian from the cornfields of Iowa, it was something else. Miami Beach on an expense account! All those unknown terrors that the nights hold in places like that. Staring me right in the face. Light the candle, mother, your little laddie is casting off into never-never land. And he might never get back alive. Ready the plasma bottles. Stand by with the stomach pump. Prepare to sweep Biscayne Bay. Tidy up those storm gutters on Collins Avenue. Seal off that shuttle to Havana. The Count is coming in. On two wings but without a prayer. And just wait until you see the Buffaloes!

And so it went. A wide-eyed, easy-to-please gang of Buffaloes and Buffalo-handlers who had the greatest and most relaxed time any bowl bunch could have. The trip was just as good as the Miami Beach brochures would have you believe every trip to Miami is, but isn't. The Buffaloes had fun. Those were the days when it didn't take much to keep a group of young men happy. And a lot of good friendship got going among the Colorados and the Clemsons, starting at the top where the rival coaches, Dal Ward and Frank Howard, were already great friends and great gentlemen. It was a fun trip and, just like it ought to be, the game was the most fun of all although it followed the same script that the 1969 Liberty Bowl game was to duplicate 13 years later.

The game was a tossup between CU's Big Eight runnersup with an overall 7-2-1 record and the Atlantic Coast champion Tigers whose record was 7-1-2. Colorado was rated as the better offensive team. Clemson was conceded an edge on defense. There were no fireworks at the start and the first 20 minutes was a punting duel with CU's long-legged sophomore, Boyd Dowler, more than holding his own in this department, sending his first kick 64 yards into the Clemson end zone. But early in the second quarter the Buffaloes got untracked and began rolling after Eddie Dove juggled a Clemson punt then returned it eight yards and CU began from its own 25 as big John Bayuk burst off tackle then lateralled to Bob Stransky for an overall 66-yard gain. That was only CU's second first down of the game and they struck quickly after that. Reserve quarterback Ralph Herbst carried for seven yards then Bayuk and Stransky took over, carrying the ball on eight of the nine plays it required to go those last 49 yards. Stransky swept right end for 26 to the Clemson 23 and Bayuk charged up the middle for 15 as John Wooten leveled a tremendous trap block and Bayuk bulled over from the two for the touchdown and Ellwin Indorf converted out of Dove's hold and it was 7-0 with 9:08 left in the half. Two minutes later it was 14-0 as Stransky intercepted a Clemson pass and returned 37 yards to the Tiger 10 from where the Buffs scored in three plays as Dowler rolled out from the six and followed his big fullback into the end zone. This time Howard Cook converted and it was 14-0 and the Buffaloes were just getting warmed up. Frank Clarke and Bayuk broke through to throw Clemson quarterback Charlie Bussey for a 10-yard loss back to the 13 on third down and Clarke then deflected the following punt and the Buffaloes got the ball at the 26 and Cook churned around right end all the way on the first play and it was beginning to look like a rout and nobody in the Colorado cheering section was too concerned when Cook missed the extra point, this time with Dove's backup man, Monte Briddle, holding. It was 20-0 with 4:02 left and the Buffaloes came roaring right back as Cook again got loose for 21 yards around right end on that old familiar single swing sweep and crashed out of bounds at the Clemson 19 with 42 seconds left. On the next play, third-string quarterback Bud Morley who was finishing up the quarter - those were in the substition rule days when a player couldn't return in a quarter once he had been taken out - floated a perfect pass to Clarke whose momentum carried him out of bounds at the one. But Morley couldn't generate any power on two quarterback sneaks and got only to a half-yard of the goal and the Buffaloes were out of time-outs and there was a lot of panic going on and they finally got a hurried snap off to Cook who fumbled the ball as the half ended. Ward and his staff were understandably upset at the Buffaloes' failure to cash in on this excellent scoring opportunity but nobody else really was. After all, hadn't the Buffaloes scored three times in nine minutes and wasn't it going to be just as wonderful in the second half?

The answer was an emphatic No! as Howard called on his long list of tobacco-spitting dressing room dramatics which even included a threat to quit coaching if the Tigers didn't stop their humiliating performance. Whatever, the shiny-domed, squatty package of southern humor who is Frank Howard said, it worked. The Tigers came out snarling and caught the Buffaloes sitting on their laurels. Clemson took the kickoff and drove 69 yards in 18 plays, the longest series in the game. On its next possession, the Tigers, who were not known for their breakaway ability and who had not generated a scrimmage run of longer than 25 yards all season, broke their fine halfback, Joel Wells, for 58 yards and suddenly it was a game again at 20-14 and the third quarter coming to an end with no sign of a Colorado awakening - the Buffaloes launched only four scrimmage plays during the period as Clemson successfully onside-kicked after its second touchdown. And when Cook fumbled and Clemson recovered at the CU 11 and scored in three plays to go ahead 21-20 with 11:12 left to play, that muffed opportunity at the end of the half suddenly looked horribly critical.

At this point, the Tigers stretched their luck and tried another onside kick. Big Wooten enveloped the ball at the CU 47 and the Buffaloes had excellent field position in the aftermath of Clemson's somewhat questionable strategy. This time the Buffaloes didn't squander their chance. Dove, a slender but slashing runner from his wingback and right halfback positions in Ward's multiple offense, had carried the ball only twice to this point. Now he got the call four straight times after Cook's initial 8-yard run to the Clemson 45. Dove responded with gains of 3, 14, 6 and 3 yards to move it to the 22 from where Bayuk smashed the rest of the way down the middle in three carries with Wooten, center Jim Uhlir, tackle Dick Stapp and guard Dave Jones supplying the big blocks. Indorf kicked the extra point and the scoring was finished for the day and so was Clemson although the Tigers got still one more chance when Dowler fumbled on a quarterback sneak and Clemson covered the ball at the CU 27. But Stransky saved the day with a perfectly-timed interception, cutting in front of the intended receiver at the 17 and continuing 18 yards upfield from where the Buffaloes controlled the ball for the remaining two minutes.

And so everybody, with the exception of the Clemson people, wound up happy and even the Clemson people could draw a lot of consolation from the fact that they had made a game of it after that disastrous second quarter. But it had been an exciting contest despite pre-game mutterings about a second-place Big Eight team meeting a club which had gotten trounced by hometown Miami 20-0 right here in this very same stadium a few weeks earlier. We Buffaloes were delirious with joy. Our men had won and had shown an offensive explosion then a clutch comeback in winning and ours was a team which had a lot of fine sophomores like Dowler and Dove and Cook and Wooten and Mondt and Herbst and Bob Salerno and Sherman Pruitt and Leroy Clark who were going to play a lot of football for the Buffaloes during the next two seasons and who would probably be back (but didn't make it.) And what about the little Italian? He got back alive but just barely, his blood thinned by the warm rays and the cool liquids he had absorbed during two torrid weeks punctuated by hot and cold flashes and a lot of groaning and rumbling from a shaky system which was already beginning to crumble from misuse. He did, in fact, collapse completely upon his return to the wintry altitude of Boulder. But a quick immersion into the bouncing fortunes of a basketball season revived him. Hurriedly, if not mercifully. And he has never forgotten the sweetest Tuesday of his life, which was New Year's Day, 1957.

No. 3: CU 41, PENN STATE 13 (BOULDER, SEPT. 26, 1970)

This was the first invasion of Boulder by a genuine, honest to God eastern power and this wasn't any normal eastern power most of whom aren't very powerful once they get out of the east and its host of unpowerful programs. Penn State was a genuine, honest to God power by anybody's sectional standards, a school which hadn't had a losing season in 31 years and which also owned the nation's longest unbeaten streak, 31, and the longest winning streak, 23. Included in that 23-game win string were five straight victories over Big Eight foes including the 27-3 humbling of CU at University Park the preceding fall and successive Orange Bowl victories over Kansas (15-14) and Missouri (10-3). When the Nittany Lions opened the season with a smashing 55-7 conquest of Navy, it looked as though they might be just as tough as ever. They had lost their dynamic quarterback Chuck Burkhart, who could do nothing very well except win and he never played in a losing game, but they did have the two backs, Lydell Mitchell and Franco Harris, who had done the Buffaloes in a year before. Plus a good nucleus of experienced hands. It figured to be one of the big early-season intersectional clashes, what with CU having victimized Alabama in the Liberty Bowl the year before and Penn State getting a lot of mileage out of its narrow triumphs over the two Big Eight kings in the past pair of Orange Bowls. Defense had been the Nittany Lion long suit in both those bowl triumphs and it had certainly been overwhelming against the Buffaloes in 1969.

The attraction was appealing enough to land the game on national television and even bring that silver-maned king of college football writers, Deacon Dan Jenkins, college football's answer to Hamilton Maule on the Sports Illustrated staff. And when you can lure

Deacon Dan away from the Darrells and the Franks and the Woodys and the Bears and all those high rollers of the college realm, you have really accomplished something. What, exactly, I am not sure of but at least you have accomplished getting Dan and his talented typewriter back out to God's country where he normally never comes unless there is something going on in the world of golf, where he is an expert, or of skiing, where he is not. The Deacon is an old friend and it was good to have him in Boulder again and we lounged through a delightful breakfast which included a lot of needed tomato juice on Jack Beattie's balcony overlooking the picturesque 15th hole at the Boulder Country Club where I have hit some of the truly great 9-wood approaches of our time. And we looked ahead to this afternoon's spectacular between east and west. And we reminisced about the old days along the frozen trails of Wengen, Switzerland and Madonna Di Campiglio, Italy when we were both novices on the international ski scene. But most of all we looked forward to the upcoming football game because if there is one thing that Deacon Dan and I have in common, it is the great delight in looking forward to an upcoming football game.

The Buffaloes were honed to a fine edge for this one. They were ready to cut themselves up some Penn State Lion. And starting quarterback Mike Cooper laid his team's head right on the chopping block on the first play of the game when he overthrew a wide-open receiver and zinged the ball right into the appreciative hands of CU safety Pat Murphy. The Buffaloes had the ball at the Penn State 40 and before you could say Joe Paterno, they had covered that distance in five plays, John Tarver slicing over from the one and Dave Haney upping the score to 7-0 with 1:30 played. On the next possession it was Mitchell who kept the Penn State predicament going, fumbling away the ball to Dave Capra at the 48. Jim Bratten, who had started the first TD drive going with an 18-yard completion to Steve Dal Porto, promptly hit Willie Nichols for 30 yards and Dave Haney wound up kicking a 35-yard field goal as the Penn State defense held. Haney got another 3-pointer late in the opening period, this one from 48 yards out, after Jim Cooch had intercepted another Cooper pass and returned it four yards to the Penn State 41. A 13-yard Bratten to Bob Masten pass set this one up as the CU quarterback found all kinds of open spots in the Penn State secondary. But tailback Ron Reiger fumbled the ball away at the CU 17 to start the second quarter and big Harris forced his way over from the six and it was still a contest, 13-7, despite the early CU domination. The Buffaloes put it to the Nittany Lion real good at this point, hammering out 71 yards in a long, steady drive which used up 19 plays and eight minutes to take a 20-7 lead into halftime on Reiger's one-yard scoring dive. But Penn State was threatening at the gun, missing a field goal after reaching the 11 and the blueclads from the coal mine country of Pennsylvania could be counted upon to come back. Hadn't they gotten up off the deck against both Kansas and Missouri in Miami?

But somebody forgot to tell Cliff Branch that the second half was supposed to be close because he caught the kickoff on the three yard line and jetted 97 yards right down the middle. If that didn't drain the remaining oxygen from the Penn State balloon, a following goal line stand which stopped the visitors at the five, after they had driven to a first and goal at the six, did. It was like pumping bullets into a dead horse after that although, really, the Nittany Lions didn't lay down and die. It was more of a case of the Buffaloes simply pumping a lot more bullets into them. Like Ward Walsh's 19-yard touchdown. And Paul Arendt's 17-yard scoring pass to Rick Kay. Actually, the Buffaloes weren't all that overwhelming in the second half despite scoring those three touchdowns. The score could have been higher had not CU thrown two interceptions and lost two fumbles.

It was a great victory. Great because it snapped the longest winning streak in the nation and because it was so convincing and because it was over the school which was the fourth-greatest winner in the history of college football and because it was on national television and because it got co-captain Phil Irwin's arms, pinned firmly around the neck of a Penn State runner, on the cover of Sports Illustrated. It was a very, very Sweet Saturday. The sweetest, by far of a season which was to harbor some sour Saturdays. Like a 21-20 upset at Kansas State seven days later and a 17-3 nosedive to Tulane on Liberty Bowl Saturday. But for the moment the Buffaloes were the kings of the west, the east, national television and just about anything else you wanted to list. How sweet it was!

No. 2: CU 20, OHIO STATE 14 (COLUMBUS, SEPT. 25, 1971)

This one almost finished in a dead heat for the No. 1 spot but lost out in a photo finish as sentimentality made the difference. But what a weekend this was. Starting with the anticipation of the battle which built up throughout the week and which was almost unbearable as our Continental charter took off full of Buffaloes and a good crew of boosters including the four leaders of our Boulder Buff Club drive, Ed Lyons, Larry Simoneau, Barry Telleen and my old Irish buddy who had so nicely surrendered his seat on that baseball trip to Honolulu three springs earlier, Danny Kelly. Plus a lot of other staunch allies like Jack Beattie, Ed Stoebe, Mack Davis, Tom Wilscam and a lot of other good men. It was going to be a great trip and everyone had girded his loins in anticipation of the Friday night and Saturday afternoon challenges and any other challenges that might jump up along the way. Everybody made it through the night but not many made it up for early morning services but I did, always being an early riser on game day except on those days when I couldn't get out of bed and besides I was having breakfast with my old All-American soul brother, John Wooten who was living in nearby Cleveland and who had laid a few bob on the Buffaloes and wanted to take a look at his investment in person. And also, Tom Brookshier was stopping over on his way from Philadelphia to Chicago where he was scheduled to do an NFL telecast the next day and I didn't want to be logy when Tom blew in. So I soft-stepped into the coffee shop at the motel and stopped to visit with Dr. George Masten, an eminent South Broadway eye doctor (and father of Robert, our tight end), who immediately prescribed a pair of darker glasses for me before sending me onward to Wooten's table. Big John and I had a very pleasant breakfast and the old Sun Devil proved he was just as quick now as he was back in 1958 as he outmaneuvered me in the race away from the check. John now weighs 260. And all you have to do John is say, hey Fred, this one's on you. You don't have to move, old buddy. You're too big. And I'm too small. And, besides, Kayo isn't around to scrutinize the expense vouchers anymore! So Big John and Turbulent Tom were the special guests, among a dozen or so others, in the KBOL broadcast booth where I was unknowingly making my final appearance as Jim Kithcart's color man and we had a great time although I may have overdone it a little bit but, dammit, Russ, Jim was a little tired from the night before, too, and I have got to step forward and take up the slack whenever my leader's tonsils start to wear down. That is the way I am built and so what if the post-game broadcast did run a little long. It was a day I never wanted to end and, besides, those line charges can't be that expensive. Especially, when we were machine-gunning great history into that old microphone.

The game itself was unbelievably CU dominated. For three quarters anyway. Woody Hayes, who is the winningest coach in the midlands if not the best loved (he was compared to Adolph Hitler and Attila the Hun in the pre-game press box chatter by one Ohio broadcaster who was obviously not a great admirer of his), was somewhat upset at the Big Eight's string of 17 straight victories over Big Ten teams. Woody pointed out that none of these 17 had come against his Buckeyes who had a little string of their own going, 19 straight wins in their massive Ohio Stadium. But I doubt that even Woody, a total gridiron realist, was prepared for the way the game went from the start. CU took the opening kickoff and quickly drove to a first down at the Buckeye 30 but lost the ball on an end zone interception at that point.

They stopped Ohio State short of a first down then brashly drove 71 yards in 10 plays to take a 6-0 lead on Johnson's 7-yard cartwheel over the goal line. Ohio State never got past midfield in the first quarter. Nor did they until their final possession of the half. In the meantime, Cliff Branch gave the Buckeyes a good look at his disappearing tail light as he sped 69 yards with a punt return and it was 13-0. This jarred the Buckeyes to life and they came grinding down the field, to a first and goal at the eight. But John Stavely and Bud Magrum and Carl Taibi and Stu Aldrich and Billy Drake and Randy Geist and a lot of other tough defensive linemen rallied there and stopped the Buckeyes at the four. Ohio State came out swinging to start the third quarter and again marched almost the length of the field to a first down at the 11. They got only as far as the two in the next four plays and they must have started getting discouraged, especially when the Buffaloes, with sophomores Johnson and Charlie Davis, biting out big chunks of yardage and Willie Nichols breaking free for a 51-yard bomb from Johnson, moved to a first down at the Buckeye two. One more touchdown and the gates might swing wide open. But Johnson, keeping and cutting over right tackle, got the ball jarred loose and Ohio State got it at the one. It was what the Buckeyes needed and they came to life again, marching all the way to the CU 38 but getting stopped by a fine defensive play from Cullen Bryant and John Stearns on a long pass into the corner of the end zone which produced an eruption from the sideline volcano which is Woody Hayes when things are not going right for his team.

The Buffaloes couldn't get a clincher, though, and Ohio State finally did drive for a touchdown to make it 13-7 with 4:28 left and started the 85,586 fans beginning to stir restlessly in anticipation of a 14-13 victory. Three plays later the Ohio State people stopped stirring restlessly in thier seats and started stirring desperately in the bottoms of their thermos bottles hoping to float one last olive to the surface before the sad exit out of the stadium as Johnson wheeled inside his right end, got a great block from Nichols and raced 39 yards into the end zone to make it 20-7. The run came after an unsccessful onside kick by the Buckeyes. If there was anything wrong with the 3-play CU 55-yard drive it was that it didn't use up enough time. There was still 3:30 left to play. Enough time for the Buckeyes to complete four out of five passes and cover 77 yards in astonishingly quick time to make it 20-14 with still 2:11 left and the clock running like the works were full of molasses. An onside kick barely was recovered by the Buffaloes. There was a whole lot of nervousness going on in the CU offense now and the Buffs couldn't move the ball and John Stearns had to come in for a pressure punt with Ohio State lining up 10 men on the line of scrimmage to try and block it. Stearns calmly lofted the ball over the mass and it rolled dead on the five. Time for six more Don Lamka passes, only two of them complete, and for Woody to stomp on his baseball cap in frustration and for all of us Buffaloes to start getting ready for the ride home and for the sweet celebrations of the second Sweetest Saturday of them all. My sturdily-glued-together $10,000 home has withstood the gale-like forces of a zillion chinook winds (I think that chinook is Indian for cyclone) but its walls have never been tested more thoroughly than by the pressure of a score or so happy Buffaloes letting off the steam which had built up during that final tense 10 minutes. But the walls stayed up, although a lot of the Buffaloes collapsed before dawn. And joy reigned supreme in the land of Buffaloes.

No. 1: CU 34, AIR FORCE 10 (BOULDER, NOV. 24, 1962)

This one was the best of all because justice was served to a nice man. Justice in the form of an overwhelming victory which let him walk out of a miserable coaching situation a winner. Which let him march out of Folsom Stadium with his head held high. And with tears of joy in his eyes. And with a dead Falcon dangling from his belt. And with the knowledge that his men thought enough of him to rally for one final massive effort to send him out a winner after he'd told them of his resignation in the dressing room before the game.

This was the farewell performance of Bud Davis as a CU head coach. And in the tradition of CU farewell performances, first shown to me by Carroll Hardy and Frank Bernardi in 1954 and to be shown to me several years later by Bob Anderson, this one by Bud and his Buffaloes was the greatest of all. I don't need to tell you the circumstances going into the season. It's fairly well detailed in the section on Bud early in this writing. The Buffalo morale had collapsed. Not to mention the defense. In the last six weeks, Iowa State had scored 57 against the Buffaloes, Oklahoma 62 and Missouri 57. A total of 336 points had spun through the opponents' windows on the nine previous scoreboards. And this one didn't figure to be much different. Ben Martin's teams could always score. They were 5-4 and had scored at least three touchdowns in six of those games, all but one of them against better defenses than CU would put up. So the Falcons were a solid 3-touchdown favorite going into this 1962 finale, played on a dark, gloomy day in Boulder. A fitting setting for the finish of the most disastrous season in modern CU football history.

IT WAS A VERY GRIM YEAR

This picture was taken in the press box just before the kickoff of the 1962 CU-Air Force game. You can tell it was a very grim year. But it didn't turn out to be a grim Saturday.

Bud had spent most of the week drafting his letter of resignation. To his great credit, he made his exit gracefully, keeping the bitterness which must have welled up high in his soul well concealed. Two of Bud's assistants, Dal Ward and Ed Farhat, who had been pretty well out of the picture most of the season because they worked with the defense and CU obviously didn't spend much time working on defense that fall, got a rare opportunity to feed some input into the game plan. They were a pair of seasoned veterans who knew that the name of the game is run then pass and not pass then run. So they went to work installing some blocking and running into the CU offense. Air Force had to be overconfident. It was almost impossible not to be when you looked at the CU record. So the Falcons may have been a little fat coming into the kickoff. The truth was, they were about to fly right into the side of a mountain. They never knew what hit them. Except that whatever it was, it was wearing a bright yellow uniform. Sunflower gold, the CU uniform maker called it. It was still and 50 degrees at the kickoff and CU won the toss and received and Air Force booted it out of the end zone. On the first play, Bill Harris took a quick pitch and sailed 17 yards around left end. But CU always was effective early in the game. Just wait until they fold up. Mavity rammed for five over tackle. Harris came back around end again for six more. And so it went. First one. Then the other. And, once, even quarterback Frank "Crazy Legs" Cesarek, whose arm was a lot quicker than his legs, kept for five. The Buffaloes marched for 80 yards most impressively. In 15 plays. Without a pass. When Cesarek lunged in from a foot out and kicked the extra point, 7:37 had elapsed. Air Force had not touched the football. They just barely touched it on the kickoff as Darryl Bloodworth fumbled it away to Harris at the Falcon 30. Right back came the suddenly-surging Buffaloes. Nine plays brought them to a fourth and goal at the three and Cesarek calmly straightened up and hit captain Ken Blair with a quick pass and it was 14-0. Only 2:53 remained in the quarter and Air Force still hadn't snapped the ball. The just-as-suddenly-aroused CU defense forced a punt from the 15 and Mavity's short runback moved it to the Falcon 48. But the Buffaloes couldn't make it three straight scores and the Falcons began to come back, missing a field goal after reaching the 26 then coming back to go 58 yards in four plays with reserve quarterback Allen McArtor firing 19 yards to halfback Dick Czarnota for the TD. Now it was 14-7 and this was more like it. CU could roll over and die any time now. But the Buffaloes came right back and got deep enough to miss a field goal from the 25 as the half ended. Quick, Willie, the oxygen! Statistically, it was not a freakish half. CU had a 12-7 lead in first downs and had 205 total yards to the Air Force's 128.

But the second half started like most second halves started that fall. Air Force moved into position for a field goal to make it 14-10 with 8:12 gone. But burly Bill Symons, a fast and bruising sophomore who had wallowed around most of the fall trying to get his feet on the ground, took the kickoff and ran 79 yards to the Falcon 19. Harris and Mavity punched it in close and, again, Cesarek dove behind his center for a half-yard touchdown. 21-10. The Buffaloes have a chance. Beginning the fourth quarter, Blair punted to safetyman Terry Isaacson who was hit hard by guard Tim Monczka and dropped the ball at the 12. Symons was on top of it like a big cat. Mavity got to the eight on first down and Symons took it over in three tries. 28-10! 12:12 left to play. Can even the Buffaloes blow this lead now? Blow it, man, they were just starting to build it up. Nick Graham promptly intercepted an Isaacson pass and returned it 11 yards to the 30. Buffalo Bill Harris got a yard then caught a quick pass over the middle from Cesarek for 14 then moved to the 13. And from there Symons just mauled his way into the end zone and it was 34-10 and the game was over although there were still more than nine minutes left to play. Folsom Stadium was in an uproar. The beleaguered Buffaloes were breathing fire. Forgotten, for the moment, were those eight topheavy losses and those 346 points and all the horrors which go along with a fall which contains eight losses and 346 enemy points. Keep putting it to those bluebirds, Buffaloes! They ain't much but they're all we got left. Win it for old Bud! Or old Dal! Or the Gipper! Or Steve Canyon! Or anybody! Mostly just win it. And win it they did. Nothing dramatic happened during those final nine minutes. Except that the game ended with the Buffaloes ahead by 34-10. Which was by far the most dramatic thing which happened all season. The Saturday night was the sweetest one of all time. Until the next one, that is. I can remember, dimly and foggily, late that night, relishing the victory with just three other men. Dal Ward, Bud Davis and Kayo Lam. At Kayo's house. And it was a most intoxicating moment in my life. And I mean, intoxicating. These were three great Buffaloes and three of the men I most admire and respect in the whole world. Because they are great guys. And great friends. And great Buffaloes. The last condition is perhaps the most important quality of all.

What can be a greater moment than drinking the heady wine of unexpected victory with great friends? That is what it is all about, dear readers. That is what it is all about.

I have had a lot of fun during my days at CU thumping out a lot of doggerel, some of it clean enough to print, most of it not. Some of it good, most of it bad. Some of it clever, most of it not. Some of it pertinent, much of it impertinent. But the meter was always fairly decent. And the right lines rhymed most of the time. And anything you write, rhyme or not, can't be all bad as long as it is about college football. There have been some polite requests that I include some of those verses in this book. There have been a lot more requests that I not include any. I yield to the majority. None will be included. Except this one. Which came soon after that Sweetest Saturday of All, Nov. 24, 1962 and summed up the Bud Davis season. And summed it up well, I thought.

Ode to the End of a Long, Tough Season
It was a rugged fall for us,
There's no use to pretend.
The start was bad, the middle worse,
But what a lovely end!
So please don't knock our battered men,
Because they weren't first-rate.
Despite their woes, our Buffaloes
Are still best in the state!

EPILOGUE

I have a confession to make. That 1962 CU-Air Force game is not the greatest game. The greatest game is the next one. Always. Great as the 25 I've described in the preceding pages were, they can't hold a candle to the one which is coming up. You can have your million yesterdays. I'll take one tomorrow. Because tomorrow is when that next great game gets played. And tomorrow is when that next Joe Romig or Bob Anderson or Frank Bernardi or Eddie Dove comes marching along in his CU uniform. And tomorrow is when I want to be present.

If I could have one wish, it would be that I could be in the press box for the next 25 years of CU football. How I'd love that! And how I'd love writing a book about those 25 seasons. Maybe we could title it, "Football, SCU-Style." SCU standing for "Senile Casotti Uncensored."

Thanks for coming along for the ride on this first one!

Fred Casotti
May 30, 1972